Lucian, *True History*

ποικιλα = subtle – lies (~~...~~ untrue
as tells he is lying about all and
exaggerates on historians lies (e.g.

πιθανως ψευδη = contradictory
true he tries to convince other

ποικιλα = subtle (need thought/
reflection like serious texts)
↳ Plato's Apology (21b) allusion
↳ proves even tho

cites allusion → contradictory

parallels between L and historian
in preface in terms of lang.

Homer's Ody
↳ hiding behind narrator (deception)
↳ better than Ody (as educated
readers)
↳ clear correlation with his
famous depiction shows we
can't rely on the preface even
it's accurate

contradiction: confesses to lying
yet professes he will tell
plausible / ~~accurate~~ truelike lies
↳ does in nature

LUCIAN
TRUE HISTORY

Introduction, Text, Translation, and Commentary

By

DISKIN CLAY

and

JAMES H. BRUSUELAS

OXFORD
UNIVERSITY PRESS

OXFORD
UNIVERSITY PRESS

Great Clarendon Street, Oxford, OX2 6DP,
United Kingdom

Oxford University Press is a department of the University of Oxford.
It furthers the University's objective of excellence in research, scholarship,
and education by publishing worldwide. Oxford is a registered trade mark of
Oxford University Press in the UK and in certain other countries

First Edition published in 2021
Impression: 5

Published in the United States of America by Oxford University Press
198 Madison Avenue, New York, NY 10016, United States of America

British Library Cataloguing in Publication Data
Data available

Data is available at the Library of Congress.

ISBN 978–0–19–878964–2 (hbk.)
ISBN 978–0–19–878965–9 (pbk.)

Printed and bound by
CPI Group (UK) Ltd, Croydon, CR0 4YY

Preface

We should begin with the words of Diskin Clay:

> This introduction and commentary grew out of the enjoyable experience of teaching selections from Lucian's *True History* for many years at Duke University, in courses for first-year graduate students (our Camp Lejeune for Greek), or, in one case, for third year undergraduates. I also used my translation of *True History* in courses I taught for our Master of Liberal Arts Program on Utopias: Ancient and Modern. My translation of *True History* 1.22–6 served as an appendix to our presentation of Iamboulos' *Island of the Sun* in Diskin Clay and Andrea Purvis, *Four Island Utopias: Being Plato's Atlantis, Euhemeros of Messene's Panchaia, Iamboulos' Island of the Sun, and Sir Francis Bacon's New Atlantis*, Newberryport, MA: Focus Publishing/R. Pullins Company, 1999 (115–17). My commentary occasionally records the debt owed to Lucian's *True History* by later writers such as Rabelais, Swift, and Borges, and occasionally I note ancient artistic illustrations of episodes in *True History*.

The above was extracted from Diskin's draft manuscript. I thought it necessary to include it here, since neither did Diskin leave a preface nor, sadly, did Andrea have the opportunity to write one before she passed. The quoted text is short and to the point. But I think it conveys something we all know well; the joy of teaching a text to which you are attached, whatever the reasons may be. I chose to write my dissertation on Lucian for a very simple reason: Lucian makes me laugh. If I was going to invest so much time in a project, time spent alone, it seemed like a good idea. Clearly Lucian made Diskin laugh too. What better way to spend time in preparing for class, or in translating a text?

My involvement in this project came at the request of Oxford University Press, while I was still a part of the Faculty of Classics at Oxford. Diskin had left a manuscript that had been read and commented upon by external reviewers. It was at that stage—as in the life of any submitted book—in which revisions, corrections, and additions were necessary. After taking in all the data, the question was whether to append content to the existing manuscript, and thus preserve Diskin's "I", or merge our voices into one coherent text. Of course, the translation was complete, and that remains entirely the work of Clay. As for the rest, the latter was chosen because it was the only way to create a pleasant reading experience. An introduction and commentary with Diskin's section and my section, even as an appendix, seemed disjointed and was potentially an awkward read. Moreover, "my" entire section would have been a very clear window into the comments and critique of the external reviewers. That did not seem good at all. So, here we are.

Boot camp. The goal was to address the needs of students, in particular those first-year graduate students who are striving to improve both their Greek and their general knowledge of Greek culture in a short period of time. Diskin had no intent on supplanting or competing with Möllendorf's *Auf der Suche nach Lukians Wahre Geschichten: Lukians Wahre Geschichten*, which remains the primary commentary used in professional scholarship. And so, the theme of students has guided me as I spent more time than anticipated in finishing the project. The comments are thus meant to be informative and concise, but not exhaustive in references; there will, of course, be some overlap with Möllendorf, as well as the very useful commentary of Georgiadou and Lamour. The reader will also find something perhaps unusual, references to Smyth's *Greek Grammar* rather than to Kühner-Gerth. Obviously this is due to the common use of Smyth in undergraduate and graduate classrooms in the United States. It also facilitates comprehension, as students might not have the German to jump into Kühner-Gerth right away. Fair enough.

Since both Diskin and I shared a great appreciation of Lucian, it is with great pleasure and gratitude that I was both selected and was able to finish this book. I give thanks to Oxford University Press, especially Hannah Chippendale, and to the external readers. R. Bracht Branham, Karen ní Mheallaigh, and Ewen Bowie must also be mentioned, as they have for many years now been indispensable as Lucianic colleagues. Chiara Meccariello, a dear friend and longtime collaborator, read various sections of the final manuscript, providing the usual corrections and insight that make my work better. The learned atmosphere of the University of Kentucky and the calm of the surrounding Lexington area—though often an unsettling quiet in the spring of 2020 due to the emergence of COVID-19 and the closure of campus—also provided a very productive environment to bring things to a close. And for always making time more interesting, especially those much-needed breaks from serious reading, I am very thankful for Alice.

James H. Brusuelas
Lexington, Kentucky

Contents

Introduction

1. Lucian's *True History*

1.1. Introducing Lucian's *True History*

In his *True History* (as it is known from the Latin title *Vera historia*) Lucian describes his brief stay on the Island of the Blest. On this island he witnessed a perpetual banquet celebrated by the heroic dead in the half-light of the other world. Not only is the pleasure of the banquet (εὐφροσύνη) enhanced by the music of choruses led by some of the greatest poets of archaic Greece, it is enhanced by the songs of birds that echo in the tremulous woods. Two springs well up in the meadow of the Elysian Field; one flows with laughter, the other with pleasure (*VH* 2.15–16). Perhaps there is no better description of the pleasure of reading Lucian and his *True History* than this.

The *True History* is the longest of Lucian's writings. No editor, translator, or reader knows quite how to describe it or fit it comfortably into a familiar genre of Greek literature: "satires" and "dialogues" only partially describe the genre or genres he wrote in. And of all ancient Greco-Roman writers Lucian is the most inventive or—as he would say—"strange" (τὸ ξενίζον). His only rivals in imagination, wit, and mimicry are perhaps Aristophanes in Greek (whose *Birds* makes its expected appearance in the *True History*) and Apuleius of the *Metamorphoses* in Latin. Petronius hugs the coast of satire.

Like Apuleius' *Metamorphoses*, a tale that has its counterpart in the Lucianic *Lucius or the Ass*,[1] Lucian's *True History* is a first-person narrative. The incredible experiences of the author's "I" stands out in both. There is a certain authority in a fictive author who is also an actor in the story.[2] But Lucian's *True History* is not an account of the transformation from a human being into an ass and from an ass back into human form, the experience we find in *Lucius or the Ass* and in Apuleius' *Metamorphoses* (or the *Golden Ass*). The *True History* describes a metamorphosis of the familiar

[1] Whether or not Lucian is the author of *Lucius or the Ass* is debated; for the opposing sides, see Whitmarsh (2010) and Nesselrath (2014).

[2] See especially, J. J. Winkler (1985) on Apuleius' *Golden Ass*.

the narrative of an unbelievable voyage "Lucian" made by sea west of the Pillars of Heracles into realms unknown or only dimly known to the Greeks. It ends with Lucian finally sighting the continent across the Ocean from "ours," "ours" meaning the lands enclosing the Mediterranean Sea (*VH* 2.27 and 2.47). Whether this continent lies opposite to the West or to the East, we are not told. The Greeks were never confined to the shores of the Mediterranean, but the Straits of Gibraltar were proverbially the limits of their known world to the West. Lucian expresses his curiosity to learn what lies beyond the Ocean and what kind of people inhabit the lands *beyond* it (*VH* 1.5). A daring curiosity indeed. Yet the concepts are quite old. The river Ocean forms the rim of the shield Hephaestus makes for Achilles in Homer's *Iliad* (18.606–7). In the *Odyssey* (4.561–9) the Elysian Field to which Menelaus will be transported in death is described only as lying at the "ends of the earth."

In the introduction to his *True History*, Lucian promises his reader a work of literature that will provide a much-needed respite from the strain of serious reading (*VH* 1.1–2). For the success of his salutary literary project Lucian depends on an exhausted reader. And to be refreshed from serious reading depends on an ability to recognize his parodies, his literary play—or even game—with Greek literature ranging from Homer to Herodotus, Ctesias of Cnidus, Aristophanes, Plato, Menippus of Gadara, Iambulus' *Islands of the Sun*, and finally even Lucian himself. Lucian knew these authors; some (Ctesias, Menippus, and Iambulus) are barely known to us today and survive only in later summaries of their writings or, in the case of Menippus, what can be reconstructed from Lucian and other authors.[3] Lucian's many slanting allusions to Greek poetry, especially comic poetry, also present a daunting task.[4] And last, but certainly not least, to take part in this process of relaxation Lucian's reader must have a mastery of Attic prose.

In this respect, Lucian's *True History* has served its purpose. It is the perfect recreational text and test for readers wearied by the readings that now constitute the canon of Greek literature. This is the truth of his *True History*. Lucian offers the pleasures of being transported not only into realms uncharted and unexpected, but also into the nearer horizons of *mimesis* (μίμησις) and *anagnoresis* (ἀναγνώρισις): that is, the pleasure that arises

[3] The main attempt to recover Menippus from Lucian is that of Rudolf Helm (1906). On the survival of Menippus in Lucian and beyond, see Joel C. Relihan (1993) 265–93.

[4] The index to vol. 4 of Macleod's edition gives the reader a conspectus of the range of Lucian's allusions. See also Householder (1941).

from recognizing the source of an allusion. This is an experience noted by Aristotle, who in the *Poetics* (*Po.* 4.1448b20) is bent on contradicting Plato's conception of poetry and all other forms of *mimesis* as standing at "three removes from reality," i.e. imperfect and of little use (*R.* 10.597e). His point is that there is an innate human pleasure in *mimesis* and the recognition of an original. One could even substitute one of the terms of the equation *mimesis* and *anagnoresis* with *anagnosis* (ἀνάγνωσις). That is, *reading* (in a text that reminds a reader of what they already know) affords a source of recognition, and there is great pleasure in this. And so, the reading of Lucian's *True History* provides delight in that it stimulates the reader to recognize the many works of Greek literature that lie concealed under the surface of its narrative, particularly Homer's *Odyssey*. This is what our author promises in his preface when he speaks of "the covert allusions to ancient poets and prose writers as well as philosophers" his reader will discover in his narrative (οὐκ ἀκωμῳδήτως ᾔνικται πρός τινας τῶν παλαιῶν ποιητῶν τε καὶ συγγραφέων καὶ φιλοσόφων, *VH* 1.2). Moreover, within these allusions there is also the charm to be discovered in his imitation and, occasionally, his parody of Attic prose and the recovery of the Attic dialect of the fifth and fourth centuries BCE in the Second Sophistic (second to early third century CE).

One should also recognize a very different kind of appeal for the reader of *True History*: Lucian's daring novelty and inventiveness—what Roman rhetorical writers called *inventio*. Lucian, for example, calls attention to the shock of this technique in his *Zeuxis* and he demonstrates his art of invention in his *Dionysus*. In the latter he describes a grove sacred to Dionysus on the left bank of the Indus (*Dionysus* 4). Here there is a spring from which old men drink during the yearly festival of Dionysus. It is called the Spring of Silenus (perhaps inspired by the Spring of Midas described in Xenophon *An.* 1.2.13). Its waters inspire the old men to eloquence or "fluidity" (εὐροία). If they do not finish speaking before the end of this one-day festival, in the following year they continue right where they left off (7). In the former, Lucian overtly addresses this kind of invention and its appeal for his audience. His technique is not simply new or refreshing but it is also "startling" or "foreign," the τὸ ξενίζον we noted above (*Zeuxis* 1–2). Lucian's combination of invention, the "foreign," and the familiar will occupy us as we turn to him as a mimetic writer. As we shall see, Lucian's *mimesis*, his imitation of and confrontation with the Greek literary past, embraces an intricate artifice.

While Lucian's allusions are many, including works that have not survived, the Syrian from Samosata indeed seems to have been attached to

Attica, Attic, and Aristophanes. The fact that the names of both authors are nearly synonymous with laughter also seems to indicate a special relationship. But even Aristophanes did not possess Lucian's range of invention. Aristophanes was topical, as were all the early comic poets of Attica, and, even in his flights of fancy, he is grounded in Athens and the Attic Dionysia. In *Peace* (421) Aristophanes' protagonist, Trygaeus, manages to ascend to heaven and the dwelling of Zeus mounted on a dung beetle (ἱπποκάνθαρος) with the help of an unsteady stage crane (72–113). In the *Birds* (411) his protagonist, Pisthetaerus, founds his Cloudcuckooland (Νεφελοκοκκυγία) midway between earth and heaven; this new foundation is supported by thin air. In his *Frogs* (405) we follow Dionysus and his slave, Xanthias, into Hades in search for Euripides, recently dead. In contrast Lucian's wit indeed has a greater range. In his *True History*, Lucian is carried up with his ship and crew to the Moon (Selene) and is introduced to the kingdoms of Endymion on the Moon and Phaethon on the Sun (which, prudently, he did not visit). As he descends to the Earth from the Moon in his airborne ship, he passes Aristophanes' Cloudcuckooland, but without landing (*VH* 1.29). This moment of aversion (strong winds kept him away) is perhaps an indication of Lucian's estimate of the more limited reach of Aristophanes' imagination; Lucian describes his visits to the Island of the Blest and The Island of the Impious (*VH* 2.5–29, 29–32), but there is no hint of Hades as an island in Aristophanes' *Frogs*. And so, Lucian, by contrast, can be described in the terms of Hellenistic geography as an exponent of ἐξωκεανισμός or reaching beyond the Ocean and therefore the known.[5]

1.2. Lucian's life

The entry Λουκιανός in the *Suda* ends with the fantastic claim that he was torn apart by dogs (λ 683 ADLER). Such was the fate of Euripides in the biographical tradition, a fate inspired by the grim end of Pentheus in his *Bacchae*, as life came to be written in imitation of literature.[6] With a single exception, all we really know about Lucian's life is what he says about himself in works in which he presents "himself" in a number of guises. The most

[5] On the broader context of the term and the expanding world picture of Lucian and his age, see Romm (1992) 211–14.

[6] Lefkowitz (^{2}2012) 90 n. 12 notes the parallel between Euripides' end and that of Lucian and Lucian's fear that he will be torn apart by the Cynics (named after dogs, κύνες) he had angered (*Peregrinus* 2).

important of these "autobiographical" passages come in *The Dream*, *The Double Indictment*, *Alexander*, *Peregrinus Proteus*, the *Apology* for accepting salaried positions, and the apologies for two works that seem to have aroused controversy: the *Fisherman*, in which he defends his shabby treatment of philosophers in *Lives on Auction*, and *In Defense of Essays in Portraiture*, which purports to be a response to criticism of his *Essays in Portraiture*.

Based on his own works, if we allow Lucian to write his own necrology, we can conclude that he was born in Samosata on the banks of the Euphrates in Syria. He is likely to have been a speaker of Aramaic (possibly Syriac), who learned Greek as a second language. Yet, even as he became a master of Greek letters and rhetoric, he was still recognized as a "Syrian" and a "barbarian."[7] Overall, the chronology is sketchy. In his youth he abandoned a short apprenticeship as a sculptor for the culture of Greek rhetoric and the theaters of the Second Sophistic—first in Ionia, then in Greece, Italy, and even in Gaul.[8] At one point he returned to his native city to display his talent. This was *The Dream*, a seemingly autobiographical piece that in our manuscripts has *Life of Lucian* as an alternative title. In *The Double Indictment* Lucian presents himself as indicted by both Rhetoric and Dialogue and brought to trial by Hermes before the Areopagus of Athens. Here he says that he is about 40 (33). It could be that in Lucian's public presentation of himself "40" represented a mid-life crisis; "mid-life" in the sense that this acme marks the date of Lucian's decision to shift from the public displays of his rhetorical powers to the creation of a new form of comic or satiric dialogue.[9] And in three works (all prologues with no sequels) Lucian represents himself as an older man who looks back on his career as the orator who had once attracted large audiences; these are *Dionysus*, *Heracles*, and *Zeuxis*.

To make matters worse or, perhaps, more interesting, within his works Lucian operates under a number of assumed names or masks, and homogeneity is wanting. Λυκῖνος and Λούκιος are not far from his Greek name Λουκιανός. Lucian also assumed the names of Parrhesiades and Tychiades, i.e. Son of Frankness and Son of Fortune. He gives the name of his

[7] *Double Indictment* 27.

[8] His boyhood in Syria, *The Dream*; his travels, *How to Write History*; his stays in Rome, *Double Indictment* (17); his time in Gaul, *Herakles* and *Amber*.

[9] It is sometimes claimed that Lucian's "conversion to philosophy" dates to his fortieth year. Lucian (Lucinus) states that he is 40 in the *Hermotimus* (13).

grandfather as Elenxikles ("Famed for his Telling Criticisms").[10] And, of course, Lucian reveals his real name in *True History*, which we assume was well known to his readers and his many audiences, when he quotes the two hexameter lines Homer composed for him during his visit to the Island of the Blest (*VH* 2.28):

> Λουκιανὸς τάδε πάντα φίλος μακάρεσσι θεοῖσιν
> εἶδέ τε καὶ πάλιν ἦλθεν φίλην ἐς πατρίδα γαῖαν.
>
> Lucian, beloved of the blessed gods, witnessed all these things and returned to his beloved fatherland.

We do not know if by "fatherland" he meant Samosata on the Euphrates, the Greek East, or mainland Greece. Λουκιανός also appears in *Alexander* (55), *Nigrinus*, and in *The Sham Sophist* or *The Solecist*. If one combines the "autobiographical" passages and these personae, this is not exactly trustworthy data upon which to construct a life.

Despite the general lack of indirect evidence (i.e. other authors) for Lucian's life and chronology, there are a few unmistakable indicators in his corpus that help date Lucian to the rule of Marcus Aurelius (emperor 161–80) and Lucius Verus, Marcus Aurelius' co-emperor in the East (161–9). Lucian's *Peregrinus* provides our first point of temporal reference. Peregrinus "Proteus" immolated himself during the Olympic festival of 165 and Lucian describes his contact with this remarkable religious figure. He also presents "himself" as a witness to the spectacle of Proteus' self-immolation (21–40).[11] Next, Lucian's essay on *How to Write History* professes to be a record of the histories written while the Parthian campaign of Lucius Verus (162–5) was still in progress. In it he mentions Avidius Cassius, who in 165–6 conquered Ctesiphon and Seleucia in Mesopotamia, but revolted against his emperor, Marcus Aurelius, and was executed (30). Then in his *Essays in Portraiture*, Lucian attempts to describe, in the "synthetic" manner of Zeuxis,[12] the beauty of Pantheia, the favorite of Lucius Verus whose campaigns to the

[10] Parrhesiades in *The Fisherman*; Tychiades in *The Parasite* and *Lover of Lies*; grandson of Elenxikles in *The Fisherman* (19). Momus would seem to be one of Lucian's masks in *Zeus Rants*.

[11] See Clay (1992) 3430–8.

[12] He speaks in the persona of "Lucinus" in opposition to the more philosophical manner of his interlocutor, Polystratus. Zeuxis produced a portrait of Helen (or Venus) for the city of Croton by abstracting her perfect form from its partial reflections of five of the young beauties of that city; see especially Pliny (*HN* 35.64) and the discussion in Whitmarsh (2001).

East took him to Smyrna, the city of Homer, and to Pantheia in Antioch on his way to Parthia. This is an essay of many fulsome compliments to this divine beauty (all sternly rejected by Pantheia), but it is a piece that we can date. Lucian speaks not only of Pantheia but also of Verus as "our great, excellent, and mild emperor" (22). Verus died in 169, eight years into his joint rule with Marcus Aurelius. Lastly, the surviving emperor died in 180 during his campaign against the Marcomanni far to the north in Pannonia. Lucian speaks of him as ὁ θεός and, therefore, dead and, as a dead Roman emperor, a god (*divus*) in his account of his visit to the sham Asclepius Glycon at Abonouteichos east of Sinope on the south cost of the Black Sea (*Alexander* 48). So, we have a date for the composition of the *Alexander* sometime after the death of Marcus Aurelius—but Marcus was still alive as Alexander gulled the credulous of Bithynia and Rome; his votaries included Alexander's father-in-law, the senator P. Mummius Sisenna Rutilianus.[13] Out of the eighty-six works in his corpus, at least four strongly indicate that Lucian was alive and writing between 160 and about 185.

The only contemporary to name Lucian was Galen (*c.*129–99 CE or later), a younger physician in the court of Marcus Aurelius, if we give Lucian the sixty years usually accorded to him (*c.*125–85 CE). By a miracle of survival, Galen's account of Lucian has come to us not directly in his commentary on the Hippocratic *Epidemics* (2.6.29), but in the Syriac translation by Hunain ibn Ishaq (808–73) of an Arabic translation from Galen's Greek; Syria, as we shall see, has been kind to Lucian. That this anecdote survives in Syriac is perhaps fitting as the only contemporary record of the writer who liked to call himself "the Syrian." Galen cites an anecdote about Lucian (Lyqiyanus) to draw a parallel to the hypothesis that there are learned interpolations to the text of Hippocrates:[14]

> Just as one of our contemporaries, Lucian, has done. This character fabricated a book in which he set down a number of dark sayings that yielded no sense whatsoever and this he ascribed to Heraclitus.... This book he gave to confederates who conveyed it to a philosopher of repute, in whom people had great trust and confidence. They asked him to comment on the book and give some interpretations. The unlucky philosopher had no inkling that they only wanted to make fun of him. He made the attempt to

[13] For summaries of the historical context, see Jones (1986) 133–48; Clay (1992) 3438–45.

[14] Published in a German translation by Gotthard Strohmaier (1976) 117–22. The translation here is by Clay.

> make sense of each of the sayings and in the attempt he felt himself to be extraordinarily clever and for this reason exposed himself to ridicule. Lucian also…fabricated expressions that were utterly meaningless and sent them to some grammarians to interpret and elucidate in order to expose them to ridicule.

This is the Lucian whose "autobiographical" writings are now employed in the writing of his life. One of the basic tenets, after all, in the writing of ancient biography was the use of an author's work to construct their lives, their character. The use of anecdotes as a vehicle to convey character, be it fictional or historical, goes back to the early writers of biography in the Peripatetic school. As an anecdote and the only contemporary indirect evidence we have, this story does just that: it portrays the Lucian we know from his work.

1.3. Lucian's "I"

Lucian's first-person narration, sometimes accompanied by a pseudonym such as the Syrian (Σῦρος) or Lykinos (Λυκῖνος), teases us. After all, for an author of such a large body of heterogeneous works, connected by a comic-satiric thread, we have no real evidence for Lucian, the author. As just mentioned, we have the preservation of an anecdote by Galen that purportedly preserves the act of a living person. And if anyone were to compose a fake compilation of nonsensical sayings of Heraclitus in order to make fun of a philosopher…well that certainly sounds like our Lucian. The "I" of Lucian has thus been a topic of great scholarly interest. Who is it? What is it? More importantly, what is the reader supposed to infer from it? This is especially true of *True History*, where we read such statements as "I will truthfully say that I'm lying" (ἓν γὰρ δὴ τοῦτο ἀληθεύσω λέγων ὅτι ψεύδομαι).

As one might guess, in interpreting Lucian's "I" the notion of autobiography lurks. In the absence of any substantial testimony for Lucian's life, we are forced to use Lucian's work as a potential source of biographical data, even if that data is refracted, exaggerated, or even fabricated. The joke then, since Lucian is so good at jokes, is perhaps on us. Just as ancient readers constructed the lives of poets from their verse—a practice that existed both before and well after the development of what we call Hellenistic biography—we too must extract what we can about Lucian's life from his corpus. That Lucian was read in such fashion in antiquity is also betrayed by the alternative title for the Syrian's most "autobiographical" work, *The Dream* or *Life of Lucian* (βίος Λουκιανοῦ). As outlined above, according to what we can cull from Lucian's works, he seems to be Syrian and his mastery of the Greek language and the practice of rhetoric sent him around the Mediterranean as both teacher and rhetorical performer; this took him as far west as Gaul and then finally, later in age, to Egypt where he worked within the imperial bureaucracy. He is the inventor of the comic dialogue, which was founded upon a mixing of three distinct Greek literary traditions (represented by four specific authors): philosophical dialogue (Plato), Cynic literature (Menippus of Gadara), and Old Comedy (Aristophanes and Eupolis). And if *The Dream* has any underlying historical veracity, before turning to a life of education and rhetorical showmanship, the results of which are on full display in this rhetor's return home to perform before his native city, he was once destined for the family business of stone masonry. Put simply, that is it.

In the big picture of Lucianic scholarship, Lucian has taken on many roles: sophist and philosopher, satirist, postclassical hack and plagiarist, rhetorical genius, a historical mine for studying the second century CE, a unique voice of Greekness in a very Roman world, and, last but not least, a literary savant. These varied roles essentially correspond to how we have evaluated the so-called Second Sophistic over time. Once seen as a period of derivative literature, pale reflections or copies in the wake of a well-established canon of Greek literature from the fifth and fourth centuries BCE, sophists, rhetors, declaimers and their Atticist culture are now not only recognized as significant players in both the imperial and provincial hierarchies, but also the purveyors of a literary output and performative culture that both affirms a sense of Greekness within the Empire and fashions their intellectual and political status. Exploring how and why scholars have constructed Lucian according to each of those roles noted above is beyond our remit here. But for the purposes of exploring the function of Lucian's first-person voice, there is a general pattern in interpreting Lucian of which to take note.

Over the course of the twentieth century, much of Lucianic scholarship was vested in understanding his works within a kind of historical vacuum. This was largely due to how one sought to find value in Lucian's work. All the comedy, the satire, the pastiche, the parody—whatever we call it—is wonderfully hilarious. Lucian makes us laugh. Be that as it may, what makes Lucian significant? For early German scholarship, notably Helm, Lucian was as an unrefined, pedestrian path to the writings of the Cynic

Menippus.[15] Forget Lucian. Just dismantle his works to find the quotations and paraphrases of now lost Cynic literature. For the French scholar Bompaire, who is largely responsible for presenting Lucian as a creative talent in his own right, the value of understanding the Syrian is in the context of imperial rhetorical education and training.[16] An artist Lucian may be, but his imitation, his second-century CE *mimesis*, is tantamount to his rhetorical training. For scholars such as Baldwin and Jones, the idea was to step away from literary traditions and to read Lucian in direct relationship to second-century society and culture.[17] One not only can mine factual data about second-century life from Lucian, but his works also reveal a general timeline for when Lucian was writing. Finally, Branham showed us why Lucian's intertwining of Greek literary traditions, whether that is philosophical dialogue, historiography, travel literature, etc., is the literary point to keep in mind.[18] It is the incongruent blending and even contradictory overlapping of these traditions that is the source of laughter. Laughter and how it is elicited is Lucian's significance. And so we see this pattern of moving from the historical-literary to the historical to a deeply literary source of human laughter. Scholarly approach to Lucian's "I" has also undergone a similar trajectory, moving from a quasi-literal autobiography to a more complex literary strategy of fictional autobiography.

Reading Lucian's first-person narration as indicative of the *real* Lucian, especially in *The Dream*, is a strategy that once had currency.[19] But as critical readers became more sensitive to Lucian's literariness and rhetorical talent, Lucian's life, as evidenced in his works, started to become unstable. We see this take shape in Gera's analysis of *The Dream*, in which the young Syrian, a very green sculptor's apprentice, must unconsciously choose between an intellectual life and that of a sculptor as he sleeps.[20] Gera rightfully reminds us of the literary use of dreams going back to Plato, Xenophon, and even in Lucian's contemporary Galen. Moreover, while Lucian's struggle between Culture and Sculpture is principally a savvy repurposing of Prodicus' "Choice of Heracles" in Xenophon's *Memorabilia*, where Virtue and Vice vie for the hero's fidelity, Gera also notes that Prodicus' tale was commonly repurposed by other authors, both Greek and Latin. In the context of intertextuality, Humble and Sidwell dig even deeper, providing an exhaustive list of intertexts going all the way back to Homer and Hesiod.[21]

15 Helm (1906). 16 Bompaire (1958). 17 Baldwin (1961); Jones (1986).
18 Branham (1989). 19 Baldwin (1961); Jones (1986). 20 Gera (1995) 237–50.
21 Humble and Sidwell (2006) 213–25.

If we add the possibility that the very artistic attributes that led to the apprenticeship in masonry may reflect the anecdotal and biographical tradition of Socrates, then the foundation of Lucian's life seems more a construct of prior literary models and *topoi* than a documentary account. Lucian is displaying his exceptional skills in the mimetic practice of the second century CE, creating something new from the cultural and literary traditions of a distant past. Yet all three scholars do not fully divorce Lucian's literary creation from the supposed *real* Lucian. The idea of autobiography is still based on one thing: the choice to become a rhetor. Based on what we scrape together about the *real* Lucian, he does not seem to have achieved great success. Despite his skill in rhetoric and his ability to engage canonical texts, he definitely did not succeed on the scale of fame and fortune as declaimers such as Herodes Atticus or Favorinus—though, ironically far more Lucian has been passed down than either of those two. This perceived lack of success tends to inform our Lucian construct. Gera attempts to establish connections between *The Dream*, the *Rhetorum praeceptor*, and *The Double Indictment* to establish a timeline for Lucian's life in terms of their composition, trying to flesh out a possible disappointment with the path he chose that perhaps led to the creation of the comic dialogue. Humble and Sidwell too see a sense of disappointment or wishful thinking. Lucian's path to fame and fortune, in the end, was nothing more than a dream. Lucian may have excelled in Greek paideia, Hellenization, or Hellenistic assimilation, but the rewards seem wanting. Lucian's wit and humour, his voice, is often tied to this supposed lack of achievement.

This idea of Hellenization, especially in the context of a native Syrian absorbing and mastering Greek Atticist culture, is also never far from Lucian. That first-person voice often depicts himself as barbarian and speaking with a barbarian tongue (βάρβαρος). Although that attribute is conveyed via the Greek language, in syntax and words that adhere to a pure Attic style, this voice is inherently not Greek. Nor, for that matter, in an Empire is it Roman. Identity and the politics therein are thus unavoidable topics of contemplation when reading Lucian. Whitmarsh and Goldhill have particularly explored this topic with customary insight. In examining the possible tensions between Lucian, Greek paideia, Second Sophistic culture, and even Rome itself, Whitmarsh observes that Lucian's masks are far too many to reveal one unified being underneath. The voice may be barbarian, but in this comedy where the gods, philosophy, intellectuals, the foundations of Greek culture, and basically everyone and everything is a target, the *real* Lucian is always beyond reach in the distance. Modelling

Lucian is thus an ongoing series of "interpretive projections."[22] Lucian is protean. Lucian is anything he needs to be to incite laughter. Lucian is hard to pin down. Goldhill too recognizes and enjoys Lucian's distance. It is that witty self-conscious "I" that explores what it means to not just be someone of status—intellectual or political—in imperial Greek culture, to pursue fame and fortune with a weaponized Greek paideia, but also the experience of becoming, visually manifesting, and emanating Greekness.[23] *The Dream* is an autobiography not vested in facts, but, as Goldhill states, is a story of "coming into culture."[24] Lucian is Syrian. Lucian is other. Lucian is too good at being Greek. Through Lucian we have a chance to view Greece and Rome from the perspective of a literary consciousness that permanently resides on the other side of the Bosphorus.

Taking identity from the cultural to the authorial, Lucian's "I" has also been the focus of narratological analysis. Here autobiography is not real, but fiction. It is, in fact, a lie. ní Mhealleigh has produced much insight regarding how Lucian pushes the limits of the contract of fictionality between reader and author. Lucian's self-conscious, reflexive "I" and his pseudonyms construct a link between narrator and author that may or may not be there.[25] Again, it is a tease. And this reality or alternative reality can have a unique impact on a given work regarding reader expectation. In the case of the *True History*, Lucian comically and rather overtly destabilizes the kind of writing associated with Greek historiography and travel literature, in which authorial presence is named, establishing an authoritative contract in terms of credibility. Simply recall the opening line of Herodotus, "This is the exposition of the inquiry of Herodotus...," or Thucydides, "Thucydides, an Athenian, wrote the history of the war between the Peloponnesians and the Athenians...." This is all reliable stuff. In the *True History* Lucian may not name himself at the outset, but eventually his first-person narration leads not to a pseudonym but to the mention of his own name, establishing a direct link between author and narrator. Yet for the reader, the presence of the *real* Lucian—yes, this is a real world account of travelling to the Moon!—is problematic, since Lucian says, "I will truthfully say that I'm lying." According to ní Mhealleigh, with that first-person voice Lucian then creates an "anti-autobiography or autobiographical lie."[26] Credibility thus gets tossed out the window. In doing so, ní Mhealleigh observes how Lucian is

[22] Whitmarsh (2001) 248–52. [23] Goldhill (2002) 60–107.
[24] Goldhill (2002) 67. [25] ní Mhealleigh (2010) 121–32.
[26] ní Mhealleigh (2010) 128–31.

good at not simply creating a fake, one based on established genres and Greek authors, but also pushes back at the mimetic privileging of the original. The copy, the re-enactment of golden age Athenian intellectual culture and writing, as ní Mhealleigh cogently argues, can in fact be even better, as false and fantastic as it may be.[27]

For ancient readers in particular, Whitmarsh has also added a fine layer of nuance into this relationship between author and narrator. The crucial aspect to bear in mind for the kind of fictional autobiography that Lucian employs is not so much about an author-narrator divide as impersonation and illusionism in a performative context.[28] The fictional "I" is more like that of an actor who instantiates and then navigates a transgression between the real (self) and the fictional (role).[29] Sophists, rhetors, and declaimers are indeed performers. And so Whitmarsh is correct to embed this notion within the kind of impersonation that is very familiar to an ancient audience going back to Homeric rhapsodes, who were enthused with Homer's spirit and thus became Homer during their performance.[30] Lucian projects himself into the *True History* constantly through his first-person narration and jarringly once through his own name. For his audience, Lucian thus assumes a literary role, one taken up before him by the likes of Herodotus, Ctesias, and others. However, as Whitmarsh states, "Lucian is the most metaleptic author"; metalepsis is Genette's term that defines this transgressive violation of narrative levels.[31] In this metaleptic play where author and narrator become one, Lucian then takes comic shots at the convention of ensuring plausibility, since the author himself disavows his own account. Lucian has pseudonyms. Lucian has masks. He is an actor playing roles that blend the real world with the fictional to self-consciously play with the very act of literary composition.

This convergence of Lucian's "I" with that of a dialogue's principal narrator and protagonist should also be understood in a comic context. One of the principal elements in Lucian's comic dialogue is Old Comedy, as typified by Aristophanes and Eupolis, and the parabasis is a seminal feature of the genre. Here we find that moment where the poet's voice intrudes upon the narrative, the play's major themes are foregrounded, and the social and historical contexts are localized. Moreover, this moment of poetic self-consciousness and self-analysis explicitly bridges the contemporary world

[27] ní Mhealleigh (2014) 234–45.
[28] Whitmarsh (2014) 239–40.
[29] Whitmarsh (2014) 239–40.
[30] Whitmarsh (2014) 238.
[31] Whitmarsh (2014) 241–2.

with the dramatic structure and action of the play, the importance of free speech and self-criticism often being the underlying theme. And very often the poet momentarily becomes the comic hero himself. Simply recall how Dicaeopolis in *Acharnians* speaks of Cleon's lawsuit against Aristophanes as his own. The poet, in fact, exposes his voice to such an extent that Hubbard, in a study devoted to the intertextual parabasis, describes it as a sort of comic autobiography. In his words, "...not because they actually portray events in the poet's life, but inasmuch as they project the poet's wishes and fantasies into a fictionalized confrontation with the political, social, and intellectual currents of his day."[32] Lucian's "I" and the parabatic "I" are indeed similar. They both merge the real world with the fictional for self-conscious and metaleptic purposes. The best example of this is probably in *Fisherman*. In metafictionally defending his treatment of philosophers in *Lives on Auction*, Lucian's first-person narration is merged with the pseudonym *Parrhesiades*, i.e. the frank or free speech (παρρησία) so dear to Old Comedy. This "I" is not unlike Aristophanes in the parabasis of *Clouds*, addressing the poor reception of the first version of the play. With his indebtedness to Old Comedy and the overall comic nature of Lucian's corpus, in borrowing this technique Lucian may have assumed the general mask of the comic hero. Lucian's first-person character, like so many comic characters and heroes of Aristophanes, is this protean figure that addresses the audience and self-consciously initiates parodic play. Lucian's "I" is essentially a vessel to be manipulated for comic, ironic, and satiric purposes.

Now, if one had to isolate a common thread in all the various kinds of interpretation mentioned thus far, the idea of autobiography, factual or fictional, has consistently appeared. Perhaps, then, we should consider the state of actual ancient biographical and autobiographical writing. One thing to bear in mind is the reality of Lucian's timeline. In the second century CE, biography, in an ancient sense, is no longer just an element or part of other generic wholes, such as historiography, but an established mode of writing. In presenting a person's life and personality, it also varies in form. Although Plutarch's *Lives* might be seen as the "classic" example, we need only look to Satyrus' *Life of Euripides*, which is composed as a dialogue, to be reminded of ancient biography's elasticity. More importantly, although the term autobiography is a coinage of the eighteenth century and thus not used in

[32] Hubbard (1991) 220.

antiquity, autobiographical modes of writing were also in currency in the imperial period. There are few observations we should take note of in context. First and foremost, Pelling rightfully observes the absence of the genre.[33] Much like the development of early biography, we see it embedded in other more distinct modes. Isocrates' *Antidosis* is a notable, and often cited, instance of early autobiography, though obviously a rhetorical speech. Pelling then specifically draws our attention to ὑπόμνημα (memoirs) and the tradition of *commentarii*. In his discussion of the early development of Latin autobiographical writing, such as the memoirs of Augustus, Sulla, and the works of Rutilius Rufus and M. Aemilius Scaurus, he notes a distinct negative connotation.[34] Both Cicero (Cicero to Lucceius, *Fam.* 5.12.8) and Tacitus (*Ag.* 1.3) convey the suspicion, criticism, and issues in credibility associated with this kind of writing.[35] Ancient biography can have an encomiastic tone, and thus in autobiographical writing there is a danger of projecting arrogance and self-praise in narrating one's own life. Pelling also specifically mentions how Plutarch seems to corroborate the idea of suspicion and lack of credibility, suggesting that Greek authors were also aware of this negative perception.[36] The overall point is that for an author clearly talented in parodying and intertwining genres, not to mention in a self-conscious fashion, the presence of actual biography or autobiography does not often enter the discussion regarding Lucian and his "I." To take one example, if we consider Lucian's *Demonax*, which reads like a philosophic βίος, Lucian seems to play with the tradition of biography in that work. However, with the absence of any established genre of autobiography, it is obviously far more difficult to assess his awareness of autobiographical modes of writing. Nevertheless, we should take into account the suspicion and issues regarding credibility that come with narrating one's own life. Lucian's first-person narration, his "I," whether we call it anti-autobiography or fictional autobiography, may have been suspicious from the outset in the minds of his audience. If so, that is perhaps just another level of self-consciousness and metaleptic play; the lie, the lack of credibility is only further intensified, further hyperbolic.

In the end, Lucian is very much a missing person. We have no biographical tradition about Lucian the author—not that it would constitute historical fact, even if we did. Instead, there is only this life rhetorically constructed from Greek literature of the past, which is characterized by a Greek voice

[33] Pelling (2009) 41–64. [34] Pelling (2009) 42. [35] Pelling (2009) 42–3.
[36] Pelling (2009) 47–58.

that is self-consciously and simultaneously Syrian, other, author, satiric, and comic. More importantly, this voice seems to exist in both the real and fictional worlds. And so the joke is, again, possibly on us. In looking for Lucian, because his first-person voice invites the reader to do so, we must navigate his comic-satiric labyrinth and experience his play with imperial Greek culture, specifically the act of literary creation in the wake of the gravitas of a now classical canon, and possibly even his own life. But as we try to get a clearer picture, as we go from one work to another, Lucian is always in the distance. His "I" and his pseudonyms float like a mirage on the horizon.

1.4. Lucian's afterlife

This fountain of wit and source of pleasure ran dry in Christian times, when Lucian come to be abominated, not for his unsparing wit and inventiveness, but for his mocking treatment of the Greek gods and—most unforgivably—of Jesus Christ. Yet, like so many pagan authors deemed useful as a model of rhetorical and Attic prose, his manuscripts continued to be copied and commented on in the Greek East.[37] His disgraceful entry in the Byzantine encyclopedia, the *Suda*, begins: "Lucian of Samosata, called the 'blasphemer' and 'reviler'—one could better say the atheist. In his dialogues there is biting satire of things sacred as the sacred is juxtaposed with the comic." To his Christian reader Lucian's greatest offense was that in his biographical sketch of *Perigrinus Proteus* he touches on Peregrinus' experiment with Christianity and blasphemes Christ himself by styling him "the crucified sophist" (*Peregrinus* 13; cf. 11): "The wretched fool! For this offense he has paid sufficient penalty and in time to come he will inherit fire eternal in the company of Satan" (*Suda* λ 683 ADLER). These words are probably those of Arethas of Caesarea in Cappadocia (appointed bishop in 902), a scholarly theologian who produced commentary on a variety of Greek authors. The

[37] The subscriptions to Books 1 and 2 in G (Vaticanus Graecus 90, tenth century) reads: "I Alexander, Bishop of Nicaea in Bythinia corrected this text with the help of 'my brother,' Jacob, Metropolitan of Larissa." They are to be found in the apparatus of Macleod I xiii on Vaticanus 90. Alexander, who became bishop of Nicaea in Asia Minor in 912, was roughly the contemporary of Arethas, who also played a role in the preservation of Lucian, "the atheist." His scholia (marginal comments) to Lucian are often not commentaries at all but invectives addressed to Lucian directly. For the considerable scholarship and library of Arethas, see Wilson (1983) 120–4.

"fire eternal" echoes the apocalyptic words of Christ in Matt. 25.41, and Arethas was a compiler of Greek commentary (scholia) on the Apocalypse.

Peregrinus was placed on the *Index librorum prohibitorum* by Pope Alexander VII in 1664 and it is torn out of MS B (Vindobonensis 123). The reaction to Lucian's description of Christ as the "crucified sophist" is directly linked to Lucian's use of the term σοφιστής. Although "sophist" was largely positive in connotation, a learned expert of some form, both Aristophanes and Plato, two very important authors for Lucian, used it in the pejorative sense of a learned "cheat" or "quibbler." Lucian employs that connotation to such an extent that sophist and cheat are practically synonymous in his corpus. It is not surprising that Arethas, if those are his words, was driven to a fit of apoplexy as he commented on the offending passage. For Lucian, perhaps the joke then is on Arethas. As he inveighed against the abominations of paganism, he in fact helped preserve the manuscripts of Lucian by selecting him as a subject of commentary (*Scholia in Lucianum* 218.20–220.21 Rabe). To his eternal glory Arethas also preserved the *Meditations* of the emperor Marcus Aurelius, who was hostile to the theatrics of Christian martyrs as contrasted with philosophical resolve in face of death (M. Ant. 11.3).

In the Renaissance and in the Enlightenment Lucian had a kinder fate. Both St. Thomas More and Erasmus translated Lucian, and, in view of his fate as Chancellor to Henry VIII, More's translation of Lucian's *Tyrannicide* is ominous. In More's *Utopia* (of 1516) Lucian's books, then in print,[38] were brought to the island of Utopia by Raphael Hythlodaeus on his fourth voyage with Amerigo Vespucci. The Utopians, who had a genetic affinity to Greek, were captivated by his "wit and pleasantry."[39] The imaginary voyages of the *True History* and *Icaromenippus* might not have had a deep influence on More's philosophical voyage to Utopia in the southern hemisphere, but Lucian's wit did. Leon Battista Alberti exploited Lucian's *Zeus Rants* and *Council of the Gods* in his *Momus* written around 1450. His *Musca* is also a parody of Lucian's *Encomium to the Fly*. A remote descendant of Lucian's *True History* is notably Cyrano de Bergerac's (1619–55) *Voyage dans la Lune* and *Histoire comique des États et Empires du Soleil*, a work published posthumously by Le Bret in 1657. Le Bret suppressed passages that he feared

[38] The *editio princeps* was printed in Florence in 1496; the Aldine in Venice in 1503.

[39] The Latin reads: *Luciani quoque facetiys ac lepore capiuntur, The Works of St. Thomas More*, vol. 4 (*Utopia*), ed. Edward S. Surtz and J. H. Hexter (1965) 182.2–3. The most revealing study of More in his relation to Lucian is that of R. Bracht Branham, "Utopian Laughter: Lucian and Thomas More," Moreana 86 (1985) 23–43.

would offend religion and consign the work of this *libertin* to the *Index librorum prohibitorum*. The omitted passages were only restored in the edition of de Bergerac's complete works in 1920.[40] Certainly Lucian's presence can be detected in Captain Lemuel Gulliver's interview with Homer and Aristotle on the phantom island of Glubbdubdrib in Swift's *Gulliver's Travels*. And, as R. Bracht Branham has reminded us, his influence on Henry Fielding was profound, not so much for his *True History* as for his *Peregrinus*.[41]

Lucian indeed has had much impact beyond Greco-Roman antiquity, and the topic is very much an open field of research. The examples provided above do not constitute an exhaustive list, but are only a general sampling. The point is that Lucian has always been a pleasure to read. In fact, Lucian's prose was such a pleasurable and relaxing read that he even made it onto a shopping list of A. S. Hunt—notably alongside such necessities as candles, a water bottle, and even a revolver—as he and B. P. Grenfell lived in the desert around the ancient city of Oxyrhynchus, extracting a countless number of papyri from the city's garbage heaps from 1896 to 1907.[42]

2. The anatomy of fiction

2.1. Lies and deception: a problem with fiction

The *True History* is a first-person narrative (διήγημα), but it is not true. Its author, who is the principal actor in his narration, abdicates all responsibility for the truth of what he describes. He says in his introduction, "So I am writing about things I have never seen or experienced or learned from others" (*VH* 1.4). As already noted, the *True History* is unique among Lucian's writings in that he, as first-person narrator, confesses "I am honest when I say that I am lying." By this confession he involves himself and his reader in the toils of the Cretan paradox—"Cretans are always liars" (Κρῆτες ἀεὶ ψεῦσται)—which is first found in the tradition of Epimenides of Crete.[43]

[40] Published a year later in *Les Oeuvres Libertins de Cyrano de Bergerac*, Paris 1921.

[41] Branham (1989) 12.

[42] The transcription by Dr. Daniela Colomo is unpublished but kept with the original in the Papyrology Rooms in the Sackler Library. The transcription was made as part of the exhibition that accompanied the twenty-fifth anniversary of the performance of Tony Harrison's *The Trackers of Oxyrhynchus* at Delphi, and even held at Oxford on November 23, 2013.

[43] DK 3 B 1.

What credit could Epimenides of Crete have expected when he said "Cretans are always liars"? In Greek, the words for to lie and a lie (ψεύδομαι / ψεῦδος) cover a broad spectrum of meaning that ranges from a mistake, a fiction, and a lie. The status of the *True History* is radically different from other first-person narratives (such as those of Euhemerus, Iambulus, and Apuleius) in that it is an avowed fiction. Yet, by the Cretan paradox, the author who claims that he is not telling the truth is telling the truth. So, what game is Lucian playing?

2.2. The anatomy of a true fiction: history and myth/history or myth?

The manuscripts for the *True History* essentially preserve two versions of the title: ἀληθῶν διηγημάτων and ἀληθοῦς ἱστορίας λόγος πρῶτος / περὶ ἀληθοῦς ἱστορίας. Photius knew the work by the first title (*Bibliotheca*, Codex 166), but there is something to be said for the second, for it reflects the language of Lucian's introduction when he says that he does not want to be the only writer not to profit from the license of writing myth (ἵνα μὴ ἄμοιρος ὦ τῆς ἐν τῷ μυθολογεῖν ἐλευθερίας). He especially mentions Ctesias of Cnidus and Herodotus in this context, who both learned the technique from Homer. Yet unlike these historians Lucian confesses that he had nothing purportedly true to relate (μηδὲν ἀληθὲς ἱστορεῖν εἶχον, *VH* 1.4), and so lying was simply the natural path to take.

Lucian's conflation of myth and history is significant. Whether or not one should do so is a topic of great interest to Strabo. Stephens and Winkler have concisely presented the geographer's position: "Strabo evidently had a good nose for fiction, and he will tolerate it as long as it knows its place and does not present itself 'in the format of factual research.'" The boundary between myth and history is not be blurred. However, if one is to mythologize, noting or admitting it up front seems to be the right thing to do, and thus Strabo gives a pass to the admittedly fanciful work of Theopompus while other historians are criticized for their writing "in the guise of history" (ἐν ἱστορίας σχήματι). Strabo, of course, had no problems with Homer—his favorite poet and poets are exempt in his distinction—but Ctesias, Herodotus, and Hellanicus notably come in for his censure.[44] Lucian, who

[44] Str. 1.2.35 and 11.6.3. For the importance of these passages in assessing ancient fiction, see Stephens and Winkler (1995) 115.

censures Ctesias, Herodotus, and even Homer, and yet treats Iambulus with indulgence, as Strabo had treated Theopompus,[45] combines Strabo's distinction of the two kinds of writing in the *True History*.

The play with this distinction is also not unique to the *True History*. Although Lucian seems to step upon the firm ground of history in his essay *On How to Write History*, there are some jarring problems. Here Lucian describes the histrionic histories that were being written during Lucius Verus' Parthian campaigns. Yet in doing so he seems to invent the contemporary historians Creperius Calpurinanus of Pompeiopolis, Callimorphus, and the absurdly entitled *Parthenonica* of Demetrius of Sagalassus. These historians likely share in the reality of Julius Capitolinus and Valcacius Gallicanus, two of the invented "historians" of the *Historia Augusta*.[46] Like a good historian, Lucian insists (as would Leopold von Ranke after him) that a historian should preserve the historical record and describe events as they actually happened (ὡς ἐπράχθη εἰπεῖν, 39, or, in Ranke's formulation, to demonstrate what actually happened: *wie es eigentlich gewesen ist*). He thus offers some precepts on how history should be written. In contrast to poetry, history will tolerate no fiction (ψεῦδος). This precept also enjoins frankness and the avoidance of flattery. The writing of history requires political understanding and a proper understanding of the art of interpretation as well. And it requires what Polybius had insisted on: αὐτοψία, "seeing with one's own eyes."[47] Lucian was not, however, a witness to the events his bogus historians describe. One of these historians had never penetrated as far east to have encountered a Syrian (24). Furthermore, our veracious author reveals his mendaciousness when he speaks of the recitations he had heard in Ionia and Achaea. One of the authors of these oratorical histories he does not name; the other is Crepereius Calpurianus of Pompeiopolis: "By the Graces, let no one doubt the truth of what I am about to say" (14–15; cf. 26). Clio, the Muse of History, perhaps should be added as the fourth of the Graces. Lucian's fiction has its grace, but this grace is masked by the plain and

[45] *VH* 1.3 and 2.31. He is forgiving towards Iambulus, whom no one could take as veracious, as is Strabo towards Theopompus in 1.2.35. Theopompus, at least, confessed that he was inserting myth into his history of Philip of Macedon.

[46] The fraud infesting the lives of the *Scriptores historiae Augustae* has been most vigorously and convincingly exposed by Ronald Syme (1971) and (1983). Robert (1980) 422–6 and Jones (1986) both attempt to vindicate the reality of some of the historians of Lucian's *How to Write History*. Kezamis (2010) 285–307 more recently considers these historians as inventions of Lucian, as does Möllendorf (2001) 117–40. On the current debate between real vs. fake, see especially *FGrHist* / *BNJ* 208; *FGrHist* / *BNJ* 210.

[47] Plb. 12.25d–28a.

honest face of truth. Be that as it may, while Lucian is clearly having fun informing the reader how to write history—in the guise of history according to Strabo—in the *True History*, seemingly aware of Strabo's *dictum*, Lucian has preemptively defused the situation. He has already explained to the reader that he is honestly fabricating his tale (*VH* 1.4). Like Theopompus, he cannot be blamed!

Admitting one's embrace of fiction or myth certainly nullifies criticism such as Strabo's. But Lucian will not let it go at that. The logical dilemma of the Cretan paradox is pushed further. In his introduction, Lucian indeed says, "I am writing things I have never seen or experienced nor learned from others. What is more, they neither really exist nor fundamentally can they exist. For this reason those who encounter my tale should have no trust in them" (*VH* 1.4). But despite the frank confession he continually undermines this premise, or at least presents it as a boundary over which he jumps back and forth. In describing the Star Wars between Endymion and Phaethon, Lucian assures his reader that he did not actually see and will not "dare" to describe the horse-cranes that failed to arrive in time to join King Endymion's forces in battle (*VH* 1.13). When he reports the number of cloud-centaurs, the allies of King Phaethon, he says, "They were so many that I feared that to some readers they would seem unbelievable" (*VH* 1.16).[48] As for the removable eyes of the Selenitai, the truth is incredible, but Lucian will describe them even at the risk of seeming to lie (*VH* 1.25). Then there is the mirror over the well in the Palace of King Endymion. It might seem incredible but, if Lucian's skeptical reader ever reaches the Moon, he will discover that he is telling the truth. Seen or not seen? Witnessed or not witnessed? Lucian claims or insinuates both positions. In general, this is how Lucian offers his readers the challenge of verifying the truth of his long description of the marvels he witnessed on the Moon: "Whoever does not believe what I have said will, if he should ever reach the Moon, know that I am telling the truth" (*VH* 1.26). Lucian is not only getting away with it, but he thus continues to throw it in the face of the reader. Like the good thief, who knows how to work with impunity, he relishes in this fact. On the Island of the Impious Lucian witnesses the terrible punishments of Herodotus and Ctesias and "those who told a falsehood in the course of their lives." He feels a warm flood of relief as he realizes that he will not share their punishment in death (*VH* 2.31). Lucian, after all, has

[48] A table of the opposing forces is given in Georgiadou and Larmour (1998) 106.

already admitted to his fabrication. A place is thus reserved for him at the symposium of the Island of the Blest (*VH* 2.28), something Voltaire appreciated as he placed him on the Elysian Fields in the company of Erasmus, known as Lucianus Batavus, and Rabelais, something that Robert Burton also admired in his *The Anatomy of Melancholy*.[49]

Beyond Lucian's metaficitional dialogue with his reader regarding the truth status of his *True History*, there are also some narrative "signposts" that continually indicate the fiction in Lucian's truth. Most notable is perhaps the painstaking circumstantial detail in the exact record of time, space, and size. Thus a bogus precision in the chronology of the distinct stages of Lucian's voyage seems circumstantial: "we sailed for seventy-nine days, then on the eightieth..." (*VH* 1.6). After Lucian sails beyond the Pillars of Heracles, a typhoon then carries Lucian and his companions aloft for seven days and seven nights. Then on the eighth...they land on the Moon (*VH* 1.10). The pattern is familiar: there is an odd number representing a steady progress and then the even number that signals the change. The pattern is best exemplified in the opening of the first book of the *Iliad*: for nine days Apollo showered his arrows of plague on the Greek army, and then on the tenth day...(1.53–4). The numbers recorded in the *True History* are also equally precise and absurd, especially when Lucian gives the numbers of the forces of Endymion and Phaethon. Not counting Phaethon, Endymion, and Lucian and his forty-eight companions and helmsman, the fantastic lunar and solar forces are tallied in units of thousands, the smallest of which is the 5,000 of the dog-nutters. The grand total for the forces of King Endymion comes to 400,000, not counting the baggage carriers (*VH* 1.13). Lucian gives the numbers for only three of the units of King Phaethon's army. They give a total of only 150,000. Then there is the precise measurement of space, beginning with the foot. Heracles' footprint on a rock on the Island of the Vine-Maidens is a *plethron* (or 100 feet) long. The stade (or *stadion* of approximately 600 feet) is also a common metric, but in Lucian so is a Cycladic island, the mast of a transport ship, an elephant, and the Colossus of Rhodes. Finally, there is often elaborate documentation, which is cited verbatim, such as the peace treaty imposed upon the defeated Selenitai (*VH* 1.20) and the letter Odysseus asked Lucian to convey to Calypso on the island of Ogygia (*VH* 2.35). Such detail, and the list could go on, while it is

[49] *Oeuvres de Voltaire* (Pléiade edition, Paris 1961) 737. Burton (1904) 405 has an appreciative comment on Rhadamanthus' present to "scoffing Lucian" of the mallow root that served him well on the island of Hydramardia (as he names it).

supposed to convey authority and credibility, is just too much in the end. The reader will undoubtedly recognize this.

All this narrative confidence and detail, which is supposed to ensure credibility, reminds one of Miguel de Cervantes's true history of Don Quixote. This he recovered from the unimpeachable source of the Arab "historian" Cid Hamete Benengeli (*historiador arabico*), who is responsible for the true history (*verdadera historia*) of Don Quixote della Mancha (I ix and I xxviii). Or for a more ancient corollary, in the beginning of Antonius Diogenes' *The Wonders beyond Thule*, the reader is told that Deinias' story comes from tablets of cypress wood found in the catacombs of Tyre by Alexander after he laid siege to the city—it has archaeological provenance![50]

2.3. Fiction vindicated: the usefulness of lies

Although Lucian confesses that he is lying and enjoys pointing out that some historians embrace myth, and thus are in fact also lying, truth does exist in his *True History*. Paradoxically, poets, the purveyors of myth, are contrasted with historians on three occasions as being more truthful. The first case of vindication comes as Lucian describes the rain of blood that fell from the sky during the war between Endymion and Phaethon. This strange event confirms the truth of Homer's description of the tears of blood that Zeus shed at the death of his son Sarpedon (*VH* 1.17; *Il.* 16.459–61). Then the actual sighting of Aristophanes' Cloudcuckooland on Lucian's descent from the Moon to Earth confirms the narrator's opinion that Aristophanes is an honest man (*VH* 1.29: καὶ ἐγὼ ἐμνήσθην Ἀριστοφάνους τοῦ ποιητοῦ, ἀνδρὸς σοφοῦ καὶ ἀληθοῦς καὶ μάτην ἐφ' οἷς ἔγραψεν ἀπιστουμένου). And Homer was not far from the truth that an Island of Dreams exists (*VH* 2.32–5); an oblique reference to the Gates of Ivory and Horn in the *Odyssey* (19.560–9). If poetry can be more truthful than history, and if poetry is a fiction, then fiction is perhaps useful.

This "truth" in fiction that Lucian illustrates ultimately brings us to the bigger question of whether or not Greco-Roman antiquity shared our modern notion of fiction. The topic has been much discussed, and Lucian certainly plays a role in it. Rather than embark on a long exhaustive survey,

[50] On such aptly labeled pseudo-documentarism in ancient fiction and its subsequent implication of complicit and savvy readers, the kind Lucian requires to find all the allusions and parody buried in the *True History*, see ní Mheallaigh (2008) 403–31.

however, let us focus on some ideas that stem from an older but still relevant work: Gill and Wiseman (eds.), *Lies and Fiction in the Ancient World*. The contributions in this volume by Wood, Gill, and Feeney have particular relevance when contemplating the "fiction" of Lucian's *True History*.

In thinking about this bigger question, both Wood and Feeney focus on the problem of writing and its truth-status. Truth and lies are indeed the first and foremost concerns. Fiction, or whatever we choose to call it, comes afterward. And so, Wood notes the underlying problem of entanglement: history can contain falsehoods or inaccuracies and a novel can be used as a historical document.[51] Feeney defines this further by asking an important question: "What do we mean when we say 'Evander, or Chloe, or Little Dorrit did this or that,' and how are these utterances different from saying 'Hitler, or Caesar, or John Major, did this or that'?"[52] Of course, this point seems lodged in both the modern notion of the act of writing fiction and the concerns of modern critics—what Austen, Hemingway, Miller, or Atwood did when sitting down to write a novel. Feeney is also keen on reminding us that our culture and that of Greco-Roman antiquity are too far separated to expect exact or explicit overlaps in cognition.[53] Still, similarity in the context of integrating the not true into a narrative is there. For Lucian's second-century CE timeline and the general context of his rhetorical education, the first-century rhetorician Quintilian is an often-cited example. His tripartite structure of narrative is very familiar to us and understandable: myth (far removed from what is true), argumentum or story (made up but retains verisimilitude), history (something that actually happened).[54] In those first two categories—though if we recall Strabo's criticism the third is not entirely exempt—the fictitious or not true ranges from the unbelievable or impossible to the familiar but never actually happened. For ancient critics, as many scholars have noted, the utmost concern was placed on the moral value and functionality of engaging in lies and deception. For Plato, as we see in the *Republic*, Gill makes the critical point to keep in mind: mimetic poetry is not simply three degrees removed from reality but truth itself, and thus it is deceptive and incapable of conveying ethical truth.[55] Thus there was no moral value in such act, and since most poetry was guilty of deception it was banned from his ideal city. But, as we will see in our discussion of Lucian and *mimesis* below, beginning with Aristotle and certainly by Lucian's time there was resistance to this position. Mimetic art, including

[51] Wood (1993) xiii. [52] Feeney (1993) 230–1. [53] Feeney (1993) 231.
[54] Feeney (1993) 232. [55] Gill (1993) 44–5.

poetry, can have a function within the environment of paideia according to Plutarch; the deceptions and negative *exempla* can be seen for what they are. More importantly, in this context of paideia, Feeney notes a passage in the *Moralia* (150d) where Plutarch conveys that it is wisdom that allows one to enjoy the mechanisms and techniques of deception found in poetry and tragedy because the wise are familiar with them[56] Again, it is familiarity and education and thus recognition of what an artist or writer is doing that is key. In Plutarch's passage it is the stereotypical dullard Thessalian that represents the other end of the spectrum, i.e. the one so stupid they actually believe the mimetic representation to be true.

This kind of game between true and not-true and how a reader or audience member engages both is indeed a link between modern notions of fiction and what Lucian is doing in the *True History*. For Feeney, he ultimately looks to Newsom's concept of duality as an accurate literary descriptor of what we see happening in ancient fiction.[57] The idea of duality centers around fictive belief and being simultaneously aware of what stabilizes and destabilizes a fictitious construct. In terms of modern film and television the "period piece" is a good example. The HBO series *Rome* implemented such accurate detail in clothing, weapons, food, and even some readable Latin graffiti that there was a strong sense of authority and authenticity in its depiction of the end of the Roman Republic. However, although the characters of Lucius Vorenus and Titus Pullo, through whose lives we experience historical events, may have names taken from actual historical records, their story arc is a fiction. Moreover, many of their death-defying actions and escapes from imminent danger particularly seem impossible. But that is precisely why we enjoy it. While we relax, like Lucian's readers, and appreciate the details, we also enjoy in recognizing the impossible and the fiction or lie within a true story (i.e. the historical fall of the Republic). Feeney also rightfully notes that just as one does not want to be like Plutarch's Thessalian, one also should not be too wise either. While one does not actually believe in Superman's powers, for example, breaking down the physics of why Superman cannot exist would not necessarily make the character more enjoyable. Lucian's truth game in the *True History* is indeed indicative of this idea of "duality," as the Syrian challenges us from the very beginning to recognize who and what he has stitched into his narrative.

[56] Feeney (1993) 236–7.

[57] Feeney (1993) 238.

Lastly, Gill's dense chapter on Plato is important because it focuses on the philosopher's concern with falsehood. Lucian knows Plato. Plato is an essential element in the creation of the comic dialogue. As noted above, Plato finds fault in the falsehood and deception of poetry because they are mechanisms that are incapable of conveying ethical truth; and so they have no place in a well-defined program of ethical education.[58] Be that as it may, there still lurks within Plato an actual usefulness of the false or not true in a context important to Lucian's program: mythmaking. Gill cogently classifies the kinds of lies in which Plato is especially interested: "deliberate lying" and "saying or believing what is in fact false."[59] But Gill also insightfully specifies Plato's other kind of lie, namely that the truth of the distant past is uncertain, and so one then makes the false appear as true as possible; these are the so-called "necessary falsehoods" or "noble lie."[60] Specifically regarding Platonic myth, Gill states, "It is characteristic of what we call Plato's myth that they present usually in narrative form accounts of subjects of which we do not, and indeed cannot, know the truth...."[61] Nevertheless, as accounts that are like the truth but may indeed be false, they still can propagate truth. The passage in the Phaedrus (275b–c), when he calls out Socrates for making up the Egyptian legend, certainly makes this clear, as Gill points out.[62] Socrates states, "what matters is not the source of such a story but the truth or falsity of the story it conveys."[63] Platonic myth, even if false, can thus be truth-like, and thus treat as true what is false because it is conveying the truth-like. Gill is right to note that there seems to be a truth game at play here, and this should be borne in mind when reading the *True History*. If Plato is making an account of something in the past as true as possible, then, although the falsehood of mimetic poetry is not suitable for conveying ethical truth, that does not mean that falsehood itself (ψεῦδος not poetry) cannot convey truth. Again Lucian knows Plato. But Plato, as a source to be recognized, is notably absent in the *True History*.

Lucian's truth game in the *True History* indeed seems perfectly at home in the strategy of postmodern writers like Barthes, Calvino, and Eco, who overtly in a metafictional way invite the reader to play with the notion of the real world around them vs. the world constructed in words on the page before them. Yet in terms of speaking backwards rather than forward in time, Lucian is perhaps just being Lucian—if one permits a tautology. As

[58] Gill (1993) 42–4. [59] Gill (1993) 52–3. [60] Gill (1993) 52.
[61] Gill (1993) 56. [62] Gill (1993) 58.
[63] With Gill's translation, see the discussion at Gill (1993) 58–9.

Branham has concisely shown, it is the overlapping of literary traditions, which always reveal incongruity, that produces the comic effect: Lucian's rhetorical laughter.[64] And so, the overlapping of defined notions of history—what Polybius and Strabo expect—with the kind of myth or tall tales evident in the histories of Herodotus or Ctesias is a classic example of Lucian's comic incongruity. But at the same time, perhaps none of this matters. Plato and Platonic myth already show that a noble lie can exist; falsehoods in words can convey general truth. Overlapping the truths and falsehoods of philosophy and history via their connection through myth comically negates one another like a good Socratic *aporia*. Perhaps this is why Plato is referenced once but largely absent in the *True History*. Bringing him in might make the overall game of recognition too obvious, too easy. Laird, after all, not only sees a connection or possible allusion to Plato in the *True History*, but argues that this work is Lucian's response to Platonic philosophical fiction—again, the irony being philosophy is supposed to be about truth.[65] Besides, like Lucian, Plato is off in the world of his own creation (*VH* 2.17), his noble lie. Looking back to the Cretan paradox, Lucian's fiction is perhaps simply an exploitation of the entanglement of the truth and lies evident in Greek literary traditions.

3. *Mimesis*

3.1. The familiar and the foreign: Lucian's creative backdrop

There is an apparent paradox in Lucian's attitude towards *mimesis, mimesis* defined as his imitation or engagement with the Greek literary past. He often asserts that he adheres to the canon of both the Attic dialect and the model of the great Athenian orators of the fifth and fourth centuries. Yet, at the same time, he recognizes that in terms of his invention there is a discordant element of the foreign and of an arresting novelty. His terms are τὸ ξενίζον, "the foreign," and καινότης, "newness" or "freshness" (*Zeuxis* 1). "Foreign" or "strangeness," in particular, is expressed by the verb ξενίζω. We find it in Demosthenes' *Against Euboulides* where he defends Euxitheus against the charge that he had no right to Athenian citizenship because his father spoke Greek with a foreign accent (ἐξένιζε, 57.18)—much like Greek

[64] Branham (1989). [65] Laird (2003) 115–27.

emmigrants who return from the United States to Greece with a foreign accent and are known as "Americans." Like many Athenians, Euxitheus was forced by circumstances to live far from Attica and on his return to Athens he spoke Greek with what seemed a foreign accent. His situation was already familiar to Solon at the beginning of the sixth century BCE.[66] But it was not as dire as that of Cavafy's *Poseidonians* (*Unpublished Poems* of 1906); his Poseidonians had immigrated to Paestum (Poseidonia) in Italy and no longer spoke Greek, as they were "exiled from Hellenism." Lucian's writing is Greek and his *mimesis*, like so many others, was acquired in the schools of rhetoric, but there is something else, something foreign there.

As Whitmarsh observes, the definition of *mimesis*, taking into consideration the idea of imitation of not simply the model but the original and thus the authentic and authoritative, intersects both the realms of philosophy (the imitation of nature by art) and rhetoric (imitation of past literary models and style).[67] For Lucian's age, the Second Sophistic, Whitmarsh has also mapped out the essential ideas and authors to keep in mind: Plutarch, Pseudo-Longinus, and Dionysius of Halicarnassus. What we see is a combination of education, inspiration, and artifice. For Plutarch, who especially positions himself against Plato's objections to poetry, there is indeed value in mimetic art. Plato may consider mimetic constructs so far removed from the original that they are imperfect and, in the case of poetry, even harmful if they depict the bad and/or unethical, but that does not mean Plato's ideas cannot be recognized. In tune with Aristotle (*Po.* 4.1448b), a mimetic representation of the bad and/or ugly does not compel imitation of the bad and/or ugly. Instead, such imitation can be useful within an environment controlled by applied paideia; in an interpretative context, especially a reading context, one can rationally recognize it as an *exemplum* of the bad.[68] Knowing, understanding, and recognition are of the utmost import when engaging mimetic art and learning from it. In Pseudo-Longinus passionate inspiration from past models may indeed be a creative motivator, but such inspiration does not necessarily entail full submission to those models. There is a give and take, even a contest, as past and present meet. Orators of the fourth century BCE may be models of composition but at the same time they should not be suffocating templates. In this contest we see not only an embrace of artifice, i.e. an intricate alteration within the mimetic representation of the original, such as the use of calculated figured speech, but

[66] F 36.11–12 West². [67] Whitmarsh (2001) 46–89.

[68] Whitmarsh (2001) 46–57.

perhaps even a contest and/or collision of culture and geopolitics; Whitmarsh is right to advise us to bear in mind that in confronting the Greek literary culture of the past an author perhaps cannot avoid its diachronic shift from freedom to submission (Macedon and then Rome).[69] And in Dionysius of Halicarnassus artifice becomes something even more than the calculated play with language. It is startlingly mechanical, as if the writer is now an engineer. Dionysius' *mimesis* is defined by an artifice that entails breaking down models to their component parts and then rebuilding by restructuring and also mixing the bits together, even if the creation, the product, is startling.[70]

For Lucian's "unruly" and even "unnatural" inventiveness, whether it is in the form and shape of the mushroom-stalkers, the phallus-navigators, or the world constructed in the belly of a whale, these concepts suggest that Lucian was engaging the discourse on *mimesis* that had been evolving over the first few centuries of the Roman period. Lucian's readers need paideia to recognize how he breaks down the Greek literary past into pieces in order to build new and comically incongruous wholes. More importantly, with the "foreign" and "strange" elements produced by a self-referencing Syrian writing in Greek, the notion of an inspirational and confrontational arena of creation seems very applicable to Lucian's writing, even if that arena is on the surface very old, very Attic.

3.2. Attic and Atticism: language as status

> Greek, Sir, is like lace; every man gets as much of it as he can.
> Samuel Johnson, quoted in the Preface to Goodwin and Gulick's
> *A Greek Grammar*

One is tempted to emend this *obiter dictum* by adding "Attic Greek." In his *Lives of the Sophists*, Philostratus mentions Hadrian of Tyre who was able, under the tutelage of Herodes Atticus, to imitate the style of any orator, save that of Herodes. Hadrian's orators delivered their speeches in the Attic dialect in Attica, bringing "classical" owls to Athens in the Second Sophistic.[71] Philostratus does not recognize Lucian of Samosata as one of his sophists, but Lucian is perhaps the greatest mimic and adaptor of his age.

[69] Whitmarsh (2001) 57–71.

[70] Whitmarsh (2001) 71–89.

[71] VS 585–590.

His talent in reproducing Greek dialect and syntax is unparalleled in the Second Sophistic. The close imitation of Herodotean Ionic in *The Goddess of Syria* (44) has even prompted some readers to reject the possibility that the Syrian Lucian could have been its author.[72] Lucian's first experience of Greek was undoubtedly the κοινή, or the common tongue spoken in the Greek East, a language that had its origins in Attic Greek and was spread to the East by the conquests of Alexander of Macedon. As it spread abroad, Attic Greek required accent markings (diacritical signs) for those learning Greek as a second language and, in the course of its extension to the East, it became much simplified, indeed "vulgar," in its vocabulary. The fine nuances of the particles and moods tended to disappear, and even the nice distinction between οὐ and μή and the delicate formula μή οὐ with the imperative ("Don't think about it and don't do it") was lost from sight. The dual number common in Homer and in Plato virtually disappears, as do the subjunctive and optative moods. Yet, as revived in the Second Sophistic, Attic Greek is resurrected, with a focus on not just style but grammar and morphology.[73] Why? When exactly the resurgence of Attic Greek began after the development and spread of Koine remains unclear. It definitely predates Lucian's age and may even reach as far back as the Hellenistic period.[74] But in the Second Sophistic it is clear that command and control of Attic was tied to a very important facet of imperial life: status. At the beginning of the third century CE, Philostratus of Lemnos, "the Athenian," composes in Attic the tedious apology Apollonius of Tyana delivers before the emperor Domitian. It is doubtful that Domitian's Greek was good enough to catch the elegance of Apollonius' reference to Thales and Anaxagoras as the "twain from Ionia"—in the long defunct dual (τὼ Ἴωνε).[75]

Lucian too lived in the age of the sophist Herodes Atticus (*c.*101–77) whose talents in "concert oratory" did not match his wealth so far as we can judge from the fact that, with one exception (his Corinthian oration), his orations do not survive. Nevertheless, Herodes is indicative of Atticism's role within the culture of the imperial elite. Herodes was not only a patron and wealthy benefactor for Athens and Asia Minor, but he also served as a Roman senator and even achieved the consulship in 143. Although Herodes was by no means solely responsible for any shift in Atticistic trends, his

[72] For a learned discussion on the debate over authorship of the *De dea Syria*, one that goes back at least to the seventeenth century, and which presents a strong case for attributing the work to Lucian, see Lightfoot (2003) 184–208.

[73] See the comprehensive discussion by Kim (2010) 468–82.

[74] Kim (2010) 472–4.

[75] Philost. *VA* 8.7.26.

wealth and influence undoubtedly helped define what cultural refinement was in the Second Sophistic by latching on to the trend or desire for a pure Atticism. In the quest for pure Attic Herodes even believed that he had discovered a Greek who still spoke Attic Greek. This was the autochthonous giant Agathion, who spoke pure Attic in the isolated plain of Attica where he was protected from foreign influences imported from the sea (ἡ μεσογεία δὲ ἄμικτος βαρβάροις οὖσα ὑγιαίνει αὐτοῖς ἡ φωνὴ καὶ ἡ γλῶττα τὴν ἄκραν Ἀτθίδα ἀποψάλλει).[76] For Lucian, whose pseudonyms often present themselves as "barbarians" in fine Attic prose, this praise of purity, the unmixed (ἄμικτος), is very noteworthy. The story seems like an anecdote, real or imagined, and Kim thus rightfully says, "Perhaps no anecdote more vividly illustrates the quasi-mythical status enjoyed by the Attic dialect in the imperial era."[77] Herodes' discovery of the uncorrupted speech of Agathion is very much like the contemporary discovery of Elizabethan English still spoken on Ocracoke Island off the coast of North Carolina—of course, any movement to speak and compose in Elizabethan English in the twenty-first century would probably result in condemnation and banishment to obscurity.

One of the most striking diagnostic features of Attic as against Ionic and other Greek dialects is the double *tau* for the double *sigma* (sometimes developing out of -γι as in πράττω from πράγιω; cf. πρᾶγμα).[78] Hence Attic shows πράττω and θάλαττα for πρήσσω and θάλασσα (except in tragedy). It is striking that when Xenophon, one of the purest writers of Attic, describes the excitement of his army, when they caught sight of the Black Sea from the height of Mt. Theches, all cry out θάλαττα (*An.* 4.7.24). The ten thousand came from many regions of Greece, yet they all cry out in Xenophon's Attic—a symptom of what is to come. In Lucian we occasionally find a non-Attic form for the double *tau*, as in ἐτασσόμεθα in *VH* I.13, where there is no disagreement in the manuscripts. Another common feature of the Attic dialect is the assimilation of the consonant cluster ρσ to ρρ as in ἄρρην for ἄρσην (male) and θάρρος for θάρσος (courage). As against Ionic, Attic shows a long α for η after ι, ε, and ρ—ἱστορία for ἱστορίη, χώρα

[76] Philost. *VS* 2.1. Herodes' Agathion seems to have been the inspiration of Lucian's lost Sostratus, a work mentioned by Lucian in his Demonax (1). Philostratus uses a similar phrase at *VA* 8.7.25 to describe Attica as the mother city of Ephesus.

[77] Kim (2010) 468.

[78] The paradox of Lucian's invention of the prosecution of sigma against tau before the jury of vowels (*The Consonants at Law*) is that his usage shows his preference for tau. Neil Hopkinson has given a good account of Lucian's Atticism in his introduction to this short dialogue (2008) 151–2, as did R. J. Deferrari (1916). For an updated position, see Kim (2010).

for χώρη. Lucian also resists the natural tendency to simplify words, like γίγνομαι, γιγνώσκω and οὐδέν to γίνομαι, γινώσκω, and οὐθέν (from οὐδ' ἕν), but he is not consistent.

In many ways the grammarians who had become the "Guardians of Culture" were the guardians of diction. In compiling their lexica they regarded Attic Greek as proper diction, since classical Athens had become the cultural model *par excellence*—they would have felt comfortable as editors of the *Dictionnaire de l'Academie Française*. To atticize (ἀττικίζειν) was to imitate fourth-century prose authors in style, orthography, vocabulary, and morphology. It is not simply that the Koine was devoid of Attic forms and usage. Quite the contrary, there was still a residue of Attic in Koine, but along with numerous postclassical additions. The Koine was also employed for literary, philosophical, and subliterary purposes. And so, to refine a literary Greek that was closer to the ancients, who were deemed classical and whose works defined the canon in education, was to construct a unique elite identity. Command and control of Attic immediately set one apart from mainstream Koine users. The idea of command and control is critical. Even amongst those who professed to know Attic, censure was not necessarily avoidable. The contest of knowledge largely came down to isolating and proscribing anything that was non-Attic, false Attic, and, of course, postclassical. The most important of Lucian's contemporaries to legislate Attic diction were Phrynichus of Bithynia, Aelius Moeris, and Julius Pollux of Naucratis. For the most part, lexica (dictionaries and glossaries) were descriptive and designed for reading texts, including Attic. Yet by the second century there is a notable focus on writing Attic. Pollux, Moeris, and Phrynichus are very much concerned with usage and prescribing what one should do, specifically in the case of grammar and morphology. Phrynichus' dictionary, for example, takes the form: "Say σκίμπους not κράββατος."[79] The offending word for bed is common in the Greek of the New Testament and gives the diminutive κρεββάτι in Modern Greek. Lucian seems to observe Phrynichus' prescriptions. He avoids κράββατος. However, since his Attic is so good, Lucian tastefully employs κλίνη in preference to σκίμπους. And Lucian's *Pseudoligista, The False Critic*, is devoted to defending an instance of his allegedly bad Attic Greek. Who knows Attic best is indeed a mark of status.

[79] XLIV (pp. 137–8) in W. G. Rutherford, *The New Phrynichus, being a revised text of the Ecloga of the Grammarian Phrynichus* (1881).

The contest, however, was not just about whose command over Attic usage was best. The Koine was still the everyday language, and so some resistance to the nitpicking over minutiae and to the insistence on what amounted to obfuscation to many was to be expected. Pollux was the tutor to Commodus (son and successor to Marcus Aurelius and emperor from 180–92) and held the Imperial Chair of Rhetoric at Athens. He was also fond of pointing out the errors of well-known sophists. Lucian, despite his own efforts to master and employ correct Attic, was not above poking fun at the degree to which the "policing" of language had reached; Pollux is clearly mocked by Lucian in *The Professor of Rhetoric* (24). And like *The False Critic* noted above, Lucian also takes aim at a variety of phonies and individuals obsessed with Attic purity in works such as the *Teacher of Rhetoric, Lexiphanes*, and the *Ignorant Book Collector*. But it is Galen, not Lucian, whose resistance seems more concerned with language as an applied tool vs. a literary vehicle. As a doctor, the language of medical texts was Koine, not to mention the language between doctor and patient. Galen not only composed his own lexicographical works, notably his *On False Attic Usage* and forty-eight-book glossary, but he also makes sure to point out how obsolete and essentially useless Attic vocabulary is for categories such as plants and animals.[80] As much as one aspect of elite and educated status was predicated upon command of Attic Greek, how useful it actually was in everyday life was noted. Even Plutarch mocks speakers who insist on using strict Attic Greek (Plut. *De aud.* 42d).

As for style, Aristotle describes the simple paratactic style of Greek prose as "beaded on a string" (λέξις εἰρομένη, *Rhetoric* 1409a). The opposing term is λέξις κατεστραμμένη (sometimes translated as "the compacted style"; Demetr. *Eloc.* 1.12–18) or the periodic style of subordinating thought. Xenophon, a model for the Second Sophistic, exhibits the "beaded style" in the narrative parts of his *Anabasis* and the "compacted style" in the speeches of his *Hellenika*. A *gradus ad Parnassum* would take the student of Attic prose from the simple opening of the *Anabasis* to the grand and convoluted opening of Demosthenes' *On the Crown*. Lucian is fond of elaborate periodic sentences as he mimics the high "Attic" style. In the *True History* he sometimes creates a parody of the style of the Attic orators, in the sense of pushing the technique to the limits of intelligibility, by creating a string of aorist participles trussed up by the main verb of the sentence in the aorist

[80] Gal. *Libr. Ord.* XIX 60–1 Müller.

tense. An early example in the *True History* comes from the narrative of the voyage beyond the Pillars of Heracles, as Lucian and his crew prepare to leave the Island of the Vine-Maidens: καὶ δὴ λαβόντες ἀμφορέας τινὰς καὶ ὑδρευσάμενοί τε ἅμα καὶ ἐκ τοῦ ποταμοῦ οἰνισάμενοι καὶ αὐτοῦ πλησίον ἐπὶ τῆς ᾐόνος αὐλισάμενοι ἕωθεν ἀνήχθημεν οὐ σφόδρα βιαίῳ πνεύματι (*VH* I.9). Here four stages of the action preparatory to setting sail are set out; the four stages are subordinated in aorist participles.

Lucian's exquisite and mimetic style reminds us of two later triumphs in bilingualism: that of Joseph Conrad in English prose and that of the greatest French poet of the twentieth century, Guillaume Apollinaire: both began by speaking and writing Polish. Like Conrad and Apollinaire, Lucian was not simply working, writing, and thinking in an "other" culture, but carving out a space within that culture by mastering its language. In the world of the Second Sophistic a rhetor has a chance at wealth, status, and even inclusion within the imperial social networks, if his rhetorical showmanship was not only something to be seen, but, more importantly, something to be heard. Greek, Attic Greek, was everything. Too little execution might convey a limited understanding. Hyper-Atticism (going overboard) might convey a lack of style or elegance, or just plain pedantry.

3.3. Lucian at play: Lucian's odyssey or stuck in literary la-la-land

With such a command and control of Attic Greek and Greek literature, Lucian is good at parody. Now, we should say that the use of the word here encompasses the multitude of terms that are typically used to describe Lucian's work: pastiche, comic, satiric, burlesque, travesty, carnival, etc. Various aspects of critical theory are also tied to such language; in grouping them together, objections can certainly be made.[81] Nevertheless, parody is given preference here not simply because of the intrinsic nature of play that these terms share, thus making it a nice umbrella, but because parody is a part of ancient discourse, especially rhetoric. The ancient terms for parody convey imitative singing or even a singer (παρῳδός), the application of

[81] On parody and satire in Lucian, see Camerotto (1998) and (2014).

serious verse to humourous ends (παρῳδή/παρῳδία), and verbal abstracts covering comic quotation and a form of stark textual re-arrangement and paraphrase (παρῳδέω/παρῳδία).[82] Textual transformation and/or imitation via rearrangement / word substitution, quotation, or paraphrase combined with a change of context are the essential concepts. Textual repurposing or recycling is often used to succinctly describe the outcome. As we saw in discussing Lucian's "I," Lucian is very self-referential, very meta-, in the context of his literary personae and the act of literary and rhetorical composition. In terms of his textual repurposing or recycling, Lucian is no different. Parody, especially of the metafictional variety, is a critical part of Lucian's *mimesis*.

In the introduction to Lucian's *True History*, as we have often noted, Lucian speaks of his veiled allusions to ancient poets, prose writers, and philosophers. Of prose writers our attention is especially drawn to Herodotus, a good liar. He accurately describes the fragrance wafting off the coast of Arabia Felix as he nears the coast of the Island of the Blest (*VH* 2.5). He also claims that he was an eye-witness to some of what he reports; Herodotus relies not only on what he has observed himself but the reports of others and his own inquiries (ὄψις, ἀκοή, ἱστορίη, 2.99.1). As for Ctesias of Cnidus, he exists only in fragments now. However, Photius' summary shows that Ctesias was in prose the "Prince of Liars." He described the man-eating *mantikora*, griffins, a river flowing with honey, the dog-headed creatures that inhabit the mountains above the river Hyparchus, and asses with horns.[83] In the *True History* we discover a river flowing with wine, springs of water, honey, and myrrh (*VH* 2.17 and 2.13), the man-eating Boukephali, and bulls with horns below their eyes. Then there is Iambulus. Since Diodorus Siculus is the only other author to mention Iambulus, it is difficult to know what Lucian had in mind. It would seem that Lucian followed Iambulus in his description of the bodies of the fantastic creatures that inhabit the Moon (the Selenitai) and the ending of his account of his travels to the Island of the Sun, finally arriving at India. Diodorus knows of Iambulus' account of his return from India and Palibothra (Patna), but does not give a condensation of it. Lucian only promises an account of his return

[82] See the entire discussion at Lelièvre (1954) 66–81.

[83] Phot. *Bibl.* Codex 72: 46b; 46b; 47b; 48b. Ctesias' *Indica* is reassembled and translated in Janick Auberger, *Ctésias: Histoires de l'orient* (Paris 1991) 103–32. Auberger also provides the images—or a bestiaire—of the beasts described by Ctesias on the two pages following xviii–xix.

from "the continent opposite ours."[84] Herodotus, Ctesias, and Iambulus are indeed critical foundations, or at least inspirations, for his *True History*. But there is still a broader conceptual framework in which Lucian is composing, especially when Lucian reaches the Moon and the Island of the Blest.

3.3.1. The Moon

The Moon, Lucian's first stop, is a fantastic place, especially against the backdrop of its war with the Sun. The combatants are strange hybrids, whose names are mostly *hapax legomena*: horse-vultures, cabbage-wings, mushroom-stalkers, horse-ants, flea-archers, to name a few. Travelling to a fantastic place filled with unbelievable creatures certainly has its origin in the journey of Odysseus in Homer's *Odyssey*, where the hero of Greek epic too encounters fantastic creatures such as witches and monsters (Calypso, the Sirens, Scylla, Charybdis, the Cyclops). But Lucian always has direct sources in mind, the ones we are supposed to recognize. For the episode of the Moon, what might those sources be?

The Moon, as ní Mheallaigh and Georgiadou and Larmour note, has a distinct tradition as an alternate world in Greek philosophical thought going back to Anaxagoras in the fifth century BCE.[85] The Pythagoreans particularly constructed a Moon that was similar to Earth but populated with fantastic beings and plant life; it was, in fact, a mirror-like body. At one point, the Moon is even referred to as a counter-earth (ἀντίχθων). This tradition is taken up by Plutarch and thus still had currency in the second century. The tradition of the Moon as an "other" or even inverse world already had a long foundation by Lucian's time; that Lucian had access to works now lost in this context is quite possible. Moreover, writing or reporting on a strange or "opposite" world is, of course, by no means unfamiliar to Greek writing. Although we need only think of Herodotus on Egypt, there is also the tradition of paradoxography that should be kept in mind, writers on the abnormal and marvelous. While early evidence exists from the Hellenistic period, such as works by Antigonus of Carystus, in the second

[84] D.S. 2.55.2–6 (Clay and Purvis (1999) 115–17) and *VH* 1.15–17; Diod. 2.61.3 (Clay and Purvis (1999) 114) and *VH* 2.47. The continent "opposite ours" might be inspired by Theopompus' continent beyond both the Ocean and the Mediterranean, *FGrHist* 115 F 75C (from Ael. *VH* 3.18; Clay and Purvis (1999) 174–5). Rhadamanthus prophesies Lucian's destination to the "other continent" on his way home at *VH* 2.27.

[85] ní Mheallaigh (2014) 216–18; and Georgiadou and Larmour (1998) 82–3.

century paradoxography was very much alive in Lucian's contemporary Phlegon of Tralles, whose writing on the weird and marvelous rivals what we see in the *True History*. Phelgon's *Book of Marvels*, for example, documents monsters, talking heads, and giants. In terms of parody and playful borrowing, by the second century there was plenty of material on which Lucian could draw. While the presence of hybrid and fantastic creatures in Ctesias' *Indica* and Iambulus seem to be Lucian's primary parodic playground, some—though there is skepticism—have also noted that Antonius Diogenes also composed an episode on the Moon in the *Wonders beyond Thule*, which may or may not have influenced Lucian.[86] But, like Ctesias, Antonius is also not well preserved. We rely on fragments and another summary by Photius. In the absence of substantial evidence upon which to make solid textual connections, it is therefore difficult to assess the depth of Lucian's play. Interpretation is thus open-ended when contemplating Lucian's hybrids and the world of his Moon. All we have is this fantastic place and the strange creatures that inhabit the *True History*, which Lucian describes with the ethnographic attention of Herodotus and with a zeal for detail reminiscent of Aristotle's naturalistic writing.

Be that as it may, in this celestial war there is one grand allusion or reference that seems clear and makes sense. As we see in Fusillo and the exhaustive compilation of allusions in the commentaries of Georgiadou and Larmour and Möllendorff, in the amplified, hyperbolic, and estranged creatures we can see a very familiar topic in Lucian's world: philosophers and philosophy.[87] Philosophers are everywhere in Lucian's corpus, and they are usually the butt of the joke. This is not surprising because the second century was inundated with philosophy. Cynicism was fashionable. There was a revival of Platonism. Epictetus' brand of Stoicism was even more applied than theoretical; it was concerned with everyday life. With this kind of everyday philosophy we particularly see the search for applied wisdom, i.e. the search to learn what is the best kind of life. Depending on the philosophic sect the answer may not only vary, but the variety of responses taken together, unfortunately, reveals nothing but contradiction; exposing contradictions and pretension (ἀλαζονεία), like his predecessors in Old Comedy, is a great part of Lucian's wicked humour. To make matters worse, with so many competing philosophic positions in general, a zero-sum game seems ridiculous, if not null and void. Regardless, competition amongst

[86] See also Nesselrath (1993).

[87] Georgiadou and Larmour (1998); Fusillo (1999); Möllendorff (2000).

the philosophical schools was fierce. As a result philosophers as combatants is not an uncommon image; it even appears in Lucian's *Symposium*. And so, in the episode on the Moon, as Fusillo observes, Lucian seems, on one level at least, to have created a mock-intellectual war of philosophy in the vein of the mock-epic *Batrachomyomachia*.[88] Many of these creatures, these *hapax legomena*, are linked to philosophy, or at least the caricatures of philosophy going back to Aristophanes. In this competition, this ἀγών, when everything is a contradiction, and thus nonsense, it should not be surprising that the combatants and their weapons are also nonsense.

The journey to the Moon in the *True History* is not the only one in Lucian's corpus. Menippus in the *Ikaromenippus* also briefly talks with Selene on his way to find the gods. So, with this celestial war, the wondrous and bizarre creatures, and Lucian's ability to venture into space, the notion of utopian and even modern science fiction has been raised in the context of the *True History*. Nesselrath has particularly noted that the deformation and transformation implicit in parody can also be linked to the general framework of ancient utopias.[89] Plato's Ur and Atlantis, for example, are beyond the known geographic world and constitute a transformed and refracted model of the known, a model that thus engages contemporary society. On Lucian's Moon, his parallel Earth, ní Mheallaigh observes that the lunar beings are very human-like in their predilection for war, imperialism, and social class; yet the Moonmen are also more pristine than humans, since they neither urinate nor defecate.[90] Furthermore, this Moon society is made up of only men, who give birth via the calf of the leg; Lucian is clearly having fun with the idea of phallocentric monogenesis, an idea which is very old, as Uranus in Hesiod conveys, who sidesteps the female role in reproduction entirely by using the blood and semen from his severed testicles to create Aphrodite. The real world thus cannot be divorced from Lucian's celestial society. Parody in some form or another is usually applied in attempting to elucidate Lucian's world and creatures. As we have already noted, at least in the context of second-century philosophy and philosophers, Lucian's Moon is a possible deformed and comically hyperbolic version of his contemporary world. Since Lucian engages Iambulus' world of the *Island of the Sun*, which is considered a part of ancient utopian fiction, Lucian's Moon is likely intertwined with ancient utopian writing. Again, the Moon is a mirror reflection of the Earth. ní Mheallaigh interestingly takes this idea even further. If the

[88] Fusillo (1999) 367.

[89] Nesselrath (1993).

[90] ní Mheallaigh (2014) 219–20.

Moon is a mirror reflection of the Earth and thus a kind of copy, then Lucian's Moon and all its life forms exist on a mimetic level as well.[91] Thus, for ní Mheallaigh, there is also a self-reflexive engagement with the ideas of original and copy, the real and the fictional, reality and false reality, and for Lucian's second-century reality the classical and the postclassical. ní Mheallaigh reminds us of the metaleptic nature of Lucian's work, in which the reader goes back and forth across the boundary between the real world and the world in the book.[92] In ní Mheallaigh's focus on fiction and fakes, we, as readers, come face to face with the disconcerting concept of a reality that is not exactly true and simultaneously not exactly false. Finally, as Georgiadou and Larmour note in their commentary, this strategy of deformation and defamiliarization of the known world via fantastic or technological proxies is also a part of the genre of science fiction. Although the Moon and aerial journeys, such as the flight of Daedalus and the hilarious trip of Trygaeus to the home of the gods in Aristophanes' *Peace*, have a long-standing place in ancient philosophy, myth, and comedy, the *True History* indeed shares literary attributes with authors like H. G. Wells, Ursula K. LeGuin, and especially works like Jules Verne's *Journey to the Centre of the Earth*.[93] This should not be surprising, however, since the *True History* and the kinds of ancient literature it draws on are the likely influencers in the early development of modern fantasy and science fiction. As interesting as science fiction is as a hermeneutic approach to reading the *True History*, we should also keep ancient readers in mind, whose cognitive reference for reading this kind of work is likely grounded in poetic performance, mythography, paradoxography, and comedy.

After Herodotus and Ctesias, Odysseus comes third and last to be named as a liar, but for Lucian he truly comes first. He is the originator and teacher of this kind of twaddle in the tall tales of his voyages that he recounts to Alcinous on the island of Scheria (*Odyssey* 9–12). This passage was so notorious in antiquity that it came to be known as the Ἀλκίνου ἀπόλογος—"the tale told to Alcinous." Plato was the first to describe it by this strange title as Socrates introduces the myth of Er that concludes the *Republic* (10 614B).[94] If Lucian protests the fabulous tales Odysseus tells to the Phaeacians on Scheria, he protests too much: "the originator and teacher of such tall

[91] ní Mheallaigh (2014) 221.

[92] ní Mheallaigh (2014) 221–6.

[93] Georgiadou and Larmour (1998) 44–8; see also Keen (2014) and (2015); Martín Rodríguez (2014); and Viglas (2016).

[94] For the history of the phrase, see J. Adam's commentary ad loc. (1965).

tales (βωμολοχία) is Homer's Odysseus who related in the court of Alcinous the slavery of the winds, human beings with only a single eye, who eat meat raw and are cannibals, beasts of many heads, and the transformations of his comrades under the influence of malefic potions" (*VH* 1.3). Lucian does not describe the slavery of the winds or a Cyclops, but he does encounter on the Moon creatures that can remove and exchange their eyes (*VH* 1.25), just as his Menippus can replace one of his eyes with the eye of an eagle in the *Icaromenippus* (14). Homer and the *Odyssey* are indeed important in the *True History*. Lucian encounters on the Moon the horse-vultures with only three heads—half those of Odysseus' Scylla (*VH* 1.11; *Od.* 12.90–1). His escape from the belly of the whale is unmistakably his version of Odysseus' escape from the cave of the Cyclops (*VH* 2.1; *Od.* 9.303–5). On his visit to Calypso's island he discovers it is just as Homer described it (*VH* 2.36). And although his companions are not transformed by a Circe, in the final episode, on his visit to the island Kobalousa, the hospitable women who greet his companions are clearly a melding of Homer's Circe (*VH* 2.46; *Od.* 10.210–547) and the Sirens, whose coast is covered with the rotting bodies of the men their song had attracted (*VH* 2.46 and *Od.* 12.37–54 and 165–200). Lucian exercises Odyssean caution with these women, who are revealed to have ass shanks instead of feminine feet. He carries a stalk of mallow, the equivalent of Odysseus' μῶλυ on Circe's island—something Rhadamanthus had the foresight to provide him with as he was leaving the Island of the Blest (*VH* 2.28 and 46; *Od.* 10.301–6). Odysseus and his journey—that is, his tall tales—are indeed a very important foundation for Lucian's *True History*.

3.3.2. The Island of the Blest

The importance of Homer in imperial Greek culture cannot be overstated. Homer stands at the core of ancient education. Knowing the *Iliad* and the *Odyssey*, having the ability to recite or quote Homer, instantly conveys that one is a part of the educated class, even perhaps a part of the elite. Of course, the inculcation of Homer as the definitive figure of Greek culture reaches far back into the archaic and classical periods, but it is in the Hellenistic period that scholars at Alexandria and Pergamum created a buzzing hive of activity, documented in papyrus commentaries and medieval scholia, over the establishment of Homer's text and the investigation of its meaning. The *Iliad* and the *Odyssey* not simply became the two monumental epics that all Greeks regarded as the fountainhead of their literature and culture, but Homer became the basis for Greek cultural identity. Homer even became the source of all knowledge, knowledge beyond the arts such as science and technology.

For any author, engaging Homer, whether that constitutes quotation, paraphrase, or some kind of parodic transformation, is significant and the act should be subject to examination. In the *True History* the *Odyssey* is the general blueprint that Lucian uses to frame his narrative and Odysseus is his example of the liar *par excellence*. The Island of the Blest particularly draws parallels and allusions to Homer's Scheria, Elysian Fields, and Odysseus' journey to the underworld; though Iambulus' *Island of the Sun* and even, according to Möllendorf, Jerusalem in the *Apocalypse of John* are present.[95] But Homer and the *Odyssey* are nowhere more present than in Lucian's Island of Blest. And this presence has been the subject of insightful analysis by Zeitlin, Kim, and ní Mhealleigh.[96] The critical facts to bear in mind are: (1) Homer and the epic heroes are physically present in this never-ending symposium and Homer's songs are sung; (2) the conversation between Lucian and Homer himself; (3) the events that essentially re-enact parts of the *Iliad*, such as the funeral games; and (4) the sequels to the *Iliad*, such as the new battle between the heroes and those of the Island of the Wicked, which even inspires Homer to compose a new epic poem. As Zeitlin observes, Lucian is very much an Odyssean type in his journey to the Moon, his escape from the belly of the whale, and his overall progression back to Earth.[97] And, in the context of sequels, there is perhaps nothing more memorable than Lucian's journey to the island of Calypso, where he delivers a letter from Odysseus that explains what happened after he left; it also expresses his wish to escape his current situation and return to her! Nevertheless, although Homer's presence is everywhere and much scholarly ink has been spilled in providing elucidation, let us focus on the overall conclusions drawn by Zeitlin, Kim, and ní Mhealleigh from Lucian's face-to-face meeting with Homer and the general epic life of Homer and his heroes on the Island of the Blest.

Lucian's face-to-face chat with Homer is both revealing and funny for one consistent reason: we are utterly wrong when it comes to Homer! Where is he from? No, not Chios or Smyrna, but Babylon. And his real name is Tigranes. What about those lines of hexameters marked as spurious

[95] Möllendorf (2005). [96] Zeitlin (2001); Kim (2010); ní Mheallaigh (2014).
[97] See also the discussion at ní Mheallaigh (2014) 227–30.

in the Alexandrian recensions? Yes, he wrote them. Zenodotus and Aristarchus are wrong. What is the significance in starting the *Iliad* with the wrath of Achilles? Well, that idea just came to him. Did he write the *Odyssey* first, as most say? No. Lastly, during this interview Lucian can clearly see that Homer is not blind. Within one brief encounter, the biographical tradition, Alexandrian textual scholarship, and literary criticism are rendered useless. On one level, for Zeitlin, the point is not that we are wrong about Homer, but that there is no real answer in the first place. By Lucian's time, although Homer is the fountainhead of Greek culture, he is also continuously refashioned to suit a Mediterranean culture that is multicultural and stretches across great swathes of territory.[98] Besides Babylonian, Homer, for example, is also said to be Chaldean, Syrian, Egyptian, and even Roman. If Homer is the foundation and fountainhead of Greek culture and identity, then Zeitlin observes that Hellenic identity is not a stable but an indeterminate concept, and within it Homer is a commodity.[99] Consequently, if Homer operates as a form of cultural capital, we should always be sensitive to whether we are dealing with identity or identification with. In culture wars, "identity" and "to identify with" are not necessarily the same thing. On another level, for Kim, Lucian's joke is grounded in the reality of Homer's reuse and refashioning over time. If Homer is what we want or need him to be at a given moment, again a commodity, then this kind of questioning and investigation is pointless.[100] Although meeting Homer is an ideal moment to settle Homeric controversies and thus further cement his credibility and cultural authority, Lucian's face-to-face meeting, as ní Mheallaigh observes, produces only another version of Homer, one that in the larger context of the *True History* is possibly just another lie or fiction.[101] Homer, like Lucian's many personae, might just be another costume.

With the presence of Homer's epic heroes, the funeral games, the theft of Helen redux, and other events, the *Iliad* is alive and well on the Island of the Blest. In combination with all the other famous individuals of the past, Branham aptly describes the scene as "the disconcerting babel of incompatible traditions that marks the postclassical from of Hellenic culture in the empire."[102] ní Mhealleigh rightfully supplements Branham by describing the scene as a kind of collection or encyclopedia or miscellany, in which imperial culture was so interested.[103] In this context, Kim makes an interesting

[98] Zeitlin (2001) 211–66. [99] Zeitlin (2001) 263–6. [100] Kim (2010) 162–8.
[101] ní Mhealleigh (2014) 237–40. [102] Branham (1989) 82.
[103] ní Mhealleigh (2014) 240–50.

observation regarding Homer and his epic characters. Unlike most of Lucian's typical characters, which are in some fashion hyperbolic and comic and convey incongruity, the Homeric characters on the Island of the Blest are essentially the same characters from the Homeric epics.[104] Moreover, they are still up to their same old tricks. As noted, for example, Helen is abducted and must be returned to Menelaus, and even Thersites seeks vindication by suing Homer for the treatment he received at the hands of Odysseus in that now famous episode (*Il.* 2.212–335). Kim ingeniously observes that, even with these re-enactments and new events, the status quo of Homer's narrative prevails. You can remove these characters from the shores of Troy and even make them fight new battles, but Achilles still thinks and operates like Achilles. Helen is still Helen—as constructed by men. There is thus no room for evolution or character development. According to Kim, this is a "closed literary world."[105] After all, Lucian's world is built on Greek paideia and the classical models of the fifth and fourth centuries constitute inert examples that are hundreds of years old. Meeting Homer and his characters is no different than reading the *Iliad*.[106] ní Mhealleigh takes this analysis even further, suggesting that not only are the Homeric characters indeed stuck in time, but also the status quo of epic is further intensified by attempts to escape Homeric narratives.[107] Odysseus' letter to Calypso, Thersites' legal action against Homer, and Helen's attempt to escape with her lover Cinyras constitute attempts to break the status quo at the level of writing and authorship.[108] Nevertheless, all end in failure. Worse still, although Homer even composes a new epic—which Lucian subsequently loses—the surviving first line is just a parodic transformation of the opening lines of both the *Iliad* and *Odyssey*.[109] By simply rewriting himself rather than truly composing something new, ní Mheallaigh suggests that not even Homer can escape himself. In this ideal literary compendium, ní Mheallaigh again reminds us that competitive interplay between mimetic and original, between fiction and reality, continues to be intertwined in Lucian's world. In the end, this is very anticlimactic, very comically disappointing. To go back to the source and only assume its personae, as is typical in rhetorical exercises (προγυμνάσματα) of the second century CE, is ultimately an inert moment of creation. For Kim, Lucian's comic premise is that Homer's legacy is simply his ability to tell a story. And this is certainly more myth (μῦθος) than history (ἱστορία).

[104] Kim (2010) 161. [105] Kim (2010) 170. [106] Kim (2010) 162–8.
[107] ní Mhealleigh (2014) 242–5. [108] ní Mhealleigh (2014) 242.
[109] ní Mhealleigh (2014) 243.

_ that is what we should take away from this model: story-telling. ., to end on ní Mhealleigh's overall point, one should perhaps make the story (model) even better (copy).

If Lucian has an overarching model for the travels described in the *True History* it is fundamentally the *Odyssey*. And although scholarly interpretation of his *mimesis* and especially his use of Homer conveys the depth of his writing, we must remember that we are still supposed to relax when we read his story. A great part of Lucian's travels is inspired by the daring of his own imagination, even if the general context of some of his episodes clearly have precedent elsewhere: the voyage up to the Moon (*VH* 1.9–29), the arrival at Lychnopolis (*VH* 1.29); the long stay in the belly of the whale (*VH* 1.30–2.2); the sea of ice and the cave Lucian and his crew excavate in it (*VH* 2.2); the sailors with feet of cork (2.4); Lucian's Island of the Blest (*VH* 2.5–29) and Islands of the Impious—only one of which is described (*VH* 2.29–32). The reader wearied by the study of "classical" texts can turn to Lucian for relaxation and encounter the nut navigators (*VH* 2.37–8); the pirates riding dolphins (*VH* 2.39); the actual landing on a halcyon nest (*VH* 2.40); the forest of tall trees growing out of the sea (*VH* 2.42–3); the bridge over the great cavern in the sea (*VH* 2.43); the carnivorous bullheads that devour three of Lucian's companions (*VH* 2.44–5); and, finally, the phallus navigators (*VH* 2.45). Lucian at play—his imagination, parody, and lies—is funny, refreshing, and discombobulating.

Reader's Guide

(1) Abbreviations, etc.

ADLER	A. Adler, *Suidae Lexicon*, Stuttgart 1989–94.
ALLEN	T. W. Allen, *Homeri Opera*, I–V, Oxford 1946 (^{1}1908).
BERGER	H. Berger, *Die geographischen Fragmente des Eratosthenes: neu gesammelt, geordnet und besprochen*, Leipzig 1880.
BERNHARDY	*Geographi Graeci Minores*, I, Leipzig 1828.
BNJ	I. Worthington (ed.), *Brill's New Jacoby*, Leiden and Boston 2006 (www.brillonline.com).
CCAG	F. Cumont and F. Boll, *Catalogus Codicum Astrologorum Graecorum*, Brussels 1898–1953.
DES PLACES	E. Des Places, *Atticus: Fragments*, Paris 1977.
DK	H. Diels and W. Kranz, *Die Fragmente der Vorsokratiker*, Zürich and Berlin ^{6}1952.
ERBSE	*Scholia Graeca in Homeri Iliadem (scholia vetera) Recensuit Hartmut Erbse*, I–VII, Berlin 1969–.
FGrHist	F. Jacoby, *Die Fragmente der Griechischen Historiker*, I–XV, Berlin; later: Leiden 1923–58.
	G. Schepens (ed.), later: S. Schorn (ed.), *Die Fragmente der Griechischen Historiker Continued.* Part IV. *Biography and Antiquarian Literature*, Leiden and Boston 1998–.
	H.-J. Gehrke and F. Maier (eds.), *Die Fragmente der Griechischen Historiker Continued.* Part V. *Die Geographen*, Leiden and Boston 2011 (www.brillonline.com).
GIGON	O. Gigon, *Aristotelis Opera (ex recensione I. Bekkeri, ed. 2)*, III: *Librorum Deperditorum Fragmenta*, Berlin and New York 1987.
GL	A. Georgiadou and D. H. J. Lamour, *Lucian's Science Fiction Novel True Histories*, Leiden, Boston, and Cologne 1998.
Goodwin	W. W. Goodwin, *Syntax of the Moods and Tenses of the Greek Verb*, New York 1965.

Gow-Page	A. S. F. Gow and D. L. Page, *The Greek Anthology. Hellenistic Epigrams*, I–II, Cambridge 1965. A. S. F. Gow and D. L. Page, *The Greek Anthology. The Garland of Philip and Some Contemporary Epigrams*, I–II, Cambridge 1968.
GP	J. D. Denniston, *The Greek Particles*, Oxford ^{2}1954.
Greene	W. C. Greene, *Scholia Platonica*, Haverford 1938.
Hausrath	A. Hausrath, *Corpus Fabularum Aesopicarum*, Leipzig 1956.
IG	*Inscriptiones Graecae*, Berlin 1873–.
K-A	R. Kassel and C. Austin, *Poetae Comici Graeci* (PCG), I–VIII, Berlin and New York, 1983–2001.
LIMC III	*Lexicon Iconographicum Mythologiae Classicae* III. *Atherion-Eros*, Zurich and Munich 1986.
LSJ	H. G. Liddell, R. Scott, H. S. Jones, and R. McKenzie, *A Greek- English Lexicon*, Oxford ^{10}1996.
Matthews	V. J. Matthews, *Antimachus of Colophon: Text and Commentary*, Leiden 1996.
PGR	A. Giannini, *Paradoxographorum Graecorum Reliquiae*, Milan 1966.
PMG	D. L. Page, *Poetae melici Graeci*, Oxford 1962.
PMGF	M. Davies, *Poetarum melicorum Graecorum fragmenta*. I. *Alcman- Stesichorus-Ibycus*. Post D. L. Page edidit M. D., Oxford 1991.
Poltera	O. Poltera, *Simonides lyricus. Testimonia und Fragmente. Einleitung, kritische Ausgabe, Übersetzung und Kommentar*. Basel 2008.
P.Oxy.	*The Oxyrhynchus Papri.*
Rabe	H. Rabe, *Scholia in Lucianum*, Leipzig 1906.
Rose	V. Rose, *Aritotelis Qui Ferebantur Librorum Fragmenta*, Leipzig ^{3}1886.
Smyth	H. W. Smyth, *Greek Grammar*, revised by Gordon Messing, Cambridge, MA 1956.
SSR	G. Giannantoni, *Socratis et Socraticorum reliquiae*, I–IV, Naples 1990.
SVF	H. von Arnim, *Stoicorum veterum fragmenta*, I–IV, Leipzig 1903–14.
TrGF	*Tragicorum Graecorum fragmenta*, Göttingen. I. B. Snell and R. Kannicht, *Didascaliae tragicae, catalogi tragicorum*

	et tragoediarum, testimonia et fragmenta tragicorum minorum, [2]1986.
	II. R. Kannnicht—B. Snell, *Fragmenta adespota, testimonia volumini 1 addenda, indices ad volumina 1 et 2*, 1981.
	III. S. Radt, *Aeschylus*, 1985.
	IV. S. Radt, *Sophocles*, [2]1999.
	V. R. Kannicht, *Euripides*, I–II, 2004.
VOIGT	E.-M. Voight, *Sappho et Alcaeus. Fragmenta*, Amsterdam 1971.
WEST[2]	M. L. West, *Iambi et elegi Graeci ante Alexandrum cantati*, I–II, Oxford [2]1989–92.

(2) Greek Measurements

Greek units of measurement are provided in transliteration. For convenience we list them here for reference, noting that one unit of measure (πῆχυς) is not quite exactly consistent for modern readers of this commentary, of whom many are likely to have longer arms than the ancient Greeks.

ὀργυιά	*c.*6 feet
πῆχυς	a cubit, *c.*18 inches (i.e. the measure between the elbow and wrist; a royal "cubit" is longer than the regular cubit by three "fingers")
πλέθρον	*c.*100 feet
στάδιον	*c.*600 feet

(3) Select Bibliography

Abdel Wahab, F. (1988), *Drama as Metaphor: Varieties of Theatrical Experience* (Egypt).

Adam, J. (1965, [1]1899), *The Republic of Plato* (Cambridge).

Anderson, G. (1976), *Lucian's Comic Fiction* (Leiden).

Auerbach, E. (1953), *Mimesis: The Representation of Reality in Western Literature*, trans. Willard R. Trask (Princeton).

Bär, S. F. (2013), "Odysseus' Letter to Calypso in Lucian's *Verae Historiae*," in O. Hodkinson, P. A. Rosenmeyer, and E. Bracke (eds.), *Epistolary Narratives in Ancient Greek Literature* (Leiden and Boston), 221–36.

Beck, R. (2007), *A Brief History of Ancient Astrology* (Oxford).

Betz, H. D. (1961), "Lukian von Samosata und das Neue Testament," in *Relgionsgeschichtliche und Paranetische Parallelen Texte und Untersuchungen der altchristlichen Literatur*, vol. 76 (Berlin).

Bickerman, E. J. (1968), *Chronology of the Ancient World* (Ithaca, NY).

von Blanckenhagen, P. H. (1992), "Stage and Actors in Plato's *Symposium*," *Greek, Roman, and Byzantine Studies* 33: 51–68.

Bompaire, J. (1958), *Lucien Écrivain: Imitation et Création* (Paris).

Bowersock, G. W. (1969), *Greek Sophists in the Roman Empire* (Oxford).

Branham, R. B. (1985), "Utopian Laughter: Lucian and Thomas More," *Moreana* 86: 23–43.

Branham, R. B. (1989), *Unruly Eloquence: Lucian and the Comedy of Traditions* (Cambridge, MA).

Branham, R. B., and Marie-Odile Goulet-Cazé (eds.) (1991), *The Cynics: The Cynic Movement and its Legacy* (Berkeley, Los Angeles, and New York).

Bulloch, A. W. (1985), *Callimachus, The Fifth Hymn: Edited with Introduction and Commentary* (Cambridge).

Camerotto, A. (1998), *Le metamorfosi della parola: studi sulla parodia in Luciano di Samosata* (Pisa).

Camerotto, A. (2014), *Gli occhi e la lingua della satira: studi sull'eroe satirico in Luciano di Samosata* (Milan).

Casson, L. (1971), *Ships and Seamanship in the Ancient World* (Princeton).

Caster, M. (1937), *Lucien et la pensée religeuse de son tempe* (Paris).

Clay, D. (1992), "Lucian of Samosata: Four Philosophical Lives (Nigrinus, Demonax, Peregrinus, Alexander Pseudomantis)," *ANRW* 36.5: 3406–50.

Clay, D. (2004), *Archilochos Heros: The Cult of Heroes in the Greek States* (Cambridge, MA).

Clay, D., and A. L. Purvis (1999), *Four Island Utopias, Being Plato's Atlantis, Euhemeros of Messene's Panchaia, Iamboulos' Islands of the Sun, and Sir Francis Bacon's New Atlantis* (Newburyport, MA).

Deriu, M. (2017), "How to Imagine a World without Women: Hyperreality in Lucian's *True Histories*," *Medea* 3.1: 1–22.

Dover, K. J. (1968), *Aristophanes Clouds: Edited with Introduction and Commentary*, repr. Oxford University Press (Oxford 1989).

Dubel, S. (1994), "Dialogue et autoportrait: les masques de Lucien," in A. Billault (ed.), *Lucien de Samosate. Actes du colloque international de Lyon organisé au Centre d'Études Romaines et Gallo-Romaines les 30 septembre–1er octobre 1993, Lyon* (Paris), 19–26.

Fauth, W. (1979), "Utopische Inseln in den *Wahren Geschichten* des Lukian," *Gymnasium* 86: 39–58.

Feeney, D. C. (1993), "Epilogue: Towards an Account of the Ancient World's Concept of Fictive Belief," in C. Gill and T. P. Wiseman (eds.), *Lies and Fiction in the Ancient World* (Exeter), 230–44.

Fowler, H. W., and F. G. Fowler ([2]1949), *The Works of Lucian of Samosata* (Oxford).

Fusillo, M. (1999), "The Mirror of the Moon: Lucian's *A True Story*—From Satire to Utopia," in S. Swain (ed.), *Oxford Readings in the Greek Novel* (Oxford), 351–81.

Georgiadou, A., and D. H. J. Larmour (1995), "The *prolaliae* to Lucian's *Verae Historiae*," *Eranos* 93: 100–12.

Georgiadou, A., and D. H. J. Larmour (1997), "Lucian's Vine-Women (*VH* 1, 6–9) and Dio's Libyan Women (*Orat.* 5): Variations on a Theme," *Mnemosyne* 50: 205–9.

Gera, D. L. (1995), "Lucian's Choice: *Somnium* 6–16," in D. Innes, H. Hine, and C. Pelling (eds.), *Ethics and Rhetoric: Classical Essays for Donald Russell on his Seventy-Fifth Birthday* (Oxford), 237–50.

Gill, C., and P. Wiseman (1993), *Lies and Fiction in the Ancient World* (Exeter).

Goldhill, S. (2001), "The Erotic Eye: Visual Stimulation and Cultural Conflict," in S. Goldhill (ed.), *Being Greek under Rome: Cultural Identity, the Second Sophistic and the Development of Empire* (Cambridge), 184–93.

Goldhill, S. (2002), *Who Needs Greek? Contests in the Cultural History of Hellenism* (Cambridge).

Grand-Clément, A. (2015), "Poikilia," in P. Destrée and P. Murray (eds.), *A Companion to Ancient Aesthetics* (Oxford), 406–21.

Graziosi, B. (2002), *Inventing Homer: The Early Reception of Epic* (Cambridge).

Habicht, C. (1988), *Pausanias' Guide to Ancient Greece* (Berkeley, Los Angeles, and London).

Hansen, W. F. (2002), *Ariadne's Thread: A Guide to International Tales Found in Classical Literature* (Ithaca, NY).

Hansen, W. F. (2003), "Strategies of Authentication in Ancient Popular Literature," in S. Panayotakis, M. Zimmerman, and W. Keulen (eds.), *The Ancient Novel and Beyond* (Leiden and Boston), 301–13.

Harmon, A. M. (1913), *Lucian, of Samosata* (Cambridge, MA).

Haslam, M. W. (1972), *Plato, Sophron, and the Dramatic Dialogue*, in *BICS* 19: 17–38.

Helm, R. (1906), *Lucian und Menipp* (Leipzig).

Helm, R. (1927), art. *Lukianos*, in *RE* XIII.2: 1725–8.

Householder, F. W. (1941), *Literary Quotation and Allusion in Lucian* (New York).

Humble, N., and K. Sidwell (2006), "Dreams of Glory: Lucian as Autobiographer," in B. McGing and J. Mossman (eds.), *The Limits of Ancient Biography* (Swansea), 213–25.

Hunter, R. (2012), *Plato and the Traditions of Ancient Literature* (Cambridge).

Jerram, C. S. (1879), *Luciani Vera Historia*, repr. Bolchazy-Carducci (Chicago 1990).

Jones, C. P. (1986), *Culture and Society in Lucian* (Cambridge, MA).

Keen, T. (2014), "*Fantastika* and the Greek and Roman Worlds," *Foundation* 118: 5–8.

Kidd, S. E. (2017), "Play in and around the Ancient Novel," *American Journal of Play* 9.3: 356–73.

Kim, L. (2010). *Homer between History and Fiction in Imperial Greek Literature* (Cambridge).

Laird, A. (2003), "Fiction as a Discourse of Philosophy in Lucian's *Verae Historiae*," in S. Panayotakis, M. Zimmerman, and W. Keulen (eds.), *The Ancient Novel and Beyond* (Leiden and Boston), 115–27.

Larmour, D. H. J. (1997). "Sex with Moonmen and Vinewomen: The Reader as Explorer in Lucian's *Vera Historia*," *Intertexts* 1.2: 131–46.

Lefkowitz, M. R. (^{2}2012), *The Lives of the Greek Poets* (Baltimore).

Lightfoot, J. (2003). *Lucian, On the Syrian Goddess* (Oxford).

Lye, S. C. (2016), *The Hypertextual Underworld: Exploring the Underworld as an Intertextual Space in Ancient Greek Literature*, Diss. Los Angeles.

Rodríguez, M. M. (2014), "From Stapledon's Star Maker to Cicero's Dream of Scipio: The Visionary Cosmic Voyage as a Speculative Genre," *Foundation* 118: 45–58.

ní Mheallaigh, K. (2008), "Pseudo-Documentarism and the Limits of Ancient Fiction," *AJP* 129.3: 403–31.

ní Mheallaigh, K. (2009), "Monumental Fallacy: The Teleology of Origins in Lucian's *Verae Historiae*," in A. Bartley (ed.), *A Lucian for our Times* (Newcastle upon Tyne), 11–28.

ní Mheallaigh, K. (2010), "The Game of the Name: Onymity and the Contract of Reading in Lucian," in F. Mestre and P. Gomez (eds.), *Lucian of Samosata: Greek Writer and Roman Citizen* (Barcelona), 121–32.

ní Mheallaigh, K. (2014), *Reading Fiction with Lucian: Fakes, Freaks and Hyperreality* (Cambridge).

von Möllendorf, P. (2000), *Auf der Suche nach Lukians Wahre Geschichten: Lukians Wahre Geschichten* (Tübingen).

von Möllendorf, P. (2005), "Christliche Apokalypsen und ihr mimetisches Potential in der paganen Bildungdkultur: ein Beitrag zu Lukians *Wahren Geschichten*," in S. Alkier and R. B. Hays (eds.), *Die Bibel im Dialog der Schriften* (Tübingen and Basel), 179–94.

Morgan, J. R. (1985), "Lucian's *True Histories* and the *Wonders beyond Thule* of Antonius Diogenes," *CQ* 35: 475–90.

Morrison, J. S., and R. T. Williams (1968), *Greek Oared Ships* (Cambridge).

Nesselrath, H.-G. (1990), "Lucian's Introductions," in D. A. Russell (ed.), *Antonine Literature* (Oxford), 111–40.

Nesselrath, H.-G. (1993), "Utopie-Parodie in Lukians *Wahren Geschichten*," in W. Ax and R. F. Glei (eds.), *Literaturparodie in Antike und Mittelalter* (Trier), 41–56.

Nesselrath, H.-G. (2002), "Homerphilologie auf der Insel der Seligen: Lukian, *VH* II 20," in M. Reichel and A. Rengakos (eds.), *Epea Pteroenta: Beiträge zur Homerforschung. Festschrift für Wolfgang Kullmann zum 75. Geburtstag* (Stuttgart), 151–62.

Nesselrath, H.-G. (2014), "Language and (in-)Authenticity: The Case of the (ps.-)Lucianic *Onos*," in J. Martínez (ed.), *Fakes and Forgers of Classical Literature: Ergo decipiatur!* (Leiden), 195–205.

Pelling, C. B. R. (ed.) (1988), *Plutarch: Life of Anthony* (Cambridge).

Relihan, J. C. (1993), *Ancient Menippean Satire* (Baltimore).

Romm, J. S. (1990), "Wax, Stone, and Promethean Clay: Lucian as Plastic Artist," *Classical Antiquity* 9: 74–98.

Romm, J. S. (1992), *The Edges of the Earth in Ancient Thought* (Princeton).

Russell, D. A. (1991), *Anthology of Greek Prose* (Oxford).

Sabnis, S. (2011), "Lucian's Lychnopolis and the Problems of Slave Surveillance," *The American Journal of Philology* 132.2: 205–42.

Savidis, G. (ed.) and E. Keeley and P. Sherrard (trans.) (1993), *C.P. Cavafy Collected Poems Revised Edition* (Princeton).

Schironi, F. (2018), *The Best of the Grammarians: Aristarchus of Samothrace on the Iliad* (Ann Arbor).

Stephens, S. A., and J. J. Winkler (1995), *Ancient Greek Novels: The Fragments* (Princeton).

Strohmaier, G. (1976), "Übersehenes zur Biographie Lukians," *Philologus* 120: 117–22.

Swain, S. (1996), *Hellenism and Empire: Language, Power, and Classicism in the Greek World, AD 50–250* (Oxford).

Tackaberry, W. H. (1930), *Lucian's Relation to Plato and the Post-Aristotelian Philosophers* (Toronto).

Tsetskhladze, T. R. (2006), "Revisting Ancient Greek Colonisation," in T. R. Tsetskhladze (ed.), *Greek Colonisation: An Account of Greek Colonies and Other Settlements Overseas* (Leiden), xxiii–lxxxiii.

Turner, P. (1958), *True History, and Lucius, or the Ass* (Bloomington, IN).

West, M. L. (1966), *Theogony: Edited with Prolegomena and Commentary* (Oxford).

Whitmarsh, T. (2001), *Greek Literature and the Roman Empire* (Oxford).

Whitmarsh, T. (2006), "True Histories: Lucian, Bakhtin, and the Pragmatics of Reception," in C. Martindale and R. F. Thomas (eds.), *Classics and the Uses of Reception* (Oxford), 104–15.

Whitmarsh, T. (2010), "The Metamorphoses of the *Ass*," in F. Mestre and P. Gómez (eds.), *Lucian of Samosata, Greek Writer and Roman Citizen* (Barcelona), 73–81.

Whitmarsh, T. (2011), *Narrative and Identity in the Ancient Greek Novel: Returning Romance* (Cambridge).

Wilson, N. G. (1983), *Scholars of Byzantium* (London).

Winkler, J. J. (1985), *Auctor and Actor: A Narratological Reading of Apuleius's The Golden Ass* (Berkeley, Los Angeles, and London).

Zeitlin, F. I. (2001), "Visions and Revisions of Homer," in S. Goldhill (ed.), *Being Greek under Rome: Cultural Identity, the Second Sophistic, and the Development of Empire* (Cambridge and New York), 195–266.

Viglas, K. (2016), "The Placement of Lucian's Novel *True History* in the Genre of Science Fiction," *Interlitteraria* 21.1: 158–71.

A Note on the Text

The Greek text of Lucian's *True History* presented here is that of M. D. Macleod in the *Oxford Classical Texts* series (Oxford 1972, vol. 1, *libelli* 13–14). In the introduction, or *praefatio*, Macleod gives an account of the two classes of manuscripts on which he bases his edition of the eighty-six writings published in his four volumes, the so-called γ and β archetypes. He also gives an account of the limited evidence, the indirect tradition, for Lucian and his writings: Lucian is known to the unfriendly Christian apologist Lactantius, the ascetic of the Egyptian desert Isidorus of Pelusium, and maybe even to the emperor Julian; Eunapius of Sardis mentions him in his *Lives of the Sophists* in the fourth century and speaks of Lucian as an author "serious only in provoking laughter" (*VS* 454); he is known to the epistolographer Aristaenetus of the fifth or sixth century; fifteen works of "the Syrian" were paraphrased in Syriac in the sixth century; Photius, twice Patriarch of Constantinople, mentions him as the author of *True Histories* and *The Ass of Lucius of Patras* in his invaluable *Bibliotheca* or *Myriobiblos*. As for Lucian's manuscript tradition, a small number of bishops have played an important role: Basil, Bishop of Pisidia in the ninth century, wrote scholia on Lucian; Arethas, who became Bishop of Caesarea in Cappadocia in the tenth century, also made marginal comments on the manuscripts of Lucian; Alexander, Bishop of Nicaea in Bithynia, corrected the text of Vaticanus Γ in the tenth century, "with the help of my beloved brother, Jacob, Metropolitan of Larissa" (so the subscription reads at the end of Γ). The interest of these churchmen was Lucian's refined (Attic) Greek, to which they aspired—not his blasphemies of Christ and the pagan gods.

Macleod's edition of the *True History* is based on five manuscripts. Γ and Ω (Γ Vaticanus 90 and Ω Marcianus 840) are of the tradition deriving from γ. Z (Vaticanus 1323), N (Parisinus 2957 until *VH* 2.14), and P (Vaticanus 76) derive from β. Macleod presents his stemmata (or family tree of manuscripts) at vol. 1, xv and xvi. For a more comprehensive description of Lucian's manuscript tradition, see the Belles Lettres edition of Bompaire (1993). In producing this commentary, the manuscripts of Lucian have not been consulted. In the translation and the text, two corrections Macleod made to *VH* 1 (p. 83.12 pro οἶς *lege* οἶα and p. 101.13 *lege* λέξω) in the *corrigenda* to volumes 1–3 in volume 4 have been incorporated. In the translation, Clay has also adopted D. M. Russell's emendation of συνιζανούσης (p. 96.29).

TEXT OF *TRUE HISTORY*

with translation by Diskin Clay

ΑΛΗΘΩΝ ΔΙΗΓΗΜΑΤΩΝ Α

(1) Ὥσπερ τοῖς ἀθλητικοῖς καὶ περὶ τὴν τῶν σωμάτων ἐπιμέλειαν ἀσχολουμένοις οὐ τῆς εὐεξίας μόνον οὐδὲ τῶν γυμνασίων φροντίς ἐστιν, ἀλλὰ καὶ τῆς κατὰ καιρὸν γινομένης ἀνέσεως—μέρος γοῦν τῆς ἀσκήσεως τὸ μέγιστον αὐτὴν ὑπολαμβάνουσιν—οὕτω δὴ καὶ τοῖς περὶ τοὺς λόγους ἐσπουδακόσιν ἡγοῦμαι προσήκειν μετὰ τὴν πολλὴν τῶν σπουδαιοτέρων ἀνάγνωσιν ἀνιέναι τε τὴν διάνοιαν καὶ (2) πρὸς τὸν ἔπειτα κάματον ἀκμαιοτέραν παρασκευάζειν. γένοιτο δ᾽ ἂν ἐμμελὴς ἡ ἀνάπαυσις αὐτοῖς, εἰ τοῖς τοιούτοις τῶν ἀναγνωσμάτων ὁμιλοῖεν, ἃ μὴ μόνον ἐκ τοῦ ἀστείου τε καὶ χαρίεντος ψιλὴν παρέξει τὴν ψυχαγωγίαν, ἀλλά τινα καὶ θεωρίαν οὐκ ἄμουσον ἐπιδείξεται, οἷόν τι καὶ περὶ τῶνδε τῶν συγγραμμάτων φρονήσειν ὑπολαμβάνω· οὐ γὰρ μόνον τὸ ξένον τῆς ὑποθέσεως οὐδὲ τὸ χαρίεν τῆς προαιρέσεως ἐπαγωγὸν ἔσται αὐτοῖς οὐδ᾽ ὅτι ψεύσματα ποικίλα πιθανῶς τε καὶ ἐναλήθως ἐξενηνόχαμεν, ἀλλ᾽ ὅτι καὶ τῶν ἱστορουμένων ἕκαστον οὐκ ἀκωμῳδήτως ᾔνικται πρός τινας τῶν παλαιῶν ποιητῶν τε καὶ συγγραφέων καὶ φιλοσόφων πολλὰ τεράστια καὶ μυθώδη συγγεγραφότων, οὓς καὶ ὀνομαστὶ ἂν ἔγραφον, εἰ μὴ καὶ αὐτῷ σοι ἐκ τῆς ἀναγνώσεως φανεῖσθαι (3) ἔμελλον <ὧν> Κτησίας ὁ Κτησιόχου ὁ Κνίδιος, ὃς συνέγραψεν

Libelli 13 et 14. ΓΩ = γ; usque ad 13 c. 14 med. ZN = β, postea PZ = β; S codicem (qui alibi quidem γ classis et Ω codicis simillimus est, his tamen in libellis multas β lectiones exhibet) ubi operae pretium visum est tantum rettuli. Titulus ἀληθῶν (ἀληθινῶν Ω) διηγημάτων ᾱ γ : ἀληθοῦς ἱστορίας λόγος πρῶτος β : περὶ ἀληθοῦς ἱστορίας κτλ. recc.; cf. Phot. *Bibl.* 166 καὶ γὰρ τοῦ περὶ ἀληθῶν διηγημάτων Λουκιανοῦ κτλ. **2** ἀσχολουμένοις Γ : ἠοκημένοις Ωβ **4** δὴ Γ^{a}β : δὲ Ω **5** τοὺς om. β **6** ἀνεῖναι Γ^{a}β **8** ἀνάπαυσις Γ^{a}β : ἀνάγνωσις γ **11** αὐτοὺς ante φρονήσειν add. E. Schwartz **15** πρός τινας ᾔνικται β **17** συγγράφοντας N : συγγεγραφότας Z **18** φαίνεσθαι β **19** lacunam ante Κτησίας postulant codd. : ὧν (vel οἷον) suppl. Bekker : ἔμελλον Κτησίας γ : ἔμελλε Κτησίας N et fort. Z cf. Phot. *Bibl.* 72 fin. ὃς γ : om. β

Book 1

INTRODUCTION: LUCIAN'S APOLOGY

(1) As is true of trainers and those whose profession it is to care for the body and whose concern is not only for exercise but the relaxation that comes at the proper time—this they consider the most important part of training—it is, in my own view, appropriate for those involved in literary studies to relax their mind after the sustained reading of serious texts and to render themselves the more vigorous for the labors to follow. (2) This relaxation would prove more fitting if literary people were to engage in the kinds of writings that provide not only pure entertainment for their wit and charm but open new vistas that are poetic. In my opinion, such readers will think that such is the case of this present composition. The novelty of my argument and the charm of my project will entertain them, not only because we have brought before the public a variety of fictions in a compelling and veracious manner, but because each of the events narrated also contains a comically covert allusion to some of the ancient poets, writers, and philosophers who have written amazing and fabulous tales. I would have entered their names in this narrative, were it not the case that they would be clear to you as you read; one such author is Ctesias of Cnidus, son of Ctesiochus, (3) who wrote an account of the regions of India and of the world there, things he had never seen himself or heard of from any reliable witness. Iambulus too

περὶ τῆς Ἰνδῶν χώρας καὶ τῶν παρ᾽ αὐτοῖς ἃ μήτε αὐτὸς εἶδεν μήτε ἄλλου ἀληθεύοντος ἤκουσεν. ἔγραψε δὲ καὶ Ἰαμβοῦλος περὶ τῶν ἐν τῇ μεγάλῃ θαλάττῃ πολλὰ παράδοξα, γνώριμον μὲν ἅπασι τὸ ψεῦδος πλασάμενος, οὐκ ἀτερπῆ δὲ ὅμως συνθεὶς τὴν ὑπόθεσιν. πολλοὶ δὲ καὶ ἄλλοι τὰ αὐτὰ τούτοις προελόμενοι συνέγραψαν ὡς δή τινας ἑαυτῶν πλάνας τε καὶ ἀποδημίας, θηρίων τε μεγέθη ἱστοροῦντες καὶ ἀνθρώπων ὠμότητας καὶ βίων καινότητας· ἀρχηγὸς δὲ αὐτοῖς καὶ διδάσκαλος τῆς τοιαύτης βωμολοχίας ὁ τοῦ Ὁμήρου Ὀδυσσεύς, τοῖς περὶ τὸν Ἀλκίνουν διηγούμενος ἀνέμων τε δουλείαν καὶ μονοφθάλμους καὶ ὠμοφάγους καὶ ἀγρίους τινὰς ἀνθρώπους, ἔτι δέ πολυκέφαλα ζῷα καὶ τὰς ὑπὸ φαρμάκων τῶν ἑταίρων μεταβολάς, οἷα πολλά ἐκεῖνος πρὸς ἰδιώτας ἀνθρώπους τοὺς Φαίακας ἐτερατεύσατο. τούτοις οὖν ἐντυχὼν ἅπασιν, τοῦ (4) ψεύσασθαι μὲν οὐ σφόδρα τοὺς ἄνδρας ἐμεμψάμην, ὁρῶν ἤδη σύνηθες ὂν τοῦτο καὶ τοῖς φιλοσοφεῖν ὑπισχνουμένοις· ἐκεῖνο δὲ αὐτῶν ἐθαύμασα, εἰ ἐνόμιζον λήσειν οὐκ ἀληθῆ συγγράφοντες. διόπερ καὶ αὐτὸς ὑπὸ κενοδοξίας ἀπολιπεῖν τι σπουδάσας τοῖς μεθ᾽ ἡμᾶς, ἵνα μὴ μόνος ἄμοιρος ὦ τῆς ἐν τῷ μυθολογεῖν ἐλευθερίας, ἐπεὶ μηδὲν ἀληθὲς ἱστορεῖν εἶχον—οὐδὲν γὰρ ἐπεπόνθειν ἀξιόλογον—ἐπὶ τὸ ψεῦδος ἐτραπόμην πολὺ τῶν ἄλλων εὐγνωμονέστερον· κἂν ἓν γὰρ δὴ τοῦτο ἀληθεύσω λέγων ὅτι ψεύδομαι. οὕτω δ᾽ ἄν μοι δοκῶ καὶ τὴν παρὰ τῶν ἄλλων κατηγορίαν ἐκφυγεῖν αὐτὸς ὁμολογῶν μηδὲν ἀληθὲς λέγειν. γράφω τοίνυν περὶ ὧν μήτε εἶδον μήτε ἔπαθον μήτε παρ᾽ ἄλλων ἐπυθόμην, ἔτι δὲ μήτε ὅλως ὄντων μήτε τὴν ἀρχὴν γενέσθαι δυναμένων. διὸ δεῖ τοὺς ἐντυγχάνοντας μηδαμῶς πιστεύειν αὐτοῖς.

Ὁρμηθεὶς γάρ ποτε ἀπὸ Ἡρακλείων στηλῶν καὶ ἀφεὶς εἰς τὸν (5) ἑσπέριον ὠκεανὸν οὐρίῳ ἀνέμῳ τὸν πλοῦν ἐποιούμην. αἰτία δέ μοι τῆς ἀποδημίας καὶ ὑπόθεσις ἡ τῆς διανοίας περιεργία καὶ πραγμάτων καινῶν ἐπιθυμία καὶ τὸ βούλεσθαι μαθεῖν τί τὸ τέλος

1 καὶ…αὐτοῖς om. N **5** τὰ αὐτὰ Γ^{a}β : τοιαῦτα γ **7** καὶ βίων καινότητας om. β **9** ἀλκίνοον Γ^{a}β **11** ἀνθρώπους om. B **16** sic Z : ἐθαύμασα εἰ ἐνόμισαν N : ἐθαύμαζον εἰ ἐνόμισαν γ ἀληθῆ συγγράψαντες N : ἀληθεύοντες Z **20** πολλῷ Γ^{a}β **21** δὴ om. N ἀληθεύων λέγω Γ^{a}β **24–5** ἔτι δὲ μηδὲ… μηδὲ β **25–6** cf. Ctesias, apud Phot. *Bibl.* 72.50 a, Antonius Diogenes, ibid. 166.109 b 28 οὐρίῳ γ : εὔρῳ β **29** ἡ γ NZ : ἦν ἡ Γ^{a} **30** τί γ : ὅτι Γ^{a}β

wrote of many wondrous things in the great sea. The fiction he invented was recognized as the fiction it is by all his readers. Nonetheless, his project affords a kind of pleasure. Many other writers made the same choice as Ctesias and Iambulus; they followed in their wake and composed what they claimed were accounts of their own wanderings and travels and they told of the beasts of monstrous size that they encountered and the savagery of humans and their strange ways of life. Their guide and the master in this kind of twaddle is Homer's Odysseus and the tales he told in the court of Alcinous: winds made slaves and feral men with only one eye who are cannibals, as well as many-headed animals and Odysseus' companions who were transformed into beasts by drugs. These were the tales he told to the Phaeacians, who were simple-minded people with no experience in such deceptive rhetoric.

(4) When I encountered all these tall tales, I did not much blame these writers for lying, since I observed that fiction is an ingrained habit even among those who profess to be philosophers. But what amazed me most was that these writers believed that no one would realize that they were writing fictions and lies. For this reason, I too, prompted by vanity, have made this effort to leave something to posterity. I did not want to be the only author who could not enjoy the license of telling tall tales. I had nothing true to relate. I have had no experiences worth recording. I turned to a fiction that is much more sensible than those of the others. I make this sole claim on the truth: I am lying. I think that by this confession I will be acquitted of the charge leveled against other writers who are made vulnerable by the very fact that *I* confess that nothing I say is true. And so, I am writing about things that I never saw myself nor actually experienced nor learned from others; things that, moreover, are not real at all nor can, fundamentally, be real. For this reason, those who open this book should believe nothing it says.

HOW OUR INTREPID AUTHOR AND HIS COMPANIONS SAILED OUT INTO THE UNKNOWN ATLANTIC SEEKING WHAT LIES BEYOND THE OCEAN

(5) Now, once upon a time, I set out to sea from the Pillars of Heracles and was headed into the Western Ocean, sailing to a fair wind. My motivation for this voyage was my curiosity and my desire to see new things. I wanted to discover what the limits of the Ocean are and what kinds of men dwell

ἐστὶν τοῦ ὠκεανοῦ καὶ τίνες οἱ πέραν κατοικοῦντες ἄνθρωποι. τούτου γέ τοι ἕνεκα πάμπολλα μὲν σιτία ἐνεβαλόμην, ἱκανὸν δὲ καὶ ὕδωρ ἐνεθέμην, πεντήκοντα δὲ τῶν ἡλικιωτῶν προσεποιησάμην τὴν αὐτὴν ἐμοὶ γνώμην ἔχοντας, ἔτι δὲ καὶ ὅπλων πολύ τι πλῆθος παρεσκευασάμην καὶ κυβερνήτν τὸν ἄριστον μισθῷ μεγάλῳ πείσας παρέλαβον καὶ τὴν ναῦν—ἄκατος δὲ ἦν—ὡς πρὸς (6) μέγαν καὶ βίαιον πλοῦν ἐκρατυνάμην. ἡμέραν οὖν καὶ νύκτα οὐρίῳ πλέοντες ἔτι τῆς γῆς ὑποφαινομένης οὐ σφόδρα βιαίως ἀνηγόμεθα, τῆς ἐπιούσης δὲ ἅμα ἡλίῳ ἀνίσχοντι ὅ τε ἄνεμος ἐπεδίδου καὶ τὸ κῦμα ηὐξάνετο καὶ ζόφος ἐπεγίνετο καὶ οὐκέτ᾽ οὐδὲ στεῖλαι τὴν ὀθόνην δυατὸν ἦν. ἐπιτρέψαντες οὖν τῷ πνέοντι καὶ παραδόντες ἑαυτοὺς ἐχειμαζόμεθα ἡμέρας ἐννέα καὶ ἑβδομήκοντα, τῇ ὀγδοηκοστῇ δὲ ἄφνω ἐκλάμψαντος ἡλίου καθορῶμεν οὐ πόρρω νῆσον ὑψηλὴν καὶ δασεῖαν, οὐ τραχεῖ περιηχουμένην τῷ κύματι καὶ γὰρ ἤδη τὸ πολὺ τῆς ζάλης κατεπαύετο.

Προσσχόντες οὖν καὶ ἀποβάντες ὡς ἂν ἐκ μακρᾶς ταλαιπωρίας πολὺν μὲν χρόνον ἐπὶ γῆς ἐκείμεθα, διαναστάντες δὲ ὅμως ἀπεκρίναμεν ἡμῶν αὐτῶν τριάκοντα μὲν φύλακας τῆς νεὼς παραμένειν, εἴκοσι δὲ σὺν ἐμοὶ ἀνελθεῖν ἐπὶ κατασκοπῇ τῶν ἐν τῇ (7) νήσῳ. προελθόντες δὲ ὅσον σταδίους τρεῖς ἀπὸ τῆς θαλάττης δι᾽ ὕλης ὁρῶμέν τινα στήλην χαλκοῦ πεποιημένην, Ἑλληνικοῖς γράμμασιν καταγεγραμμένην, ἀμυδροῖς δὲ καὶ ἐκτετριμμένοις, λέγουσαν Ἄχρι τούτων Ἡρακλῆς καὶ Διόνυσος ἀφίκοντο. ἦν δὲ καὶ ἴχνη δύο πλησίον ἐπὶ πέτρας, τὸ μὲν πλεθριαῖον, τὸ δὲ ἔλαττον —ἐμοὶ δοκεῖν, τὸ μὲν τοῦ Διονύσου, τὸ μικρότερον, θάτερον δὲ Ἡρακλέους. προσκυνήσαντες δ᾽ οὖν προῇμεν· οὔπω δὲ πολὺ παρῇμεν καὶ ἐφιστάμεθα ποταμῷ οἶνον ῥέοντι ὁμοιότατον μάλιστα

2 μὲν om. β **2–3** δὲ καὶ] τε N **6** ἄκατος SZ : ἀκάτας ΓΩΝ **7** μὲν οὖν Γ[a]β **8** οὐρίῳ ἀνέμῳ Γ[a]β : sed cf. 46.15 **9** τῇ ἐπιούσῃ β **10** ἐνεγίνετο Z : ἐγίγνετο N **12** πνέοντι γ : πνεύματι β; cf. 26.3 ἑαυτοὺς γN : ἑαυτοὺς τῇ τύχῃ Z **13** cf. Diod. 2.55 **17** προσσχόντες S : προσχόντες ΓΩβ **18** χρόνον ἐπὶ γῆς γ : ἐπὶ τῆς γῆς χρόνον Z : ἐπὶ γῆς χρόνον N **20** ἐπανελθεῖν β **23** δὲ Z : τε γ : om. N **24** λέγουσαν Γ[a]β : λέγουσιν γ **27** cf. Hdt. 4.82 δ᾽ οὖν γ : οὖν Γ[d]β **27–8** οὔπω … παρῇμεν om. β, delere voluit Γ[a] **28** ὁμοιοτάτῳ codd. : corr. Du Soul

beyond it. Now, for this expedition, I loaded a ship with abundant provisions and I put on board an adequate supply of water. I enlisted fifty men of my own age, who shared my ambition. I also supplied myself with a good number of weapons and took on the most experienced helmsman, offering him a very good wage. I strengthened the ship—it was a light costal vessel—thinking of the long and stormy voyage that lay before us.

OUR AUTHOR RELATES HIS ADVENTURES ON VINELAND OR THE ISLAND OF THE VINE-MAIDENS

We landed, disembarked, and lay down upon the solid ground at the end of an exhausting voyage. Despite our exhaustion, we managed to get up on our feet. We appointed thirty men to guard the ship and twenty to accompany me and explore the island. (7) When we had advanced through the woods some three stades from the sea, we saw a stele of bronze inscribed in Greek characters that were faint and worn. The inscription read: HERACLES AND DIONYSUS REACHED THIS FAR. Nearby there were two footprints on the rock. One was a *plethron* long; the other was somewhat smaller. I thought that the smaller was that of Dionysus and the other that of Heracles. We bowed down to worship them and went on our way. When we had gone on a little further, we reached a river of wine. The wine was very

οἱόσπερ ὁ Χῖός ἐστιν. ἄφθονον δὲ ἦν τὸ ῥεῦμα καὶ πολύ, ὥστε ἐνιαχοῦ καὶ ναυσίπορον εἶναι δύνασθαι. ἐπεὶ οὖν ἡμῖν πολὺ μᾶλλον πιστεύειν τῷ ἐπὶ τῆς στήλης ἐπιγράμματι, ὁρῶσι τὰ σημεῖα τῆς Διονύσου ἐπιδημίας. δόξαν δέ μοι καὶ ὅθεν ἄρχεται ὁ ποταμὸς καταμαθεῖν, ἀνῄειν παρὰ τὸ ῥεῦμα, καὶ πηγὴν μὲν οὐδεμίαν εὗρον αὐτοῦ, πολλὰς δὲ καὶ μεγάλας ἀμπέλους, πλήρεις βοτρύων, παρὰ δὲ τὴν ῥίζαν ἑκάστην ἀπέρρει σταγὼν οἴνου διαυγοῦς, ἀφ᾽ ὧν ἐγίνετο ὁ ποταμός. ἦν δὲ καὶ ἰχθῦς ἐν αὐτῷ πολλοὺς ἰδεῖν, οἴνῳ μάλιστα καὶ τὴν χρόαν καὶ τὴν γεῦσιν προσεοικότας· ἡμεῖς γοῦν ἀγρεύσαντες αὐτῶν τινας καὶ ἐμφαγόντες ἐμεθύσθημεν· ἀμέλει καὶ ἀνατεμόντες αὐτοὺς εὑρίσκομεν τρυγὸς μεστούς. ὕστερον μέντοι ἐπινοήσαντες τοὺς ἄλλους ἰχθῦς, τοὺς ἀπὸ τοῦ ὕδατος παραμιγνύντες ἐκεράννυμεν τὸ σφοδρὸν τῆς οἰνοφαγίας.

Τότε δὲ τὸν ποταμὸν διαπεράσαντες ᾗ διαβατὸς ἦν, εὕρομεν (8) ἀμπέλων χρῆμα τεράστιον· τὸ μὲν γὰρ ἀπὸ τῆς γῆς, ὁ στέλεχος αὐτὸς εὐερνὴς καὶ παχύς, τὸ δὲ ἄνω γυναῖκες ἦσαν, ὅσον ἐκ τῶν λαγόνων ἅπαντα ἔχουσαι τέλεια—τοιαύτην παρ᾽ ἡμῖν τὴν Δάφνην γράφουσιν ἄρτι τοῦ Ἀπόλλωνος καταλαμβάνοντος ἀποδενδρουμένην. ἀπὸ δὲ τῶν δακτύλων ἄκρων ἐξεφύοντο αὐταῖς οἱ κλάδοι καὶ μεστοὶ ἦσαν βοτρύων. καὶ μὴν καὶ τὰς κεφαλὰς ἐκόμων ἕλιξί τε καὶ φύλλοις καὶ βότρυσι. προσελθόντας δέ ἡμας ἠσπάζοντο καὶ ἐδεξιοῦντο, αἱ μὲν Λύδιον, αἱ δ᾽ Ἰνδικήν, αἱ πλεῖσται δὲ τὴν Ἑλλάδα φωνὴν προϊέμεναι. καὶ ἐφίλουν δὲ ἡμᾶς τοῖς στόμασιν· ὁ δὲ φιληθεὶς αὐτίκα ἐμέθυεν καὶ παράφορος ἦν. δρέπεσθαι μέντοι οὐ παρεῖχον τοῦ καρποῦ, ἀλλ᾽ ἤλγουν καὶ ἐβόων ἀποσπωμένου. αἱ δὲ καὶ μίγνυσθαι ἡμῖν ἐπεθύμουν· καὶ δύο τινὲς τῶν ἑταίρων πλησιάσαντες αὐταῖς οὐκέτι ἀπελύοντο, ἀλλ᾽ ἐκ τῶν αἰδοίων ἐδέδεντο· συνεφύοντο γὰρ καὶ συνερριζοῦντο. καὶ ἤδη αὐτοῖως κλάδοι ἐπεφύκεσαν οἱ δάκτυλοι, καὶ ταῖς ἕλιξι περιπλεκόμενοι ὅσον οὐδέπω καὶ αὐτοὶ καρποφορήσειν ἔμελλον.

1 οἱόσπερ γ : οἷος β cf. Ctes., apud Phot. *Bibl.* 72.46 a τὸ om. β **2** ναυσιπόρον γ **7** ἑκάστης ἀνέρρει Γ^aβ **9** χροιὰν β **12–13** τοὺς ἀπὸ τοῦ ὕδατος Γ^aβ : τοῦ ὕδατος γ : del. Nilén; cf. *HSCP* 67, 275–6 **13** παραμιγνύναι Sommerbrodt οἰνοφλυγίας recc. **14** περάσαντες β **15** στελεὸς β **20** μεσταὶ Γ^aβ **21** προσελθοῦσαι γ **22** καὶ γ : τε καὶ β **26** δὲ καὶ γ δὲ β **29** ἐπεφύκεσαν γ : ἦσαν Γ^aβ ταῖς Γ^aβ : τοῖς γ

like the wine of the island of Chios. It flowed in a deep current so that in some places it was navigable. The sight of this river convinced us more firmly of the truth of the inscription on the stele, for we saw the evidence that Dionysus had indeed visited the island. I decided to discover the source of the river and followed it upstream. I did not discover the springs that fed it, but I did find many tall vines laden with grapes. From the base of each vine stock there flowed a drop of translucent wine. These vine stocks were the source of the river. We saw many fish in its waters. In the colour of their skin and in their taste they were just like wine. Naturally, we caught some of these and, once we ate them, we got drunk. In fact, when we gutted them, we found that they were full of lees. And later we observed that by mixing these fish with the others, those from pure water, we cut the strength of the edible wine.

(**8**) Then, when we had crossed the river where it was fordable, we found a great profusion of vines. The part that was attached to the earth, the vine stock, was luxuriant and thick, but in the upper part of the vines were women, all perfectly formed from the groin up. They were like the paintings of Daphne being transformed into a tree, just at the moment when Apollo had taken hold of her. Branches grew out from the tips of their fingers and they were heavy with grapes. And, what is more, their hair was plaited with tendrils, vine leaves, and grapes. When we approached these vine-women, they greeted us warmly and addressed us. Some spoke the language of Lydia; some the language of India; but most spoke Greek. They kissed us on the mouth. And as soon as one of us received a kiss, he became drunk and could not walk straight. Yet they would not allow us to pluck their fruit. But, as we attempted to pluck it, they felt pain and cried out. Some of them even wanted to have sex with us. Two of my companions who got involved with them could not manage to get free, but became attached to them by their private parts, as they became fused and rooted with them. As this happened, their fingers grew into small shoots and the tendrils twisted about them so tightly that they were about to bear fruit.

(9) καταλιπόντες δὲ αὐτοὺς ἐπὶ ναῦν ἐφεύγομεν καὶ τοῖς ἀπολειφθεῖσιν διηγούμεθα ἐλθόντες τά τε ἄλλα καὶ τῶν ἑταίρων τὴν ἀμπελομιξίαν. καὶ δὴ λαβόντες ἀμφορέας τινὰς καὶ ὑδρευσάμενοί τε ἅμα καὶ ἐκ τοῦ ποταμοῦ οἰνισάμενοι καὶ αὐτοῦ πλησίον ἐπὶ τῆς ᾐόνος αὐλισάμενοι ἕωθεν ἀνήχθημεν οὐ σφόδρα βιαίῳ πνεύματι.

Περὶ μεσημβρίαν δὲ οὐκέτι τῆς νήσου φαινομένης ἄφνω τυφὼν ἐπιγενόμενος καὶ περιδινήσας τὴν ναῦν καὶ μετεωρίσας ὅσον ἐπὶ σταδίους τριακοσίους οὐκέτι καθῆκεν εἰς τὸ πέλαγος, ἀλλ᾽ ἄνω μετέωρον ἐξηρτημένην ἄνεμος ἐμπεσὼν τοῖς ἱστίοις ἔφερεν κολπώσας (10) τὴν ὀθόνην. ἑπτὰ δὲ ἡμέρας καὶ τὰς ἴσας νύκτας ἀεροδρομήσαντες, ὀγδόῃ καθορῶμεν γῆν τινα μεγάλην ἐν τῷ ἀέρι καθάπερ νῆσον, λαμπρὰν καὶ σφαιροειδῆ καὶ φωτὶ μεγάλῳ καταλαμπομένην· προσενεχθέντες δὲ αὐτῇ καὶ ὁρμισάμενοι ἀπέβημεν, ἐπισκοποῦντες δὲ τὴν χώραν εὑρίσκομεν οἰκουμένην τε καὶ γεωργουμένην. ἡμέρας μὲν οὖν οὐδὲν αὐτόθεν ἑωρῶμεν, νυκτὸς δὲ ἐπιγενομένης ἐφαίνοντο ἡμῖν καὶ ἄλλαι πολλαὶ νῆσοι πλησίον, αἱ μὲν μείζους, αἱ δὲ μικρότεραι, πυρὶ τὴν χρόαν προσεοικυῖαι, καὶ ἄλλη δέ τις γῆ κάτω, καὶ πόλεις ἐν αὑτῇ καὶ ποταμοὺς ἔχουσα καὶ πελάγη καὶ ὕλας καὶ ὄρη. ταύτην οὖν τὴν καθ᾽ ἡμᾶς οἰκουμένην εἰκάζομεν.

(11) Δόξαν δὲ ἡμῖν καὶ ἔτι πορρωτέρω προελθεῖν, συνελήφθημεν τοῖς Ἱππογύποις παρ᾽ αὐτοῖς καλουμένοις ἀπαντήσαντες. οἱ δὲ Ἱππόγυποι οὗτοί εἰσιν ἄνδρες ἐπὶ γυπῶν μεγάλων ὀχούμενοι καὶ καθάπερ ἵπποις τοῖς ὀρνέοις χρώμενοι· μεγάλοι γὰρ οἱ γῦπες καὶ ὡς ἐπίπαν τρικέφαλοι. μάθοι δ᾽ ἄν τις τὸ μέγεθος αὐτῶν ἐντεῦθεν· νεὼς γὰρ μεγάλης φορτίδος ἱστοῦ ἕκαστον τῶν πτερῶν μακρότερον καὶ παχύτερον φέρουσι. τούτοις οὖν τοῖς Ἱππογύποις προστέτακται περιπετομένοις τὴν γῆν, εἴ τις εὑρεθείη ξένος, ἀνάγειν ὡς τὸν βασιλέα. καὶ δὴ καὶ ἡμᾶς συλλαβόντες ἀνάγουσιν ὡς αὐτόν. ὁ δὲ θεασάμενος καὶ ἀπὸ τῆς στολῆς εἰκάσας, Ἕλληνες

2–3 τὴν συμπλοκὴν καὶ ἀμπελομιξίαν N **3** δὴ om. β **4–5** καὶ αὐτοῦ... αὐλισάμενοι om. β **5** ἕωθεν γ : τῇ ἑτέρᾳ Z : ἕτερα N **7–8** ὅσον... οὐκέτι γZ : οὐ N **8** σταδίους τριακοσίους Γ : τριακοσίους σταδίους Ω : σταδίους τρισχιλίους Γ^{a}Z καθῆκεν Γ^{a}β : κατέθηκεν γ **15** καθεωρῶμεν Γ^{a}β **16** πολλαὶ om. ΩSN **17** χροιὰν γ **18** αὐτῇ codd. : corr. Jacobitz **29** ἄγειν Γ^{a}β ὡς β : εἰς γ ἄγουσιν Γ^{a}β **30** ὡς β : εἰς γ

A STILL MORE INCREDIBLE ADVENTURE: OUR AUTHOR, HIS COMPANIONS AND SHIP ARE CARRIED UP TO THE MOON

(9) We abandoned our two companions and fled to our ship. When we reached it, we told those we had left there all that had happened to us and most importantly the invination[1] of our companions. Then, we took some amphoras and filled them with water. Others we filled with wine from the river. We camped out near the promontory and, come dawn, we set out to sea with a moderate breeze. About midday, as the island had fallen out of sight, a violent hurricane arose suddenly and spun the ship about and, lifting it up some three hundred stades, did not settle it back on the sea. Rather a wind struck the sails of the ship as it was carried in the air and swept it along as it was suspended in the sky. (10) For seven days and seven nights we coursed through the air and on the eighth day we saw a great land in the sky that looked like an island. It was bright, spherical, and illuminated by an intense light. We approached it and, coming to anchor, we discovered that it was inhabited and cultivated. Now, during daylight hours we could see nothing from the island, but, as night fell, we could see many other islands nearby, some larger, some smaller. Their surface seemed to be glowing with fire. Below, another land could be seen, with cities and rivers and seas and forests. We guessed that this must be our own inhabited world.

LUCIAN AND HIS COMPANIONS LAND ON THE MOON AND ARE BROUGHT BEFORE KING ENDYMION

(11) We decided to advance further inland, but we encountered creatures they call horse-vultures and they arrested us. The so-called horse-vultures are men mounted on giant vultures who ride the vultures as horses. These vultures are enormous. Most have three heads. You can judge their size by this comparison: each of their wings is longer and thicker than the main mast of a large cargo ship. These horse-vultures are under orders to fly about the land and, should they discover a stranger, they must lead him to their king. And, indeed, when they arrested us, they brought us to their king. He examined us and could tell from our clothing that we were Greek. "So strangers," he said, "you must be Greeks?" We said that we were Greeks.

[1] The word in Greek is ἀμπελομιξίαν, or vine sex.

ἄρα, ἔφη, ὑμεῖς, ὦ ξένοι; συμφησάντων δέ, Πῶς οὖν ἀφίκεσθε, ἔφη, τοσοῦτον ἀέρα διελθόντες; καὶ ἡμεῖς τὸ πᾶν αὐτῷ διηγούμεθα· καὶ ὅς ἀρξάμενος τὸ καθ᾽ αὑτὸν ἡμῖν διεξῄει, ὡς καὶ αὐτὸς ἄνθρωπος ὢν τοὔνομα Ἐνδυμίων ἀπὸ τῆς ἡμετέρας γῆς καθεύδων ἀναρπασθείη ποτὲ καὶ ἀφικόμενος βασιλεύσειε τῆς χώρας· εἶναι δὲ τὴν γῆν ἐκείνην ἔλεγε τὴν ἡμῖν κάτω φαινομένην σελήνην. ἀλλὰ θαρρεῖν τε παρεκελεύετο καὶ μηδένα κίνδυνον ὑφορᾶσθαι· πάντα γὰρ ἡμῖν παρέσεσθαι ὧν δεόμεθα. Ἢν δὲ καὶ κατορθώσω, ἔφη, (12) τὸν πόλεμον ὃν ἐκφέρω νῦν πρὸς τοὺς τὸν ἥλιον κατοικοῦντας, ἁπάντων εὐδαιμονέστατα παρ᾽ ἐμοὶ καταβιώσεσθε. καὶ ἡμεῖς ἠρόμεθα τίνες εἶεν οἱ πολέμιοι καὶ τὴν αἰτίαν τῆς διαφορᾶς· Ὁ δὲ Φαέθων, φησίν, ὁ τῶν ἐν τῷ ἡλίῳ κατοικούντων βασιλεύς—οἰκεῖται γὰρ δὴ κἀκεῖνος ὥσπερ καὶ ἡ σελήνη—πολὺν ἤδη πρὸς ἡμᾶς πολεμεῖ χρόνον. ἤρξατο δὲ ἐξ αἰτίας τοιαύτης τῶν ἐν τῇ ἀρχῇ τῇ ἐμῇ ποτε τοὺς ἀπορωτάτους συναγαγὼν ἐβουλήθην ἀποικίαν ἐς τὸν Ἑωσφόρον στεῖλαι, ὄντα ἔρημον καὶ ὑπὸ μηδενὸς κατοικούμενον ὁ τοίνυν Φαέθων φθονήσας ἐκώλυσε τὴν ἀποικίαν κατὰ μέσον τὸν πόρον ἀπαντήσας ἐπὶ τῶν Ἱππομυρμήκων. τότε μὲν οὖν νικηθέντες—οὐ γὰρ ἦμεν ἀντίπαλοι τῇ παρασκευῇ—ἀνεχωρήσαμεν· νῦν δὲ βούλομαι αὖθις ἐξενεγκεῖν τὸν πόλεμον καὶ ἀποστεῖλαι τὴν ἀποικίαν. ἢν οὖν ἐθέλητε, κοινωνήσατέ μοι τοῦ στόλου, γῦπας δὲ ὑμῖν ἐγὼ παρέξω τῶν βασιλικῶν ἕνα ἑκάστῳ καὶ τὴν ἄλλην ὅπλισιν· αὔριον δὲ ποιησόμεθα τὴν ἔξοδον. Οὕτως, ἔφην ἐγώ, γιγνέσθω, ἐπειδή σοι δοκεῖ.

Τότε μὲν οὖν παρ᾽ αὐτῷ ἑστιαθέντες ἐμείναμεν, ἕωθεν δὲ (13) διαναστάντες ἐτασσόμεθα· καὶ γὰρ οἱ σκοποὶ ἐσήμαινον πλησίον εἶναι τοὺς πολεμίους. τὸ μὲν οὖν πλῆθος τῆς στρατιᾶς δέκα μυριάδες ἐγένοντο ἄνευ τῶν σκευοφόρων καὶ τῶν μηχανοποιῶν καὶ τῶν πεζῶν καὶ τῶν ξένων συμμάχων· τούτων δὲ ὀκτακισμύριοι μὲν ἦσαν οἱ Ἱππόγυποι, δισμύριοι δὲ οἱ ἐπὶ τῶν Λαχανοπτέρων. ὄρνεον δὲ καὶ τοῦτό ἐστι μέγιστον, ἀντὶ τῶν πτερῶν λαχάνοις πάντῃ λάσιον, τὰ δὲ ὠκύπτερα ἔχει θριδακίνῃς φύλλοις

1 οὖν Γ^{a}β : om. γ 3 καὶ ὅς] ὁ δὲ Ω καθ᾽ ἑαυτὸν Ωβ 5 βασιλεύει Ω 10 καταβιώσετε Γ^{a}β (κατα om. N) 11 τίνες γ : τίνες τε Γ^{a}β 12 ὁ τῶν γ : τῶν Γ^{a}β 17 ἐκώλυε Ω et fort. Γ´ 21 ἀποστεῖλαι γ : παραγγεῖλαι Γ^{a}β οὖν om. NΓ^{x} 26–7 πλησίον εἶναι ἐσήμαινον β

Then he asked us: "How did you travel over so great an expanse of sky to reach our island?" We told him the whole story. And he began to tell us his own story. Once upon a time, he himself was a human being. One night he was sleeping and was caught up and taken from our Earth. Upon arrival he became king of the land. And he said that that land is the Moon that shines down on us. He told us to relax and not to worry about any danger. They had everything we needed. (12) "And if," he said, "I am victorious in the war that I am now waging against the inhabitants of the Sun, your life will be a paradise." We asked him who his enemies were and what was the cause of the war. "Phaethon," he said, "the king of the nations of the Sun—you should know that the Sun is inhabited, as is the Moon—has been waging war with us for a long time now. His motive for starting the war was this: I wanted to gather together the poorest of the inhabitants of my kingdom and ship them off to found a colony on Venus, since Venus was then virgin territory and had no inhabitants. Phaethon became jealous and prevented the passage of the colony by meeting us midway with troops mounted on horse-ants. We were defeated in this engagement. We lacked the resources to match his and we retreated. But I am now resolved to wage war against him once again and to transport a colony there. Now, if you are willing to join me in this expedition, I will provide each and every one of you with a horse-vulture from the royal stables and all the necessary equipment for war. Tomorrow, we will set out from the Moon." "Just as you say," said I, "we have decided to join you."

STAR WARS: THE GREAT BATTLE OF THE MOON AND SUN

(13) We then dined and remained with the king. But at dawn we arose and fell into battle formation. The king's scouts were beginning to signal the approach of the enemy. The total number of King Endymion's army came to 100,000 troops, not counting the baggage carriers, the engineers, the foot soldiers, and the allies. Of the allies, 80,000 were horse-vultures and 20,000 were mounted on cabbage-wings. These are huge birds. They have no real wings but sprouts of cabbage grow all over their body. Their quills are just

μάλιστα προσεικότα. ἐπὶ δὲ τούτοις οἱ Κεγχροβόλοι ἐτετάχατο καὶ οἱ Σκοροδομάχοι. ἦλθον δὲ αὐτῷ καὶ ἀπὸ τῆς ἄρκτου σύμμαχοι, τρισμύριοι μὲν Ψυλλοτοξόται, πεντακισμύριοι δὲ Ἀνεμοδρόμοι· τούτων δὲ οἱ μὲν Ψυλλοτοξόται ἐπὶ ψυλλῶν μεγάλων ἱππάζονται, ὅθεν καὶ τὴν προσηγορίαν ἔχουσιν· μέγεθος δὲ τῶν ψυλλῶν ὅσον δώδεκα ἐλέφαντες· οἱ δὲ Ἀνεμοδρόμοι πεζοὶ μέν εἰσιν, φέρονται δὲ ἐν τῷ ἀέρι ἄνευ πτερῶν· ὁ δὲ τρόπος τῆς φορᾶς τοιόσδε. χιτῶνας ποδήρεις ὑπεζωσμένοι κολπώσαντες αὐτοὺς τῷ ἀνέμῳ καθάπερ ἱστία φέρονται ὥσπερ τὰ σκάφη. τὰ πολλὰ δ᾽ οἱ τοιοῦτοι ἐν ταῖς μάχαις πελτασταί εἰσιν. ἐλέγοντο δὲ καὶ ἀπὸ τῶν ὑπὲρ τὴν Καππαδοκίαν ἀστέρων ἥξειν Στρουθοβάλανοι μὲν ἑπτακισμύριοι, Ἱππογέρανοι δὲ πεντακισχίλιοι. τούτους ἐγὼ οὐκ ἐθεασάμην· οὐ γὰρ ἀφίκοντο. διόπερ οὐδὲ γράψαι τὰς φύσεις αὐτῶν ἐτόλμησα· τεράστια γὰρ καὶ ἄπιστα περὶ αὐτῶν ἐλέγετο.

(14) Αὕτη μὲν ἡ τοῦ Ἐνδυμίωνος δύναμις ἦν. σκευὴ δὲ πάντων ἡ αὐτή· κράνη μὲν ἀπὸ τῶν κυάμων, μεγάλοι γὰρ παρ᾽ αὐτοῖς οἱ κύαμοι καὶ καρτεροί· θώρακες δὲ φολιδωτοὶ πάντες θέμινοι· τὰ γὰρ λέπη τῶν θέρμων συρράπτοντες ποιοῦνται θώρακας, ἄρρηκτον δὲ ἐκεῖ γίνεται τοῦ θέρμου τὸ λέπος ὥσπερ κέρας ἀσπίδες δὲ καὶ ξίφη οἷα τὰ Ἑλληνικά. (15) ἐπειδὴ δὲ καιρὸς ἦν, ἐτάξαντο ὧδε· τὸ μὲν δεξιὸν κέρας εἶχον οἱ Ἱππόγυποι καὶ ὁ βασιλεὺς τοὺς ἀρίστους περὶ αὐτὸν ἔχων· καὶ ἡμεῖς ἐν τούτοις ἦμεν· τὸ δὲ εὐώνυμον οἱ Λαχανόπτεροι· τὸ μέσον δὲ οἱ σύμμαχοι ὡς ἑκάστοις ἐδόκει. τὸ δὲ πεζὸν ἦσαν μὲν ἀμφὶ τὰς ἑξακισχιλίας μυριάδας, ἐτάχθησαν δὲ οὕτως. ἀράχναι παρ᾽ αὐτοῖς πολλοὶ καὶ μεγάλοι γίγνονται, πολὺ τῶν Κυκλάδων νήσων ἕκαστος μείζων. τούτοις προσέταξεν διυφῆναι τὸν μεταξὺ τῆς σελήνης καὶ τοῦ Ἑωσφόρου ἀέρα. ὡς δὲ τάχιστα ἐξειργάσαντο καὶ πεδίον ἐποίησαν, ἐπὶ τούτου παρέταξε τὸ πεζόν· ἡγεῖτο δὲ αὐτῶν Νυκτερίων ὁ Εὐδιάνακτος τρίτος αὐτός.

1 τούτων β κεγχρόβολοι (-βωλοι Γ) γ ἐτετ. γ 2 καὶ οἱ Γ^{a}β : καὶ γ 3–4 πεντακισμύριοι . . . Ψυλλοτοξόται om. β 4 ἐπὶ γ : οἳ ἐπὶ β μεγίστων N 5 δὲ τῶν γ : τῶν β 7 ἐν om. N ἄνευ τῶν πτερῶν β 8 ὑποζωσάμενοι γ αὑτοὺς β 9 φαίνονται Ω 12 πεντακισχίλιοι γZ : ἑπτακισχίλιοι N 15 ἡ τοῦ Ἐνδ. γ : τοῦ Ἐνδ. ἡ β ἦν om. β 16 ab οἱ suppetit P; vide p. 82 20 ἐπειδὴ γ : ἐπεὶ β 23 ἕκαστοι (om. ἐδόκει) Z 29 εὐδίνακτος β 30 αὐτός β : οὗτος γ

like lettuce leaves. Next to them were the millet-slingers and the garlic-brigade. And in addition 30,000 flea-archers and 50,000 air-runners who were allies from the constellation of the Bear[2] arrived to assist king Endymion. Of these allies the flea-archers were mounted on the great fleas that give them their name. In size, these fleas measure approximately twelve elephants. The air-runners are foot soldiers and they fly through the air without wings. They are fitted with tunics that reach to their feet; by flapping these in the wind as sails they are borne along just like ships. In battle the air-runners function for the most part as light-armed troops. It is said that 70,000 ostrich-acorners and 50,000 horse-cranes came from the constellations over Cappadocia. I did not see them myself, and this is why I do not presume to describe their appearance. What was said about them is in fact quite astonishing and incredible.

(14) Such were the forces of Endymion. The equipment of his troops was uniform. Their helmets were of beans—you should know that on the Moon there are large, hard beans. Their breastplates were of lupines covered with scales—by stitching together lupine blades they make breastplates; on the Moon the blade of a lupine is unbreakable, like horn. Their shields and swords are like Greek shields and swords. (15) On command, they fell into formation in the following order: the horse-vultures took the right wing on which the king is stationed accompanied by the nobility, including ourselves. The cabbage-wings took the left wing. The allies chose their own positions at the center. The foot soldiers numbered about six million and they fell into formation in the following way. On the Moon there are many giant spiders, each far bigger than any of the islands of the Cyclades. They were under orders to weave a web in the space between the Moon and Venus. They accomplished their task quickly and wove a plain on which the

[2] The Big Dipper (Ursa Maior) in the northern hemisphere.

Τῶν δὲ πολεμίων τὸ μὲν εὐώνυμον εἶχον οἱ Ἱππομύρμηκες καὶ (16) ἐν αὐτοῖς ὁ Φαέθων· θηρία δέ ἐστι μέγιστα, ὑπόπτερα, τοῖς παρ᾽ ἡμῖν μύρμηξι προσεοικότα πλὴν τοῦ μεγέθους· ὁ γὰρ μέγιστος αὐτῶν καὶ δίπλεθρος ἦν. ἐμάχοντο δὲ οὐ μόνον οἱ ἐπ᾽ αὐτῶν, ἀλλὰ καὶ αὐτοὶ μάλιστα τοῖς κέρασιν· ἐλέγοντο δὲ οὗτοι εἶναι ἀμφὶ τὰς πέντε μυριάδας. ἐπὶ δὲ τοῦ δεξιοῦ αὐτῶν ἐτάχθησαν οἱ Ἀεροκώνωπες, ὄντες καὶ οὗτοι ἀμφὶ τὰς πέντε μυριάδας, πάντες τοξόται κώνωψι μεγάλοις ἐποχούμενοι· μετὰ δὲ τούτους οἱ Ἀεροκόρδακες, ψιλοί τε ὄντες καὶ πεζοί, πλὴν μάχιμοί γε καὶ οὗτοι· πόρρωθεν γὰρ ἐσφενδόνων ῥαφανῖδας ὑπερμεγέθεις, καὶ ὁ βληθεὶς οὐδὲ ὀλίγον ἀντέχειν ἐδύνατο, ἀπέθνῃσκε δὲ δυσωδίας τινὸς τῷ τραύματι ἐγγινομένης· ἐλέγοντο δὲ χρίειν τὰ βέλη μαλάχης ἰῷ. ἐχόμενοι δὲ αὐτῶν ἐτάχθησαν οἱ Καυλομύκητες, ὁπλῖται ὄντες καὶ ἀγχέμαχοι, τὸ πλῆθος μύριοι· ἐκλήθησαν δὲ Καυλομύκητες, ὅτι ἀσπίσι μὲν μυκητίναις ἐχρῶντο, δόρασι δὲ καυλίνοις τοῖς ἀπὸ τῶν ἀσπαράγων. πλησίον δὲ αὐτῶν οἱ Κυνοβάλανοι ἔστησαν, οὓς ἔπεμψαν αὐτῷ οἱ τὸν Σείριον κατοικοῦντες, πεντακισχίλιοι [καὶ οὗτοι] ἄνδρες κυνοπρόσωποι ἐπὶ βαλάνων πτερωτῶν μαχόμενοι. ἐλέγοντο δὲ κἀκείνῳ ὑστερίζειν τῶν συμμάχων οὕς τε ἀπὸ τοῦ Γαλαξίου μετεπέμπετο σφενδονήτας καὶ οἱ Νεφελοκένταυροι. ἀλλ᾽ ἐκεῖνοι μὲν τῆς μάχης ἤδη κεκριμένης ἀφίκοντο, ὡς μήποτε ὤφελον· οἱ σφενδονῆται δὲ οὐδὲ ὅλως παρεγένοντο, διόπερ φασὶν ὕστερον αὐτοῖς ὀργισθέντα τὸν Φαέθοντα πυρπολῆσαι τὴν χώραν.

Τοιαύτῃ μὲν καὶ ὁ Φαέθων ἐπῄει παρασκευῇ. συμμίξαντες δὲ (17) ἐπειδὴ τὰ σημεῖα ἤρθη καὶ ὠγκήσαντο ἑκατέρων οἱ ὄνοι—τούτοις γὰρ ἀντὶ σαλπιστῶν χρῶνται—ἐμάχοντο. καὶ τὸ μὲν εὐώνυμον τῶν Ἡλιωτῶν αὐτίκα ἔφυγεν οὐδ᾽ εἰς χεῖρας δεξάμενον τοὺς

5 οὗτοι Γ^{a}β : καὶ αὐτοὶ γ **6–7** Ἀεροκώνωπες] Ἀεροκόρακες N **9** lacunam ante ψιλοὶ statuit Gesner **11** ὀλίγον γ : ἐπ᾽ ὀλίγον β ἠδύνατο β δὲ β : δέ, καὶ γ δυσωδίας γ : δυσοσμίας β **12** ἐγγινομένης ΓΩ : ἐπιγινομένης SZ : ἐπιγενομένης PN **13–14** ὁπλῖται…μύριοι om.β **14** καλοῦνται δὲ καυλομύκητες PZ : om. N **15** μυκητίνοις β **17–18** καὶ οὗτοι del. Nilén : οὗτοι καὶ Castiglioni : fortasse, lacuna post ἀσπαράγων vel αὐτῶν statuta, retinendum **19** κἀκείνω Z : κἀκείνων γPN : om. S τε Γ^{a}β : γε γ **20** δὲ post νεφ. add. γ **23** αὐτ. ὕστ. B **24** καὶ ὁ γ : καὶ β : ὁ P^{x} : οὖν ὁ conieci κατασκευῇ Ω **25** ἐπειδὴ] ἐπεὶ N **26** σαλπίγγων Γ **27** ἔφυγον γ cf. Xen. *An.* 4.3.31

king positioned his infantry. Their commander was Nucterion, son of Eudianax; he was assisted by two others.

(16) Among the forces of the enemy, the horse-ants occupied the left wing with King Phaethon. These are huge winged beasts that resemble ants on our Earth, except for their size. The largest of these can reach a length of 200 feet. Not only are their riders warriors, but they are warriors themselves and they fight with their antennae especially. It was reported that there were about 50,000 of these. The air-mosquitoes formed on the right wing. There were about 50,000 of these too, all archers mounted on giant mosquitoes. In their rear followed the air-trotters. They had no armour and came on foot, but they too engaged in the battle. They fitted outsized radishes on their slings. Whoever they struck could not survive for long; he died a slow death from the stench that arose from the wound. It was said that they daubed their missals with mallow juice. Behind these advanced the mushroom-stalkers; 10,000 heavily armed troops that fight at close quarters. They are called mushroom-stalkers because they fight with mushroom shields. Their spears are shafts of asparagus. The dog-nutters were positioned next to them. They were dispatched by the people of the Dog Star, or Sirius. These warriors had dog faces and they fought mounted on winged acorns. They numbered 5,000. It was said that some allies arrived too late to help Phaethon. These were the cloud-centaurs and the slingers Phaethon had summoned from the Milky Way. The cloud-centaurs arrived when the battle had already been decided, so they could be of no help. The slingers never arrived at all. They say that afterwards King Phaethon was outraged at the conduct of the cloud-centaurs and scorched their land.

(17) These were the forces of King Phaethon as he advanced in formation. Once the banners had been unfurled and the donkeys on each side had brayed—they employ donkeys rather than trumpets for battle signals—they joined battle. The left wing of the Heliotai[3] turned tail at once and did not

[3] People of the Sun (*Helios*), exactly parallel to Selenitai, people of the Moon (Selene).

Ἱππογύπους, καὶ ἡμεῖς εἰπόμεθα κτείνοντες· τὸ δεξιὸν δὲ αὐτῶν ἐκράτει τοῦ ἐπὶ τῷ ἡμετέρῳ εὐωνύμου, καὶ ἐπεξῆλθον οἱ Ἀεροκώνωπες διώκοντες ἄχρι πρὸς τοὺς πεζούς. ἐνταῦθα δὲ κἀκείνων ἐπιβοηθούντων ἔφυγον ἐγκλίναντες, καὶ μάλιστα ἐπεὶ ᾔσθοντο τοὺς ἐπὶ τῷ εὐωνύμῳ σφῶν νενικημένους. τῆς δὲ τροπῆς λαμπρᾶς γεγενημένης πολλοὶ μὲν ζῶντες ἡλίσκοντο, πολλοὶ δὲ καὶ ἀνῃροῦντο, καὶ τὸ αἷμα ἔρρει πολὺ μὲν ἐπὶ τῶν νεφῶν, ὥστε αὐτὰ βάπτεσθαι καὶ ἐρυθρὰ φαίνεσθαι, οἷα παρ᾽ ἡμῖν δυομένου τοῦ ἡλίου φαίνεται, πολὺ δὲ καὶ εἰς τὴν γῆν κατέσταζεν, ὥστε με εἰκάζειν μὴ ἄρα τοιούτου τινὸς καὶ πάλαι ἄνω γενομένου Ὅμηρος ὑπέλαβεν αἵματι ὗσαι τὸν Δία ἐπὶ τῷ τοῦ Σαρπηδόνος θανάτῳ.

(18) Ἀναστρέψαντες δὲ ἀπὸ τῆς διώξεως δύο τρόπαια ἐστήσαμεν, τὸ μὲν ἐπὶ τῶν ἀραχνίων τῆς πεζομαχίας, τὸ δὲ τῆς ἀερομαχίας ἐπὶ τῶν νεφῶν. ἄρτι δὲ τούτων γινομένων ἠγγέλλοντο ὑπὸ τῶν σκοπῶν οἱ Νεφελοκένταυροι προσελαύνοντες, οὓς ἔδει πρὸ τῆς μάχης ἐλθεῖν τῷ Φαέθοντι. καὶ δὴ ἐφαίνοντο προσιόντες, θέαμα παραδοξότατον, ἐξ ἵππων πτερωτῶν καὶ ἀνθρώπων συγκείμενοι· μέγεθος δὲ τῶν μὲν ἀνθρώπων ὅσον τοῦ Ῥοδίων κολοσσοῦ ἐξ ἡμισείας ἐς τὸ ἄνω, τῶν δὲ ἵππων ὅσον νεὼς μεγάλης φορτίδος. τὸ μέντοι πλῆθος αὐτῶν οὐκ ἀνέγραψα, μή τῳ καὶ ἄπιστον δόξῃ— τοσοῦτον ἦν. ἡγεῖτο δὲ αὐτῶν ὁ ἐκ τοῦ ζῳδιακοῦ τοξότης. ἐπεὶ δὲ ᾔσθοντο τοὺς φίλους νενικημένους, ἐπὶ μὲν τὸν Φαέθοντα ἔπεμπον ἀγγελίαν αὖθις ἐπιέναι, αὐτοὶ δὲ διαταξάμενοι τεταραγμένοις ἐπιπίπτουσι τοῖς Σεληνίταις, ἀτάκτως περὶ τὴν δίωξιν καὶ τὰ λάφυρα διεσκεδασμένοις· καὶ πάντας μὲν τρέπουσιν, αὐτὸν δὲ τὸν βασιλέα καταδιώκουσι πρὸς τὴν πόλιν καὶ τὰ πλεῖστα τῶν ὀρνέων αὐτοῦ κτείνουσιν· ἀνέσπασαν δὲ καὶ τὰ τρόπαια καὶ κατέδραμον ἅπαν τὸ ὑπὸ τῶν ἀραχνῶν πεδίον ὑφασμένον, ἐμὲ δὲ καὶ δύο τινὰς τῶν ἑταίρων ἐζώγρησαν. ἤδη δὲ παρῆν καὶ ὁ Φαέθων καὶ αὖθις ἄλλα τρόπαια ὑπ᾽ ἐκείνων ἵστατο.

4 ἔφυγον Γ^{a}β : ἔπαυσαν γ   ἐπικλ. Γ^{a}β : ἐκκλ. S; cf. 4.4   5 σφῶν Γ^{a}β : σαφῶς γ   6 γενομένης β; cf. Th. 7.55   9 φαίνονται ... κατέσταξαν β   10 *Il.* 16.459   11 τοῦ om. β   17–18 συγκείμενοι ... ἀνθρώπων om. β   18 ῥοδίου PN; cf. 24.12   21 ἡγεῖτο δὲ αὐτοῦ Γ^{a}β   23 ἀπιέναι Ω   24 ἐμπίπτουσι Ω   σεληνήταις ut passim ZP   ἀτάκτως E. Schwartz : ἀτάκτοις γ : om. β   30 ἵσταντο β

even join combat with the horse-vultures. We pursued them and killed them. But their right wing began to prevail over our left wing. The air-mosquitoes pursued and advanced right up to the infantry. But with the aid of the infantry, they broke rank and fled, especially when they saw that the troops on their left wing had been defeated. Following on that brilliant victory, many troops were taken captive, but many were killed. And streams of blood poured down upon the clouds so that they became saturated and turned red, just as clouds turn red when the Sun is setting on the Earth. This prompted me to conclude that long ago a meteorological phenomenon such as this made Homer believe that Zeus "rained blood" at the death of Sarpedon.

(18) When we broke off our pursuit of the enemy, we erected two trophies: one for the infantry battle on the spider web, the other for the air war upon the clouds. While all this was going on, our scouts announced the approach of the cloud-centaurs. These troops should have joined Phaethon before the battle. As they drew near to us, they presented the strangest sight. They were a combination of a winged horse and a human being. The human part from the middle up was about the height of the Colossus of Rhodes; the horse quarters were about the size of a large transport ship. I will not record their numbers. They were so many that I fear that to some the number would seem unbelievable. Their commander was the archer of the Zodiac, Sagittarius. Once they saw that the friendly forces had been defeated, they sent a message to Phaethon asking him to renew his attack. The cloud-centaurs drew up in formation and fell upon the Selenitai, who had broken rank and scattered in their disorderly pursuit of the enemy and booty. They drove them into retreat and pursued King Endymion himself back to his city and slaughtered most of his birds. They demolished his trophies and overran the entire plain the spiders had woven. They took me and two of my companions captive. King Phaethon had made his appearance by now and the enemies were setting up their own trophies.

Ἡμεῖς μὲν οὖν ἀπηγόμεθα ἐς τὸν ἥλιον αὐθημερὸν τὼ χεῖρε ὀπίσω δεθέντες ἀραχνίου ἀποκόμματι. οἱ δὲ πολιορκεῖν μὲν οὐκ (19) ἔγνωσαν τὴν πόλιν, ἀναστρέψαντες δὲ τὸ μεταξὺ τοῦ ἀέρος ἀπετείχιζον, ὥστε μηκέτι τὰς αὐγὰς ἀπὸ τοῦ ἡλίου πρὸς τὴν σελήνην διήκειν. τὸ δὲ τεῖχος ἦν διπλοῦν, νεφελωτόν· ὥστε σαφὴς ἔκλειψις τῆς σελήνης ἐγεγόνει καὶ νυκτὶ διηνεκεῖ πᾶσα κατείχετο. πιεζόμενος δὲ τούτοις ὁ Ἐνδυμίων πέμψας ἱκέτευε καθαιρεῖν τὸ οἰκοδόμημα καὶ μὴ σφᾶς περιορᾶν ἐν σκότῳ βιοτεύοντας, ὑπισχνεῖτο δὲ καὶ φόρους τελέσειν καὶ σύμμαχος ἔσεσθαι καὶ μηκέτι πολεμήσειν, καὶ ὁμήρους ἐπὶ τούτοις δοῦναι ἤθελεν. οἱ δὲ περὶ τὸν Φαέθοντα γενομένης δὶς ἐκκλησίας τῇ προτεραίᾳ μὲν οὐδὲν παρέλυσαν τῆς ὀργῆς, τῇ ὑστεραίᾳ δὲ μετέγνωσαν, καὶ ἐγένετο ἡ εἰρήνη ἐπὶ τούτοις·

Κατὰ τάδε συνθήκας ἐποιήσαντο Ἡλιῶται καὶ οἱ σύμμαχοι (20) πρὸς Σεληνίτας καὶ τοὺς συμμάχους, ἐπὶ τῷ καταλῦσαι μὲν Ἡλιώτας τὸ διατείχισμα καὶ μηκέτι ἐς τὴν σελήνην ἐσβάλλειν, ἀποδοῦναι δὲ καὶ τοὺς αἰχμαλώτους ῥητοῦ ἕκαστον χρήματος, τοὺς δὲ Σεληνίτας ἀφεῖναι μὲν αὐτονόμους τούς γε ἄλλους ἀστέρας, ὅπλα δὲ μὴ ἐπιφέρειν τοῖς Ἡλιώταις, συμμαχεῖν δὲ τῇ ἀλλήλων, ἥν τις ἐπίῃ· φόρον δὲ ὑποτελεῖν ἑκάστου ἔτους τὸν βασιλέα τῶν Σεληνιτῶν τῷ βασιλεῖ τῶν Ἡλιωτῶν δρόσου ἀμφορέας μυρίους, καὶ ὁμήρους δὲ σφῶν αὐτῶν δοῦναι μυρίους, τὴν δὲ ἀποικίαν τὴν ἐς τὸν Ἑωσφόρον κοινῇ ποιεῖσθαι, καὶ μετέχειν τῶν ἄλλων τὸν βουλόμενον· ἐγγράψαι δὲ τὰς συνθήκας στήλῃ ἠλεκτρίνῃ καὶ ἀναστῆσαι ἐν μέσῳ τῷ ἀέρι ἐπὶ τοῖς μεθορίοις. ὤμοσαν δὲ Ἡλιωτῶν μὲν Πυρωνίδης καὶ Θερείτης καὶ Φλόγιος, Σεληνιτῶν δὲ Νύκτωρ καὶ Μήνιος καὶ Πολυλάμπης.

Τοιαύτη μὲν ἡ εἰρήνη ἐγένετο· εὐθὺς δὲ τὸ τεῖχος καθῃρεῖτο (21) καὶ ἡμᾶς τοὺς αἰχμαλώτους ἀπέδοσαν. ἐπεὶ δὲ ἀφικόμεθα ἐς τὴν σελήνην, ὑπηντίαζον ἡμᾶς καὶ ἠσπάζοντο μετὰ δακρύων οἵ τε

9 τελέσαι ZN **10** ἐπὶ τούτῳ β **11–12** cf. Th. 1.44.1, 3.36 **12** ὁρμῆς N **13** ἡ om. SN **14** οἱ ἡλ. β, sed cf. Th. 5.18.1 **15** μὲν γ : μὲν τοὺς Γ[a]β **17** ῥητῶν … χρημάτων β **18** γε ἄλλους Γ : γε ἀλλήλους Ω : om. β : πλανητοὺς E. Schwartz **19** τοὺς Σεληνίτας μηδὲ τοῖς Σεληνίταις τοὺς Ἡλιώτας ante συμμαχεῖν add. E. Schwartz **20** τῇ ἀλλήλων] ἀλλήλοις N **26** ὤμοσαν δὲ γ : ὤμοσαν β Θερείτης E. Schwartz : θερίτης γ : θερέστης β : θερίστης recc. **28** ἡ om. PN

Now, that same day we were taken to the Sun with our hands tied behind our backs by strands of spider web. (19) The forces of the Sun decided against besieging the city, but turned back and built a wall between the Sun and the Moon to prevent the rays of the Sun from reaching the Moon. The wall was a double circuit constructed of cloud. As a result, there was a perceptible eclipse of the Moon and it was overwhelmed by the deepest night. Oppressed by this wall and darkness Endymion sent a delegation to entreat Phaethon to demolish it and not to suffer them to lead their lives in utter darkness. He promised that he would pay tribute, enter into an alliance with the Sun, and never again wage war against Phaethon. And, in addition, he said that he was willing to surrender hostages. Phaethon and the Heliotai held two assemblies, but on the first day they could not manage to assuage their anger. However, on the following day they changed their minds and peace was concluded on the following terms.

THE PEACE TREATY IMPOSED ON THE SELENITAI BY THE VICTORIOUS HELIOTAI

(20) On the following conditions, this is the treaty the Heliotai and their allies made with the Selenitai and their allies. The Heliotai will demolish the intervening wall and will never in the future attack the Selenitai. They will return each of their prisoners at an agreed sum of ransom. For their part, the Selenitai will leave the other stars autonomous and will not bear arms against the Heliotai. In case of attack, they will come to the aid of the other party. The king of the Selenitai will pay as an annual tribute to the king of the Heliotai 10,000 amphoras of dew and he will give 10,000 hostages of his own people. They should colonize the morning star, Venus, in a common enterprise in which colonists of the Sun and Moon will take part. This treaty is to be inscribed in a stele of amber in the common boundary between the Sun and the Moon—the thin air between the two planets. As representatives of the people of the Sun, Pyronides, Therites, and Phlogius swore an oath. For the people of the Moon, Nuctor, Menius, and Polylampes.

(21) Such were the terms of the peace treaty. The wall between Sun and Moon was immediately razed, and the Heliotai returned those whom they had taken as prisoners. When we returned to the Moon, Endymion himself

ἑταῖροι καὶ ὁ Ἐνδυμίων αὐτός. καὶ ὁ μὲν ἠξίου μεῖναί τε παρ᾽ αὐτῷ καὶ κοινωνεῖν τῆς ἀποικίας, ὑπισχνούμενος δώσειν πρὸς γάμον τὸν ἑαυτοῦ παῖδα· γυναῖκες γὰρ οὐκ εἰσὶ παρ᾽ αὐτοῖς. ἐγὼ δὲ οὐδαμῶς ἐπειθόμην, ἀλλ᾽ ἠξίουν ἀποπεμφθῆναι κάτω ἐς τὴν θάλατταν. ὡς δὲ ἔγνω ἀδύνατον ὂν πείθειν, ἀποπέμπει ἡμᾶς ἑστιάσας ἑπτὰ ἡμέρας.

(22) Ἃ δὲ ἐν τῷ μεταξὺ διατρίβων ἐν τῇ σελήνῃ κατενόησα καινὰ καὶ παράδοξα, ταῦτα βούλομαι εἰπεῖν. πρῶτα μὲν τὸ μὴ ἐκ γυναικῶν γεννᾶσθαι αὐτούς, ἀλλ᾽ ἀπὸ τῶν ἀρρένων· γάμοις γὰρ τοῖς ἄρρεσι χρῶνται καὶ οὐδὲ ὄνομα γυναικὸς ὅλως ἴσασι. μέχρι μὲν οὖν πέντε καὶ εἴκοσι ἐτῶν γαμεῖται ἕκαστος, ἀπὸ δὲ τούτων γαμεῖ αὐτός· κύουσι δὲ οὐκ ἐν τῇ νηδύϊ, ἀλλ᾽ ἐν ταῖς γαστροκνημίαις· ἐπειδὰν γὰρ συλλάβῃ τὸ ἔμβρυον, παχύνεται ἡ κνήμη, καὶ χρόνῳ ὕστερον ἀνατεμόντες ἐξάγουσι νεκρά, ἐκθέντες δὲ αὐτὰ πρὸς τὸν ἄνεμον κεχηνότα ζῳοποιοῦσιν. δοκεῖ δέ μοι καὶ ἐς τοὺς Ἕλληνας ἐκεῖθεν ἥκειν τῆς γαστροκνημίας τοὔνομα, ὅτι παρ᾽ ἐκείνοις ἀντὶ γαστρὸς κυοφορεῖ. μεῖζον δὲ τούτου ἄλλο διηγήσομαι. γένος ἐστὶ παρ᾽ αὐτοῖς ἀνθρώπων οἱ καλούμενοι Δενδρῖται, γίνεται δὲ τὸν τρόπον τοῦτον. ὄρχιν ἀνθρώπου τὸν δεξιὸν ἀποτεμόντες ἐν γῇ φυτεύουσιν, ἐκ δὲ αὐτοῦ δένδρον ἀναφύεται μέγιστον, σάρκινον, οἷον φαλλός· ἔχει δὲ καὶ κλάδους καὶ φύλλα· ὁ δὲ καρπός ἐστι βάλανοι πηχυαῖοι τὸ μέγεθος. ἐπειδὰν οὖν πεπανθῶσιν, τρυγήσαντες αὐτὰς ἐκκολάπτουσι τοὺς ἀνθρώπους. αἰδοῖα μέντοι πρόσθετα ἔχουσιν, οἱ μὲν ἐλεφάντινα, οἱ δὲ πένητες αὐτῶν ξύλινα, καὶ διὰ τούτων ὀχεύουσι καὶ πλησιάζουσι τοῖς γαμέταις (23) τοῖς ἑαυτῶν. ἐπειδὰν δὲ γηράσῃ ὁ ἄνθρωπος, οὐκ ἀποθνῄσκει, ἀλλ᾽ ὥσπερ καπνὸς διαλυόμενος ἀὴρ γίνεται. τροφὴ δὲ πᾶσιν ἡ αὐτή· ἐπειδὰν γὰρ πῦρ ἀνακαύσωσιν, βατράχους ὀπτῶσιν ἐπὶ τῶν ἀνθράκων· πολλοὶ δὲ παρ᾽ αὐτοῖς εἰσιν ἐν τῷ ἀέρι πετόμενοι· ὀπτωμένων δὲ περικαθεσθέντες ὥσπερ δὴ περὶ τράπεζαν κάπτουσιν

1 ὁ (ante Ἐνδυμίων) om. β   με ante μεῖναι add. Herwerden μεῖναί τε γ : μείναντά με β   **2** καὶ om. β   **5** ὂν om. β   **9** ἀρσένων β γὰρ γ : δὲ β   **10** ἄρσεσι β   **11** εἴκοσιν β   **14** θέντες β   **15** καὶ ἐς γ : εἰς β   **17** ἄλλο om. β   **23** ἐγκολάπτουσι β **24** προσθετὰ γ   **26** τοῖς ἑαυτῶν Γ[a]β : ἑαυτῶν γ   **30** περικαθεσθέντες γ : περικαθεζόμενοι β; cf. 18.11, 46.25   δὴ β : ἂν γ κάπτουσιν Γ[a] : κάπτουσι Z : λάπτουσι γPN; cf. Hdt. 1.202

and our companions welcomed us with a tearful embrace. Endymion entreated us to remain on the Moon and to take part in the expedition to colonize the Morning Star. He promised me his own son as a bride—there are no women on the Moon. But I would not be persuaded. I entreated the king to let us return to the sea below. When he realized that he could not win me over, he feasted us for seven days and then sent us away.

THE SELENITAI DESCRIBED

(22) I want to tell of the strange and extraordinary things I observed on the Moon in the time before my departure. The very first thing to report is that the inhabitants of the Moon are not born of women but of males. The Selenitai mate with males and are completely innocent of the word "woman." Up until the age of 25 they are brides but afterwards they are grooms. They do not conceive in a womb but in the calf of the leg. When the embryo begins to develop, the calf begins to swell and with the passage of time they make an incision and draw the fetus out dead. But they revive the fetus by exposing it to the wind with its mouth open. Now I think this must be the derivation of the Greek medical term *gastroknemia*. It is in the back of the knee and not the stomach that the fetus of the Selenitai develops.

I can top this with another report. On the Moon there is a species of humans, the so-called Dendritai or tree-people. They are produced in the following manner. They cut off the right testicle of a person and plant it in the ground. A towering tree springs up from it. It is fleshy and somewhat like a phallus and it has branches and leaves. It produces nuts that are about a half yard in length. When these ripen, human beings hatch out from them. Moreover, these Dendritai have prosthetic genitals. Some have ivory genitals, but the poor have wood peckers. These are the organs with which they mount their partners and have sex.

(23) When a Selenites grows old, he does not die but dissolves into thin air, like smoke. They all have the same diet. They build a wood fire and, once the fire subsides, they roast frogs over the coals—there are many frogs flying through the air on the Moon. As the frogs are roasting the Selenitai sit around the fire, as at a table, and breathe in the smoke as it wafts upward and enjoy

τὸν ἀναθυμιώμενον καπνὸν καὶ εὐωχοῦνται. σίτῳ μὲν δὴ τρέφονται τοιούτῳ· ποτὸν δὲ αὐτοῖς ἐστιν ἀὴρ ἀποθλιβόμενος εἰς κύλικα καὶ ὑγρὸν ἀνιεὶς ὥσπερ δρόσον. οὐ μὴν ἀπουροῦσίν γε καὶ ἀφοδεύουσιν, ἀλλ' οὐδὲ τέτρηνται ἧπερ ἡμεῖς, οὐδὲ τὴν συνουσίαν οἱ παῖδες ἐν ταῖς ἕδραις παρέχουσιν, ἀλλ' ἐν ταῖς ἰγνύσιν ὑπὲρ τὴν γαστροκνημίαν· ἐκεῖ γάρ εἰσι τετρημένοι.

Καλὸς δὲ νομίζεται παρ' αὐτοῖς ἤν πού τις φαλακρὸς καὶ ἄκομος ᾖ, τοὺς δὲ κομήτας καὶ μυσάττονται. ἐπὶ δὲ τῶν κομητῶν ἀστέρων τοὐναντίον τοὺς κομήτας καλοὺς νομίζουσιν· ἐπεδήμουν γάρ τινες, οἳ καὶ περὶ ἐκείνων διηγοῦντο. καὶ μὴν καὶ γένεια φύουσιν μικρὸν ὑπὲρ τὰ γόνατα. καὶ ὄνυχας ἐν τοῖς ποσὶν οὐκ ἔχουσιν, ἀλλὰ πάντες εἰσὶν μονοδάκτυλοι. ὑπὲρ δὲ τὰς πυγὰς ἑκάστῳ αὐτῶν κράμβη ἐκπέφυκε μακρὰ ὥσπερ οὐρά, θάλλουσα ἐς ἀεὶ καὶ ὑπτίου ἀναπίπτοντος οὐ κατακλωμένη. ἀπομύττονται (24)
δὲ μέλι δριμύτατον· κἀπειδὰν ἢ πονῶσιν ἢ γυμνάζωνται, γάλακτι πᾶν τὸ σῶμα ἱδροῦσιν, ὥστε καὶ τυροὺς ἀπ' αὐτοῦ πήγνυνται, ὀλίγον τοῦ μέλιτος ἐπιστάξαντες· ἔλαιον δὲ ποιοῦνται, ἀπὸ τῶν κρομμύων πάνυ λιπαρόν τε καὶ εὐῶδες ὥσπερ μύρον. ἀμπέλους δὲ πολλὰς ἔχουσιν ὑδροφόρους· αἱ γὰρ ῥᾶγες τῶν βοτρύων εἰσὶν ὥσπερ χάλαζα, καί, ἐμοὶ δοκεῖν, ἐπειδὰν ἐμπεσὼν ἄνεμος διασείσῃ τὰς ἀμπέλους ἐκείνας, τότε πρὸς ἡμᾶς καταπίπτει ἡ χάλαζα διαρραγέντων τῶν βοτρύων. τῇ μέντοι γαστρὶ ὅσα πήρᾳ, χρῶνται τιθέντες ἐν αὐτῇ ὅσων δέονται· ἀνοικτὴ γὰρ αὐτοῖς αὕτη καὶ πάλιν κλειστή ἐστιν· ἐντέρων δὲ οὐδὲν ὑπάρχειν αὐτῇ φαίνεται, ἢ τοῦτο μόνον, ὅτι δασεῖα πᾶσα ἔντοσθε καὶ λάσιός ἐστιν, ὥστε καὶ τὰ νεογνά, ἐπειδὰν ῥιγώσῃ, ἐς ταύτην ὑποδύεται.

1–2 τρέφονται γ : χρῶνται Γ^{a}β **3** καὶ^{2} ΓΩ : οὐ S : οὐδὲ β : om. N **4** ἧπερ γ : ὥσπερ β ἡμεῖς, οὐδὲ β : ἡμεῖς ἀλλ' οὐδὲ γ **5** οἱ] ὥσπερ οἱ N ἕδραῖς γ : πυγαῖς β ἰγνύσιν Ωsβ, confirm. schol. : ἰγνύαις ΓΝ **7** που γ : πάντα β **15** ἢ πονῶσιν γ : ὑπνωῶσιν β **16** ἱδροῦσιν SZN : ἀλείφουσιν γP πήγνυνται Γ^{a}β : πήγνυσθαι γ **20** ἐμοὶ E. Schwartz : μοι codd. δοκεῖ codd. : corr. Dindorf **22** διαρραγέντων γ : αἱ ῥάγες Γ^{a}β **24** αὕτη Ω^{x} αὐτὴ ΓS : ταύτη Ω^{1} καὶ αὐτὴ Γ^{a}β ἔντερον δὲ οὐδὲ ἧπαρ ἐν γ : ἔντερον δὲ οὐδὲν οὐδὲ ἧπαρ ἐν Γ^{a}β : corr. E. Schwartz **25** πᾶσα SNss. Γ^{2} : om. ΩΓ^{1} : πάντα β **26** ῥιγώσῃ γZ : ῥιγῶσιν PN : ῥῖγος ᾖ Nilén **26–7** ὑποδύονται N

the smoky feast. This is their food. Their drink is air that has been condensed and poured into a drinking vessel and that sublimates as a dewy moisture. They do not urinate or relieve themselves as we do. They have no bodily apertures like ours. Nor do young men offer their buttocks to their lovers. Above the calf of the leg they have an opening around the back of the knee and thigh.

On the Moon true beauty is regarded as baldness and hairlessness. They loathe men with long hair. The opposite is true on the inhabited stars called "comets." Out there people with long hair are considered good-looking. I know this from some visitors from the comets who spoke of their admiration for long hair. Another thing to report is that the Selenitai grow beards just above their knees. They have no toes on their feet, but they all have only a single toe for a foot. Just above their buttocks sprouts a head of cabbage. This is quite long and serves as a kind of tail. It is always lush and will not break even when they fall on their backsides. **(24)** The mucus from their noses is extremely tart honey. When they work hard or exercise, a film of milk covers their entire bodies like sweat. They make cheese from this and sprinkle some drops of honey on it. They press oil from onions, which is rich, bright, and as fragrant as perfume. They have many vines whose grapes yield water. Their seeds are like hailstones and it was my impression that, when a gust of wind buffets these vines, the grapes burst open and hail falls down to earth. They use their stomachs as pouches and they put everything they need inside of them, as they can open their stomachs up and close them tight. There are no entrails visible within. All you can see inside is a thick fur lining. Their newborn babes slip into these pouches when they are cold.

(25) Ἐσθὴς δὲ τοῖς μὲν πλουσίοις ὑαλίνη μαλθακή, τοῖς πένησι δὲ χαλκῆ ὑφαντή· πολύχαλκα γὰρ τὰ ἐκεῖ χωρία, καὶ ἐργάζονται τὸν χαλκὸν ὕδατι ὑποβρέξαντες ὥσπερ τὰ ἔρια. περὶ μέντοι τῶν ὀφθαλμῶν, οἵους ἔχουσιν, ὀκνῶ μὲν εἰπεῖν, μή τίς με νομίσῃ ψεύδεσθαι διὰ τὸ ἄπιστον τοῦ λόγου. ὅμως δὲ καὶ τοῦτο ἐρῶ· τοὺς ὀφθαλμοὺς περιαιρετοὺς ἔχουσι, καὶ ὁ βουλόμενος ἐξελὼν τοὺς αὑτοῦ φυλάττει ἔστ᾽ ἂν δεηθῇ ἰδεῖν· οὕτω δὲ ἐνθέμενος ὁρᾷ· καὶ πολλοὶ τοὺς σφετέρους ἀπολέσαντες παρ᾽ ἄλλων χρησάμενοι ὁρῶσιν. εἰσὶ δ᾽ οἳ καὶ πολλοὺς ἀποθέτους ἔχουσιν, οἱ πλούσιοι. τὰ ὦτα δὲ πλατάνων φύλλα ἐστὶν αὐτοῖς πλήν γε τοῖς ἀπὸ τῶν (26) βαλάνων· ἐκεῖνοι γὰρ μόνοι ξύλινα ἔχουσιν. καὶ μὴν καὶ ἄλλο θαῦμα ἐν τοῖς βασιλείοις ἐθεασάμην· κάτοπτρον μέγιστον κεῖται ὑπὲρ φρέατος οὐ πάνυ βαθέος. ἂν μὲν οὖν εἰς τὸ φρέαρ καταβῇ τις, ἀκούει πάντων τῶν παρ᾽ ἡμῖν ἐν τῇ γῇ λεγομένων, ἐὰν δὲ εἰς τὸ κάτοπτρον ἀποβλέψῃ, πάσας μὲν πόλεις, πάντα δὲ ἔθνη ὁρᾷ ὥσπερ ἐφεστὼς ἑκάστοις· τότε καὶ τοὺς οἰκείους ἐγὼ ἐθεασάμην καὶ πᾶσαν τὴν πατρίδα, εἰ δὲ κἀκεῖνοι ἐμὲ ἑώρων, οὐκέτι ἔχω τὸ ἀσφαλὲς εἰπεῖν. ὅστις δὲ ταῦτα μὴ πιστεύει οὕτως ἔχειν, ἄν ποτε καὶ αὐτὸς ἐκεῖσε ἀφίκηται, εἴσεται ὡς ἀληθῆ λέγω.

(27) Τότε δ᾽ οὖν ἀσπασάμενοι τὸν βασιλέα καὶ τοὺς ἀμφ᾽ αὐτόν, ἐμβάντες ἀνήχθημεν· ἐμοὶ δὲ καὶ δῶρα ἔδωκεν ὁ Ἐνδυμίων, δύο μὲν τῶν ὑαλίνων χιτώνων, πέντε δὲ χαλκοῦς, καὶ πανοπλίαν θερμίνην, ἃ πάντα ἐν τῷ κήτει κατέλιπον. συνέπεμψε δὲ ἡμῖν καὶ Ἱππογύπους χιλίους παραπέμψοντας ἄχρι σταδίων πεντακοσίων. (28) ἐν δὲ τῷ παράπλῳ πολλὰς μὲν καὶ ἄλλας χώρας παρημείψαμεν, προσέσχομεν δὲ καὶ τῷ Ἑωσφόρῳ ἄρτι συνοικιζομένῳ, καὶ ἀποβάντες ὑδρευσάμεθα. ἐμβάντες δὲ εἰς τὸν ζῳδιακὸν ἐν ἀριστερᾷ παρῄειμεν τὸν ἥλιον, ἐν χρῷ τὴν γῆν παραπλέοντες· οὐ γὰρ ἀπέβημεν καίτοι πολλὰ τῶν ἑταίρων ἐπιθυμούντων, ἀλλ᾽ ὁ ἄνεμος οὐκ ἐφῆκεν. ἐθεώμεθα μέντοι τὴν χώραν εὐθαλῆ τε καὶ πίονα καὶ εὔυδρον καὶ πολλῶν ἀγαθῶν μεστήν. ἰδόντες δ᾽ ἡμᾶς οἱ Νεφελοκένταυροι, μισθοφοροῦντες παρὰ τῷ Φαέθοντι, ἐπέπτησαν ἐπὶ

3 ὑποβρέξαντες γ : ἀποβρέξαντες β 4 οἵους γ : οὓς β 7 ἂν γ : ἂν πάλιν β 12 θαῦμα γ : θέαμα β 14 ἂν δὲ β 17 ἐμὲ β : με γ 18 ταῦτα μὴ πιστεύει ΓΖΝ : μὴ πιστεύει ταῦτα ΩSP 19 καὶ αὐτὸς Γ^{a}β : αὐτὸς γ 30 ἐφῆκεν ΩSβ : ἀφῆκεν ΓΝ 32 ἐπέστησαν β

(25) The well-to-do among them wear garments of the supplest glass; the poor wear clothes of woven bronze. Their country is rich in copper deposits, and they work their bronze by sprinkling it with water as if it were wool. My reader might think that I am telling lies, because what I have to report is so incredible. Even so, I will say something about their eyes. They can take their eyes out. Whoever wants to can remove his eyes and store them away until he needs them. And once he puts them back, presto! He can see again. Many of the Selenitai misplace theirs and have to borrow their neighbour's eyes. There are those too who have a large collection of eyes. These are the wealthy. For ears they have plane-leaves. The exception is the case of the Dendritai, who come from the nuts I have described. These and these alone have wooden ears.

(26) I observed still another wonder on the Moon in the palace of King Endymion. There is an enormous mirror there positioned over a well of no great depth. Now, if you were to go down into this well, you could hear all that was being said on the Earth below. And, if you look up to the mirror, you can see all the cities and peoples of the world, just as if you were standing right there. When I looked up, I could see my friends and relatives and all my native land. But I cannot say for certain if they could see me too. If anyone does not believe what I say, he will know that what I am saying is true if ever he travels to these regions himself.

(27) We then embraced the king and his retinue, boarded our ship, and sailed away. As a parting gift, King Endymion gave me two glass tunics, five *chitons* of bronze, and a full suit of lupine armour (helmet, breastplate, greaves, sword, and lance)—I left everything in the whale. He dispatched as an escort 1,000 horse-vultures who were to accompany us for a distance of five hundred stades. (28) We traversed many lands and we headed in the direction of the Morning Star, which was then being colonized. We landed on it and took on a supply of drinking water. Then, as we made our course to the Zodiac, we hugged the coast of the Sun, as we passed it portside. We did not land on the Island of the Sun, although my companions were very eager to. The wind would not permit it. Even at a distance, we could observe that the land was rich, very fertile, and well watered, and abundant in good things. But, when the cloud-centaurs caught sight of us, they swooped down

τὴν ναῦν, καὶ μαθόντες ἐνσπόνδους ἀνεχώρησαν. ἤδη δὲ καὶ οἱ (29) Ἱππόγυποι ἀπεληλύθεσαν.

Πλεύσαντες δὲ τὴν ἐπιοῦσαν νύκτα καὶ ἡμέραν, περὶ ἑσπέραν ἀφικόμεθα ἐς τὴν Λυχνόπολιν καλουμένην, ἤδη τὸν κάτω πλοῦν διώκοντες. ἡ δὲ πόλις αὕτη κεῖται μεταξὺ τοῦ Πλειάδων καὶ τοῦ Ὑάδων ἀέρος, ταπεινοτέρα μέντοι πολὺ τοῦ ζῳδιακοῦ. ἀποβάντες δὲ ἄνθρωπον μὲν οὐδένα εὕρομεν, λύχνους δὲ πολλοὺς περιθέοντας καὶ ἐν τῇ ἀγορᾷ καὶ περὶ τὸν λιμένα διατρίβοντας, τοὺς μὲν μικροὺς καὶ ὥσπερ πένητας, ὀλίγους δὲ τῶν μεγάλων καὶ δυνατῶν πάνυ λαμπροὺς καὶ περιφανεῖς. οἰκήσεις δὲ αὐτοῖς καὶ λυχνεῶνες ἰδίᾳ ἑκάστῳ πεποίηντο, καὶ αὐτοὶ ὀνόματα εἶχον, ὥσπερ οἱ ἄνθρωποι, καὶ φωνὴν προϊεμένων ἠκούομεν, καὶ οὐδὲν ἡμᾶς ἠδίκουν, ἀλλὰ καὶ ἐπὶ ξένια ἐκάλουν· ἡμεῖς δὲ ὅμως ἐφοβούμεθα, καὶ οὔτε δειπνῆσαι οὔτε ὑπνῶσαί τις ἡμῶν ἐτόλμησεν ἀρχεῖα δὲ αὐτοῖς ἐν μέσῃ τῇ πόλει πεποίηται, ἔνθα ὁ ἄρχων αὐτῶν διὰ νυκτὸς ὅλης κάθηται ὀνομαστὶ καλῶν ἕκαστον· ὃς δ᾽ ἂν μὴ ὑπακούσῃ, καταδικάζεται ἀποθανεῖν ὡς λιπὼν τὴν τάξιν· ὁ δὲ θάνατός ἐστι σβεσθῆναι. παρεστῶτες δὲ ἡμεῖς ἑωρῶμεν τά γινόμενα καὶ ἠκούομεν ἅμα τῶν λύχνων ἀπολογουμένων καὶ τὰς αἰτίας λεγόντων δι᾽ ἃς ἐβράδυνον. ἔνθα καὶ τὸν ἡμέτερον λύχνον ἐγνώρισα, καὶ προσειπὼν αὐτὸν περὶ τῶν κατ᾽ οἶκον ἐπυνθανόμην ὅπως ἔχοιεν· ὁ δέ μοι ἅπαντα ἐκεῖνα διηγήσατο.

Τὴν μὲν οὖν νύκτα ἐκείνην αὐτοῦ ἐμείναμεν, τῇ δὲ ἐπιούσῃ ἄραντες ἐπλέομεν ἤδη πλησίον τῶν νεφῶν· ἔνθα δὴ καὶ τὴν Νεφελοκοκκυγίαν πόλιν ἰδόντες ἐθαυμάσαμεν, οὐ μέντοι ἐπέβημεν αὐτῆς· οὐ γὰρ εἴα τὸ πνεῦμα. βασιλεύειν μέντοι αὐτῶν ἐλέγετο Κόρωνος ὁ Κοττυφίωνος. Καὶ ἐγὼ ἐμνήσθην

1 ἀπεχώρησαν β **4** τὸν κατάπλουν N **5–6** <ἐπὶ τοῦ> μεταξὺ τῶν Πλειάδων καὶ τῶν Ὑάδων ἀέρος E. Schwartz : μεταξύ που Πλειάδων καὶ Ὑάδων ἀέριος Nilén **5** καὶ τοῦ β : καὶ τῶν γ **6** πολὺ γ : om. β **12** ὥσπερ γ : ὥσπερ εἰπεῖν SZNP : ὡσπερεὶ Γ^{a}? et β?, cf. c. 40 **13** ξενίας γP : ζενία ZN : ξενίαι Γ^{a}S : ξενίαν recc. : corr. Cobet, cf. 14.36, 24.23, 52.6 **16** δι᾽ ὅλης νυκτὸς β **17** ἐπακούσῃ γ **18** ἡμεῖς γ : καὶ ἡμεῖς Γ^{a}β **22** ἅπαντα ἐκεῖνα γ : πάντα β **23** τῇ ἐπιούσῃ δὲ β **24** ἤδη om. β **25** cf. Aristoph. *Aves* 819 **27** κορωνὸς codd. : corr. Dindorf, cf. *Il.* 2.746 etc. κοττυφίωνος Γ^{a}N^{2}P^{2} : κοττοφίωνος ΓSP^{1}N^{1} : κιττοφίωνος Ω : κοτσοφίωνος Z

upon us and our ship (since they were King Phaethon's mercenaries) and, when they learned that we were protected by the truce, they moved off.

OUR AUTHOR AND HIS COMPANIONS LEAVE THE MOON AND DESCEND BACK DOWN ONTO THE SEA

(**29**) The horse-vultures had already left us. We sailed on the next night and day, on a downward course, and near dusk we arrived at a city called Lychnopolis. This city is situated in the air between the Hyades and the Pleiades. Yet it is located far beneath the Zodiac. When we came ashore, we discovered no human beings, only lamps racing about in the agora and whiling away their time in the harbor. Some of these lamps were very tiny and it appeared that they belonged to the lower class. Others were brilliant and they cast their light far and wide. They belonged to the great and powerful. They all possessed their own private lampfolds, one separate from the other. The lamps all had names, just like human beings. We could hear them speaking. They did nothing to harm us, but welcomed us most hospitably. Even so, we were alarmed and none of us dared to either eat or sleep. Their city hall was constructed in the center of the city. In this building the ruler took his seat during the entire night and he addressed each light by its proper name. If a lamp disobeyed his orders, he was condemned to death as a deserter. The manner of death was by being snuffed out. As we stood there, we could observe everything that was going on. We could hear the lamps making their excuses and explaining why they were delayed. I spotted our own lamp in this place. I spoke to it and asked it about news from home. He told me about everything.

We spent the night there. The next day we set sail and were on our way. We had already arrived near the clouds of the Earth. In this space we were amazed to catch sight of Cloudcuckooland. The wind did not permit us to land upon it. Yet we learned that the king of the city was called Koronos, son of Kottyphion. This brought the poet Aristophanes to mind, a person of

Ἀριστοφάνους τοῦ ποιητοῦ, ἀνδρὸς σοφοῦ καὶ ἀληθοῦς καὶ μάτην ἐφ᾽ οἷς ἔγραψεν ἀπιστουμένου. Τρίτῃ δὲ ἀπὸ ταύτης ἡμέρᾳ καὶ τὸν ὠκεανὸν ἤδη σαφῶς ἑωρῶμεν, γῆν δὲ οὐδαμοῦ, πλήν γε τῶν ἐν τῷ ἀέρι· καὶ αὗται δὲ πυρώδεις καὶ ὑπεραυγεῖς ἐφαντάζοντο. τῇ τετάρτῃ δὲ περὶ μεσημβρίαν μαλακῶς ἐνδιδόντος τοῦ πνεύματος (30) καὶ συνιζάνοντος ἐπὶ τὴν θάλατταν κατετέθημεν. ὡς δὲ τοῦ ὕδατος ἐψαύσαμεν, θαυμασίως ὑπερηδόμεθα καὶ ὑπερεχαίρομεν καὶ πᾶσαν ἐκ τῶν παρόντων εὐφροσύνην ἐποιούμεθα καὶ ἀπορρίψαντες ἐνηχόμεθα· καὶ γὰρ ἔτυχε γαλήνη οὖσα καὶ εὐσταθοῦν τὸ πέλαγος.

Ἔοικε δὲ ἀρχὴ κακῶν μειζόνων γίνεσθαι πολλάκις ἡ πρὸς τὸ βέλτιον μεταβολή· καὶ γὰρ ἡμεῖς δύο μόνας ἡμέρας ἐν εὐδίᾳ πλεύσαντες, τῆς τρίτης ὑποφαινούσης πρὸς ἀνίσχοντα τὸν ἥλιον ἄφνω ὁρῶμεν θηρία καὶ κήτη πολλὰ μὲν καὶ ἄλλα, ἓν δὲ μέγιστον ἁπάντων ὅσον σταδίων χιλίων καὶ πεντακοσίων τὸ μέγεθος· ἐπῄει δὲ κεχηνὸς καὶ πρὸ πολλοῦ ταράττον τὴν θάλατταν ἀφρῷ τε περικλυζόμενον καὶ τοὺς ὀδόντας ἐκφαῖνον πολὺ τῶν παρ᾽ ἡμῖν φαλλῶν ὑψηλοτέρους, ὀξεῖς δὲ πάντας ὥσπερ σκόλοπας καὶ λευκοὺς ὥσπερ ἐλεφαντίνους. ἡμεῖς μὲν οὖν τὸ ὕστατον ἀλλήλους προσειπόντες καὶ περιβαλόντες ἐμένομεν· τὸ δὲ ἤδη παρῆν καὶ ἀναρροφῆσαν ἡμᾶς αὐτῇ νηῒ κατέπιεν. οὐ μέντοι ἔφθη συναράξαι τοῖς ὀδοῦσιν, ἀλλὰ διὰ τῶν ἀραιωμάτων ἡ ναῦς ἐς τὸ ἔσω (31) διεξέπεσεν. ἐπεὶ δὲ ἔνδον ἦμεν, τὸ μὲν πρῶτον σκότος ἦν καὶ οὐδὲν ἑωρῶμεν, ὕστερον δὲ αὐτοῦ ἀναχανόντος εἴδομεν κύτος μέγα καὶ πάντῃ πλατὺ καὶ ὑψηλόν, ἱκανὸν μυριάνδρῳ πόλει ἐνοικεῖν. ἔκειντο δὲ ἐν μέσῳ καὶ μικροὶ ἰχθύες καὶ ἄλλα πολλὰ θηρία συγκεκομμένα, καὶ πλοίων ἱστία καὶ ἄγκυραι, καὶ ἀνθρώπων ὀστέα καὶ φορτία, κατὰ μέσον δὲ καὶ γῆ καὶ λόφοι ἦσαν, ἐμοὶ δοκεῖν, ἐκ τῆς ἰλύος ἣν κατέπινε συνιζάνουσα. ὕλη γοῦν ἐπ᾽

3 γῆν γ : γῇ β   τῶν β : τὴν γ   **4** αὗται γ : αὐταὶ β   ἠδὴ (post πυρώδεις) add. β   **6** κατετέθημεν Γ^{a}β : κατέθημεν Γ : κατέθηκεν Ω : καθείθημεν Richards   **7** θαυμάσιον ὡς β **8** πᾶσαν ἐκ τῶν παρόντων εὐφροσύνην γ : δεῖπνον πᾶσιν ἐκ τῶν παρόντων β; cf. c. 32   **8–9** ἀπορρίψαντες Γ^{a}β : ἀποβάντες γ   **12** εὐδίᾳ γ : ὕδατι β   **14** μέγιστον γ : μόνον Γ^{a}β   **18** cf. 44.16, 28   **24** ἐγχανόντος N   κῆτος β   **26** ἔκειντο δὲ SΓ^{x} : ἔκειτο δὲ γ : τὸ δ᾽ β   μεγάλοι καὶ (ante μικροὶ) inser. E. Schwartz   **29** συνιζάνουσαν ΩS : συνιζανούσης Russell : συνιζάνοντα temptavi

great talent and veracity whose writings are not believed—for no good reason at all. On the third day after we had departed from Cloudcuckooland, we were already within clear sight of the Ocean. But land was nowhere to be seen, only the islands in the air. These gave the appearance of burning and radiating heat. On the fourth day, about noon, the wind began to slacken and we set down upon the sea. (**30**) As we made contact with the water, we were overwhelmed by a feeling of joy and intense pleasure and we celebrated by feasting on all the provisions we had on board. We stripped down and went for a swim. As it happened the sea was calm and motionless.

THE AUTHOR DESCRIBES HOW HIS RETURN TO EARTH AND THE SEA WAS NO SALVATION BUT A CATASTROPHE IN THE BELLY OF THE WHALE

Often it seems that any change for the better is in fact the beginning of even greater ills. And so it was. We had sailed for only two days on a calm sea, when to the East and the rising Sun on the dawn of the third day we suddenly came within sight of monstrous creatures, whales and many other beasts. The largest of all measured just about 1,500 stades. This beast headed for us and roiled the sea, creating a wake in front of it and baring teeth taller by far than the phalluses in Greece. His teeth were as sharp as stakes and as white as ivory. We said a final farewell to one another, embraced, and braced for its onslaught. But he swallowed the ship whole and did not manage to crush us with his teeth. Our ship just slipped through the openings of his teeth and fell inside. (**31**) Once we found ourselves inside the creature, everything was dark and at first we could see nothing. But, then, when he opened his mouth, we could see a great chamber and a high, level plateau, large enough to hold a city of ten thousand inhabitants. Small and large fish were swimming in the middle of this chamber and there were other creatures that had been chewed to bits, as well as ships' masts, anchors, human bones, and cargo. But in the middle there was land and hills. My thought was that this land must be the sediment of the mud the monster swallowed.

αὐτῆς καὶ δένδρα παντοῖα ἐπεφύκει καὶ λάχανα ἐβεβλαστήκει, καὶ ἐῴκει πάντα ἐξειργασμένοις· περίμετρον δὲ τῆς γῆς στάδιοι διακόσιοι καὶ τεσσαράκοντα. ἦν δὲ ἰδεῖν καὶ ὄρνεα θαλάττια, λάρους καὶ ἀλκυόνας, ἐπὶ τῶν δένδρων νεοττεύοντα.

Τότε μὲν οὖν ἐπὶ πολὺ ἐδακρύομεν, ὕστερον δὲ ἀναστήσαντες (32) τοὺς ἑταίρους τὴν μὲν ναῦν ὑπεστηρίξαμεν, αὐτοὶ δὲ τὰ πυρεῖα συντρίψαντες καὶ ἀνακαύσαντες δεῖπνον ἐκ τῶν παρόντων ἐποιούμεθα. παρέκειτο δὲ ἄφθονα καὶ παντοδαπὰ κρέα τῶν ἰχθύων, καὶ ὕδωρ ἔτι τὸ ἐκ τοῦ Ἑωσφόρου εἴχομεν. τῇ ἐπιούσῃ δὲ διαναστάντες, εἴ ποτε ἀναχάνοι τὸ κῆτος, ἑωρῶμεν ἄλλοτε μὲν ὄρη, ἄλλοτε δὲ μόνον τὸν οὐρανόν, πολλάκις δὲ καὶ νήσους· καὶ γὰρ ᾐσθανόμεθα φερομένου αὐτοῦ ὀξέως πρὸς πᾶν μέρος τῆς θαλάττης. ἐπεὶ δὲ ἤδη ἐθάδες τῇ διατριβῇ ἐγενόμεθα, λαβὼν ἑπτὰ τῶν ἑταίρων ἐβάδιζον ἐς τὴν ὕλην περισκοπήσασθαι τὰ πάντα βουλόμενος. οὔπω δὲ πέντε ὅλους διελθὼν σταδίους εὗρον ἱερὸν Ποσειδῶνος, ὡς ἐδήλου ἡ ἐπιγραφή, καὶ μετ᾽ οὐ πολὺ καὶ τάφους πολλοὺς καὶ στήλας ἐπ᾽ αὐτῶν πλησίον τε πηγὴν ὕδατος διαγυοῦς, ἔτι δὲ καὶ κυνὸς ὑλακὴν ἠκούομεν καὶ καπνὸς ἐφαίνετο πόρρωθεν καί τινα καὶ ἔπαυλιν εἰκάζομεν.

Σπουδῇ οὖν βαδίζοντες ἐφιστάμεθα πρεσβύτῃ καὶ νεανίσκῳ (33) μάλα προθύμως πρασιάν τινα ἐργαζομένοις καὶ ὕδωρ ἀπὸ τῆς πηγῆς ἐπ᾽ αὐτὴν διοχετεύουσιν· ἡσθέντες οὖν ἅμα καὶ φοβηθέντες ἔστημεν· κἀκεῖνοι δὲ ταὐτὸ ἡμῖν ὡς τὸ εἰκὸς παθόντες ἄναυδοι παρειστήκεσαν· χρόνῳ δὲ ὁ πρεσβύτης ἔφη, Τίνες ὑμεῖς ἄρα ἐστέ, ὦ ξένοι; πότερον τῶν ἐναλίων δαιμόνων ἢ ἄνθρωποι δυστυχεῖς ἡμῖν παραπλήσιοι; καὶ γὰρ ἡμεῖς ἄνθρωποι ὄντες καὶ ἐν γῇ τραφέντες νῦν θαλάττιοι γεγόναμεν καὶ συννηχόμεθα τῷ περιέχοντι τούτῳ θηρίῳ, οὐδ᾽ ὃ πάσχομεν ἀκριβῶς εἰδότες· τεθνάναι μὲν γὰρ εἰκάζομεν, ζῆν δὲ πιστεύομεν. πρὸς ταῦτα ἐγὼ εἶπον· Καὶ ἡμεῖς τοι ἄνθρωποι νεήλυδές ἐσμεν, ὦ πάτερ, αὐτῷ σκάφει πρῴην καταποθέντες, προήλθομεν δὲ νῦν βουλόμενοι μαθεῖν τὰ ἐν

2 περίμετρος β **3** ὄρνεα τὰ θαλάττια β **5** ἀναστήσας Γ^{a}β **9** ἀναστάντες ΩS **12** ἐπεὶ γ : ἐπειδὴ β; cf. 14.2 **13** ἤδη om. β ἐγιγνόμεθα β **14** περισκέψασθαι β **15** ὅλους πέντε β **16** ἡ γραφὴ γ **23** ταυτὸν β **24** παρεστήκεσαν Γ^{a}β **25** πότερον ἔφη τῶν β **28** ὃ β : ἃ γ **30** ἐσμεν γ et post ὦ πάτερ β : μὲν Bekker

In any case, there was vegetation on the land and every species of tree grew on it and a crop of vegetables had sprouted up. It all seemed cultivated. The plateau was 240 stades in circumference. Birds could be seen there, cormorants and halcyons, nesting in its trees.

(32) It was then that we broke into tears and we wept for a long time. But after a while we roused our companions and propped our ship up. We rubbed sticks together, lit a fire, and managed to make a meal out of what provisions we had on hand. On board we had countless fish of every species and the water we had brought on from the Morning Star. The next morning we got up and, whenever the whale opened its mouth, we could sometimes see mountains and then only sky, but often we could see islands as well. And we could perceive that the creature was moving rapidly over the sea in every direction. Once we had grown accustomed to this manner of life, I chose six of our companions and, since I wanted to explore the entire island, I made my way into the wood. I had not gone for more than five stades into it when I discovered a sanctuary of Poseidon, as the inscription there made clear. A little further on I discovered many graves with steles marking them and nearby a spring of clear water. Soon we could hear a dog barking, and in the distance a wisp of smoke appeared and we surmised that someone was living there.

(33) So we hurried along and came upon an old man and a boy industriously at work in a garden, irrigating it with water from a spring. Delighted, but at the same time terrified, we stopped in our tracks. And they, it seems, had the same reaction and stood in front of us without saying a word. But, after a while, the old man said: "Tell me friends, who are you? Are you divinities that live in the sea or unfortunate human beings, like ourselves? As for us, we are human beings and we grew up on solid land, but now we have become denizens of the sea and swim about in it not really knowing what is happening to us. We guess that we must be dead, but we think that we are alive." To this I answered: "Father, we too are human beings. We have just arrived here, after we were swallowed yesterday along with our ship. And we have come here now because we want to explore these woods,

τῇ ὕλῃ ὥς ἔχει· πολλὴ γάρ τις καὶ λάσιος ἐφαίνετο. δαίμων δέ τις, ὡς ἔοικεν, ἡμᾶς ἤγαγεν σέ τε ὀψομένους καὶ εἰσομένους ὅτι μὴ μόνοι ἐν τῷ δὲ καθείργμεθα τῷ θηρίῳ· ἀλλὰ φράσον γε ἡμῖν τὴν σαυτοῦ τύχην, ὅστις τε ὢν καὶ ὅπως δεῦρο εἰσῆλθες. ὁ δὲ οὐ πρότερον ἔφη ἐρεῖν οὐδὲ πεύσεσθαι παρ᾽ ἡμῶν, πρὶν ξενίων τῶν παρόντων μεταδοῦναι, καὶ λαβὼν ἡμᾶς ἦγεν ἐπὶ τὴν οἰκίαν—ἐπεποίητο δὲ αὐτάρκη καὶ στιβάδας ἐνῳκοδόμητο καὶ τὰ ἄλλα ἐξήρτιστο—παραθεὶς δὲ ἡμῖν λάχανά τε καὶ ἀκρόδρυα καὶ ἰχθῦς, ἔτι δὲ καὶ οἶνον ἐγχέας, ἐπειδὴ ἱκανῶς ἐκορέσθημεν, ἐπυνθάνετο ἃ πεπόνθειμεν· κἀγὼ πάντα ἑξῆς διηγησάμην, τόν τε χειμῶνα καὶ τὰ ἐν τῇ νήσῳ καὶ τὸν ἐν τῷ ἀέρι πλοῦν καὶ τὸν πόλεμον καὶ τὰ ἄλλα μέχρι τῆς εἰς τὸ κῆτος καταδύσεως.

(34) Ὁ δὲ ὑπερθαυμάσας καὶ αὐτὸς ἐν μέρει τὰ καθ᾽ αὑτὸν διεξῄει λέγων, Τὸ μὲν γένος εἰμί, ὦ ξένοι, Κύπριος, ὁρμηθεὶς δὲ κατ᾽ ἐμπορίαν ἀπὸ τῆς πατρίδος μετὰ παιδός, ὃν ὁρᾶτε, καὶ ἄλλων πολλῶν οἰκετῶν ἔπλεον εἰς Ἰταλίαν ποικίλον φόρτον κομίζων ἐπὶ νεὼς μεγάλης, ἣν ἐπὶ στόματι τοῦ κήτους διαλελυμένην ἴσως ἑωράκατε. μέχρι μὲν οὖν Σικελίας εὐτυχῶς διεπλεύσαμεν· ἐκεῖθεν δὲ ἁρπασθέντες ἀνέμῳ σφοδρῷ τριταῖοι ἐς τὸν ὠκεανὸν ἀπηνέχθημεν, ἔνθα τῷ κήτει περιτυχόντες καὶ αὔτανδροι καταποθέντες δύο ἡμεῖς μόνοι τῶν ἄλλων ἀποθανόντων ἐσώθημεν. θάψαντες δὲ τοὺς ἑταίρους καὶ ναὸν τῷ Ποσειδῶνι δειμάμενοι τουτονὶ τὸν βίον ζῶμεν, λάχανα μὲν κηπεύοντες, ἰχθῦς δὲ σιτούμενοι καὶ ἀκρόδρυα. πολλὴ δέ, ὡς ὁρᾶτε, ἡ ὕλη, καὶ μὴν καὶ ἀμπέλους ἔχει πολλάς, ἀφ᾽ ὧν ἡδύτατος οἶνος γεννᾶται· καὶ τὴν πηγὴν δὲ ἴσως εἴδετε καλλίστου καὶ ψυχροτάτου ὕδατος. εὐνὴν δὲ ἀπὸ τῶν φύλλων ποιούμεθα, καὶ πῦρ ἄφθονον καίομεν, καὶ ὄρνεα δὲ θηρεύομεν τὰ εἰσπετόμενα, καὶ ζῶντας ἰχθῦς ἀγρεύομεν ἐξιόντες ἐπὶ τὰ βραγχία τοῦ θηρίου, ἔνθα καὶ λουόμεθα, ὁπόταν ἐπιθυμήσωμεν. καὶ μὴν καὶ λίμνη οὐ πόρρω ἐστὶν σταδίων εἴκοσι

2 ἤγαγεν Γ^{a}β : ἦγεν γ   3 γε γ : om. β   4 σεαυτοῦ β   7 στιβάδες ἐνῳκοδόμηντο N   8 ἐζήρτυτο Cobet   9 ἔτι δὲ β : ἔτι τε γ   10 πεπόνθειμεν γN : πεπόνθοιμεν P : πεπόνθαμεν Z   14–15 ἀπὸ τῆς πατρίδος κατ᾽ ἐμπορίαν Γ   15 μετὰ τοῦ παιδός Cobet   16 φορτίον β   19–20 ἀπήχθημεν β   20 καὶ αὔτανδροι καταποθέντες om. β   21 μόνοι om. β   25 ἡδύτατος γ : ἥδιστος β γεννᾶται γ : γίνεται β   28 δὲ post ζῶντας add. ΩS   30 ἁλμυρὰ post ἐστιν add. B

which appear large and thick. It seems that some divinit[illegible] see you and to learn that we are not the only ones trappe[illegible] But, tell us: What is your unfortunate story? Who are you[illegible] get here?" He refused to answer our questions and would [illegible] ourselves before he entertained us, as best he could. He le[illegible] ings. He had made for himself an independent house and b[illegible]ing for it and fitted it out with everything else that was needed. He set out for us a meal of vegetables, acorns, and fish. And he even poured wine for us. Once we had eaten our fill, he began to ask us about our adventures. And we related everything that had happened to us—about the storm at sea and our visit to the Island of the Vine-Maidens and our navigating the air and the war and the rest of our story until our sinking into the whale.

(34) He was utterly amazed by this and in turn he told his own tale: "Friends, I come from Cyprus. I left my island for a trading expedition with the boy you see here. I set sail for Italy with cargo on a large ship. Perhaps you saw its wreckage at the mouth of the whale. We had prosperous sailing until we arrived at Sicily. But there a violent wind caught us and in three days' time we were swept out into the Ocean. Out on the Ocean we encountered this whale and we were swallowed along with our ship. Of the entire crew we are the only survivors. All the others met their end. Once we had buried our companions and built a temple to Poseidon, we came to lead the kind of life you see before you—working our garden and eating fish and acorns. The woods, as you can see, are extensive and, let me tell you, they have many vines that produce the sweetest wine. And perhaps on your way here you saw the spring of excellent, cold water. We make our beds on leaves and we go out to the gullet of the beast where we catch live fish. There we

τὴν περίμετρον, ἰχθῦς ἔχουσα παντοδαπούς, ἐν ᾗ καὶ νηχόμεθα καὶ πλέομεν ἐπὶ σκάφους μικροῦ, ὃ ἐγὼ ἐναυπηγησάμην. ἔτη δέ ἐστιν ἡμῖν τῆς καταπόσεως ταῦτα ἑπτὰ καὶ εἴκοσι. καὶ τὰ μὲν (35) ἄλλα ἴσως φέρειν δυνάμεθα, οἱ δὲ γείτονες ἡμῶν καὶ πάροικοι σφόδρα χαλεποὶ καὶ βαρεῖς εἰσιν, ἄμικτοί τε ὄντες καὶ ἄγριοι. Ἦ γάρ, ἔφην ἐγώ, καὶ ἄλλοι τινές εἰσιν ἐν τῷ κήτει; Πολλοὶ μὲν οὖν, ἔφη, καὶ ἄξενοι καὶ τὰς μορφὰς ἀλλόκοτοι· τὰ μὲν γὰρ ἑσπέρια καὶ οὐραῖα τῆς ὕλης Ταριχᾶνες οἰκοῦσιν, ἔθνος ἐγχελυωπὸν καὶ καραβοπρόσωπον, μάχιμον καὶ θρασὺ καὶ ὠμοφάγον· τὰ δὲ τῆς ἑτέρας πλευρᾶς κατὰ τὸν δεξιὸν τοῖχον Τριτωνομένδητες, τὰ μὲν ἄνω ἀνθρώποις ἐοικότες, τὰ δὲ κάτω τοῖς γαλεώταις, ἧττον μέντοι ἄδικοί εἰσιν τῶν ἄλλων· τὰ λαιὰ δὲ Καρκινόχειρες καὶ Θυννοκέφαλοι συμμαχίαν τε καὶ φιλίαν πρὸς ἑαυτοὺς πεποιημένοι· τὴν δὲ μεσόγαιαν νέμονται Παγουρίδαι και Ψηττόποδες, γένος μάχιμον καὶ δρομικώτατον· τὰ ἑῷα δέ, τὰ πρὸς αὐτῷ τῷ στόματι, τὰ πολλὰ μὲν ἔρημά ἐστι, προσκλυζόμενα τῇ θαλάττῃ· ὅμως δὲ ἐγὼ ταῦτα ἔχω φόρον τοῖς Ψηττόποσιν ὑποτελῶν ἑκάστου ἔτους ὄστρεια πεντακόσια. τοιαύτη μὲν ἡ χώρα ἐστίν· ὑμᾶς δὲ χρὴ (36) ὁρᾶν ὅπως δυνησόμεθα τοσούτοις ἔθνεσι μάχεσθαι καὶ ὅπως βιοτεύσομεν. Πόσοι δέ, ἔφην ἐγώ, πάντες οὗτοί εἰσιν; Πλείους, ἔφη, τῶν χιλίων. Ὅπλα δὲ τίνα ἐστὶν αὐτοῖς; Οὐδέν, ἔφη, πλὴν τὰ ὀστᾶ τῶν ἰχθύων. Οὐκοῦν, ἔφην ἐγώ, ἄριστα ἂν ἔχοι διὰ μάχης ἐλθεῖν αὐτοῖς, ἅτε οὖσιν ἀνόπλοις αὐτούς γε ὡπλισμένους· εἰ γὰρ κρατήσομεν αὐτῶν, ἀδεῶς τὸν λοιπὸν βίον οἰκήσομεν.

Ἔδοξε ταῦτα, καὶ ἀπελθόντες ἐπὶ ναῦν παρεσκευαζόμεθα. αἰτία δὲ τοῦ πολέμου ἔμελλεν ἔσεσθαι τοῦ φόρου ἡ οὐκ ἀπόδοσις, ἤδη τῆς προθεσμίας ἐνεστώσης. καὶ δὴ οἱ μὲν ἔπεμπαν ἀπαιτοῦντες τὸν δασμόν· ὁ δὲ ὑπεροπτικῶς ἀποκρινάμενος ἀπεδίωξε τοὺς ἀγγέλους. πρῶτοι οὖν οἱ Ψηττόποδες καὶ οἱ Παγουρίδαι

2 ἐναυπηγησάμην Γ^{a}β : ναυπηγησάμην γ **3** ἡμῖν ἐστιν β **4** ἡμῶν γ : ἡμῖν β **8** καὶ οὐραῖα post τῆς ὕλης habet Γ : om. Ω **10** μὲν om. β **13** ἑαυτοὺς γ : αὐτοὺς β **14** et infra παγουράδαι β : ψιττόποδες γ **14** μαχικὸν γ **15** τὰ ἕω δέ β **16–17** ταῦτα ἐγὼ ἔχω β **17** τοῖς om. β **19** δυνησώμεθα Γ **20** βιοτεύσομεν β : βιοτεύσωμεν γ : οὗτοι πάντες β **21** ἐστὶν γ : εἰσὶν β **23** γε β : om. γ **24** τὸν λοιπὸν βίον γ : τὸ λοιπὸν β **27–8** τὸν δασμὸν ἀπαιτοῦντες β **28** ἀποκρινόμενος β

take baths, whenever we want to or need to. Let me say too that there is a lake not far from us some twenty stades in diameter and holding all kinds of fish. We swim in it and we have a small boat to sail on it. I built the boat myself. We reckon that this is the twenty-seventh year since the swallowing."

THE GREAT BATTLE IN THE BELLY OF THE WHALE DESCRIBED

(35) "We could, possibly, have managed to put up with all this, but our neighbours near and far are absolutely impossible to deal with. They annoy us greatly and are unsociable creatures." "So," I inquired, "there are other people living in the whale?" "Yes," he said, "many; they have no sense of hospitality and are very strange-looking. The gefulte-fishers live in the western or tail end of the forest. They are a breed of eel-eyed and crab-faced creatures and are very bellicose and provocative. And they eat meat raw! On the right flank of the whale live the triton-lizards. Above, they look like humans, but below they look like spotted lizards. Even so, they cause us less harm than the others. On the right flank dwell the crab-claws and the tuna-heads. They have come to an understanding and have entered into a military alliance with one another. The sole-feet and crab-tails inhabit the inland plain. They are a bellicose nation and they move with incredible speed. The East, the region closest to the whale's mouth itself, is for the most part uninhabited, since it is inundated by sea water. Even so, this is where I live. I pay the sole-feet an annual tribute of five hundred oysters. Now you have a description of this country. (36) We who live here must think carefully about how we should wage war with inhabitants like these and we must think of our own livelihood." I asked: "How many enemies do you have?" He answered: "More than a thousand." "Do they have any weapons?" "None," he answered, "only fish bones." "Tell me then," I asked, "would it not be best to attack them since we have weapons and they have none? If we defeat them, we can live without fear in the future."

We decided on war. We returned to our ship and made our preparations. The cause of the war proved to be the "non-payment" of tribute. The due date had already arrived. And, in fact, the sole-feet had sent a mission to demand the tribute. The Cypriot treated their demand with contempt and drove the messengers away. Now, at first, the sole-feet and crab-tails were

χαλεπαίνοντες τῷ Σκινθάρῳ—τοῦτο γὰρ ἐκαλεῖτο—μετὰ πολλοῦ (37) θορύβου ἐπῄεσαν. ἡμεῖς δὲ τὴν ἔφοδον ὑποπτεύοντες ἐξοπλισάμενοι ἀνεμένομεν, λόχον τινὰ προτάξαντες ἀνδρῶν πέντε καὶ εἴκοσι. προείρητο δὲ τοῖς ἐν τῇ ἐνέδρᾳ, ἐπειδὰν ἴδωσι παρεληλυθότας τοὺς πολεμίους, ἐπανίστασθαι· καὶ οὕτως ἐποίησαν. ἐπαναστάντες γὰρ κατόπιν ἔκοπτον αὐτούς, καὶ ἡμεῖς δὲ αὐτοὶ πέντε καὶ εἴκοσι τὸν ἀριθμὸν ὄντες—καὶ γὰρ ὁ Σκίνθαρος καὶ ὁ παῖς αὐτοῦ συνεστρατεύοντο—ὑπηντιάζομεν, καὶ συμμίξαντες θυμῷ καὶ ῥώμῃ διεκινδυνεύομεν. τέλος δὲ τροπὴν αὐτῶν ποιησάμενοι κατεδιώξαμεν ἄχρι πρὸς τοὺς φωλεούς, ἀπέθανον δὲ τῶν μὲν πολεμίων ἑβδομήκοντα καὶ ἑκατόν, ἡμῶν δὲ εἷς [καὶ] ὁ κυβερνήτης, τρίγλης (38) πλευρᾷ διαπαρεὶς τὸ μετάφρενον. ἐκείνην μὲν οὖν τὴν ἡμέραν καὶ τὴν νύκτα ἐπηυλισάμεθα τῇ μάχῃ καὶ τρόπαιον ἐστήσαμεν ῥάχιν ξηρὰν δελφῖνος ἀναπήξαντες. τῇ ὑστεραίᾳ δὲ καὶ οἱ ἄλλοι αἰσθόμενοι παρῆσαν, τὸ μὲν δεξιὸν κέρας ἔχοντες οἱ Ταριχᾶνες—ἡγεῖτο δὲ αὐτῶν Πήλαμος—τὸ δὲ εὐώνυμον οἱ Θυννοκέφαλοι, τὸ μέσον δὲ οἱ Καρκινόχειρες· οἱ γὰρ Τριτωνομένδητες τὴν ἡσυχίαν ἦγον οὐδετέροις συμμαχεῖν προαιρούμενοι. ἡμεῖς δὲ προαπαντήσαντες αὐτοῖς παρὰ τὸ Ποσειδώνιον συνεμίξαμεν πολλῇ βοῇ χρώμενοι, ἀντήχει δὲ τὸ κῆτος ὥσπερ τὰ σπήλαια. τρεψάμενοι δὲ αὐτούς, ἅτε γυμνῆτας ὄντας, καὶ καταδιώξαντες ἐς τὴν ὕλην τὸ λοιπὸν (39) ἐπεκρατοῦμεν τῆς γῆς. καὶ μετ᾽ οὐ πολὺ κήρυκας ἀποστείλαντες νεκρούς τε ἀνῃροῦντο καὶ περὶ φιλίας διελέγοντο· ἡμῖν δὲ οὐκ ἐδόκει σπένδεσθαι, ἀλλὰ τῇ ὑστεραίᾳ χωρήσαντες ἐπ᾽ αὐτοὺς πάντας ἄρδην ἐξεκόψαμεν πλὴν τῶν Τριτωνομενδήτων. οὗτοι δέ, ὡς εἶδον τὰ γινόμενα, διαδράντες ἐκ τῶν βραγχίων ἀφῆκαν αὑτοὺς εἰς τὴν θάλατταν. ἡμεῖς δὲ τὴν χώραν ἐπελθόντες ἔρημον ἤδη οὖσαν τῶν πολεμίων τὸ λοιπὸν ἀδεῶς κατῳκοῦμεν, τὰ πολλὰ γυμνασίοις τε καὶ κυνηγεσίοις χρώμενοι καὶ ἀμπελουργοῦντες καὶ τὸν καρπὸν συγκομιζόμενοι τὸν ἐκ τῶν δένδρων, καὶ ὅλως

2 ἐποπτεύοντες ΩS ἐξαυλισάμενοι β 3 ἀνδρῶν om. β 4 εἴρητο β 5–6 γὰρ…αὐτούς om. β 6 καὶ ἡμεῖς δὲ γ : τε ἡμεῖς καὶ β 7 καὶ γὰρ β : καὶ γὰρ καὶ γ 8 ἠντιάζομεν β 11 καὶ (post εἷς) del. Schmieder 19 ποσειδωνεῖον γ : προσεμίξαμεν β 20 κῆτος codd. : κύτος Wesseling 21 γυμνήτας β : ὄντας om. β 26 διαδραμόντες β

very annoyed with Scintharus—this was his name—and began against us with a great clamor. (37) Anticipating their attack, we ha our armour and prepared to face it. We fell into a formation of twenty-five men. And we ordered our other troops, who were lying in ambush, to attack the enemy from behind once they had passed by. They followed their orders and attacked them from the rear and cut them down. We, for our part, the twenty-five of us—Scintharus and his son had joined us in the battle—went on the attack and fought them with might and main, at the risk of our lives. Finally, we put them to flight and pursued them to their lairs. Of the enemy we counted 170 dead. On our side there was a single casualty, our helmsman, who was stabbed in the back by the rib of a red mullet.

(38) That day and that night we pitched camp on the field of battle. As a trophy we fixed in the ground the dry spine of a dolphin. The other creatures that lived inside the whale learned what had happened and appeared before us. The gefulte-fishers occupied the right wing and the tuna-heads the left. The crab-claws occupied the middle. The triton-lizards wanted to remain neutral and keep out of the fray. We met the enemy outside the sanctuary of Poseidon with thunderous battle cries that echoed in the belly of the whale as if it were a cavern. We routed them, since they were unarmed. We pursued them as far as the woods and gained control of the rest of the land. (39) It was not long before they sent heralds out to us and began to recover their dead and initiate negotiations about a treaty of friendship; but we decided to refuse a truce. On the next day we marched against them and slaughtered all of them, except for the triton-lizards. When they saw what was happening, they skittered right through the gills of the whale and plunged into the sea. We, for our part, occupied the land, now free of enemies and from that time on we lived without fear. We spent most of our time in exercising and hunting and working our vineyards and gathering fruit from our trees. All in all, we were the picture of men caught in a vast

ἐῴκειμεν τοῖς ἐν δεσμωτηρίῳ μεγάλῳ καὶ ἀφύκτῳ τρυφῶσι καὶ λελυμένοις.

Ἐνιαυτὸν μὲν οὖν καὶ μῆνας ὀκτὼ τοῦτον διήγομεν τὸν τρόπον. τῷ δ᾽ ἐνάτῳ μηνὶ πέμπτῃ ἱσταμένου, περὶ τὴν δευτέραν τοῦ (40) στόματος ἄνοιξιν—ἅπαξ γὰρ δὴ τοῦτο κατὰ τὴν ὥραν ἑκάστην ἐποίει τὸ κῆτος, ὥστε ἡμᾶς πρὸς τὰς ἀνοίξεις τεκμαίρεσθαι τὰς ὥρας—περὶ οὖν τὴν δευτέραν, ὥσπερ ἔφην, ἄνοιξιν, ἄφνω βοή τε πολλὴ καὶ θόρυβος ἠκούετο καὶ ὥσπερ κελεύσματα καὶ εἰρεσίαι· ταραχθέντες οὖν ἀνειρπύσαμεν ἐπ᾽ αὐτὸ τὸ στόμα τοῦ θηρίου καὶ στάντες ἐνδοτέρω τῶν ὀδόντων καθεωρῶμεν ἁπάντων ὧν ἐγὼ εἶδον θεαμάτων παραδοξότατον, ἄνδρας μεγάλους, ὅσον ἡμισταδιαίους τὰς ἡλικίας, ἐπὶ νήσων μεγάλων προσπλέοντας ὥσπερ ἐπὶ τριήρων. οἶδα μὲν οὖν ἀπίστοις ἐοικότα ἱστορήσων, λέξω δὲ ὅμως. νῆσοι ἦσαν ἐπιμήκεις μέν, οὐ πάνυ δὲ ὑψηλαί, ὅσον ἑκατὸν σταδίων ἑκάστη τὸ περίμετρον· ἐπὶ δὲ αὐτῶν ἔπλεον τῶν ἀνδρῶν ἐκείνων ἀμφὶ τοὺς εἴκοσι καὶ ἑκατόν· τούτων δὲ οἱ μὲν παρ᾽ ἑκάτερα τῆς νήσου καθήμενοι ἐφεξῆς ἐκωπηλάτουν κυπαρίττοις μεγάλαις αὐτοκλάδοις καὶ αὐτοκόμοις ὥσπερ ἐρετμοῖς, κατόπιν δὲ ἐπὶ τῆς πρύμνης, ὡς ἐδόκει, κυβερνήτης ἐπὶ λόφου ὑψηλοῦ εἱστήκει χάλκεον ἔχων πηδάλιον πεντασταδιαῖον τὸ μῆκος· ἐπὶ δὲ τῆς πρῴρας ὅσον τετταράκοντα ὡπλισμένοι αὐτῶν ἐμάχοντο, πάντα ἐοικότες ἀνθρώποις πλὴν τῆς κόμης· αὕτη δὲ πῦρ ἦν καὶ ἐκάετο, ὥστε οὐδὲ κορύθων ἐδέοντο. ἀντὶ δὲ ἱστίων ὁ ἄνεμος ἐμπίπτων τῇ ὕλῃ, πολλῇ οὔσῃ ἐν ἑκάστῃ, ἐκόλπου τε ταύτην καὶ ἔφερε τὴν νῆσον ᾗ ἐθέλοι ὁ κυβερνήτης· κελευστὴς δὲ ἐφειστήκει αὐτοῖς, καὶ Πρὸς τὴν εἰρεσίαν ὀξέως ἐκινοῦντο ὥσπερ τὰ μακρὰ τῶν πλοίων.

τὸ μὲν οὖν πρῶτον δύο ἢ τρεῖς ἑωρῶμεν, ὕστερον δὲ ἐφάνησαν (41) ὅσον ἑξακόσιοι, καὶ διαστάντες ἐπολέμουν καὶ ἐναυμάχουν. πολλαὶ μὲν οὖν ἀντίπρῳροι συνηράσσοντο ἀλλήλαις, πολλαὶ δὲ καὶ ἐμβληθεῖσαι κατεδύοντο, αἱ δὲ συμπλεκόμενοι καρτερῶς

3 διηγάγομεν γ 7 πολλὴ om. ΩS 10 ἐνδοτέρω γ : ἐντὸς β 11 ἡμισταδίους γ 13 οὖν om. β 14 μὲν om. β 15 τὴν περίμετρον Γ[a]β 17–18 αὐτ. μεγ. β 18 ὡσπερεὶ β 20 χαλκοῦν β 22 ἐκαίετο β 23 ὁ (ante ἄνεμος) om. β 24–5 ταύτην . . . νῆσον Γ : αὐτὴν . . . νῆσον β : τὴν νῆσον καὶ ἔφερε ταύτην ΩS 25 ᾗ] οἱ P 28 ἑξακόσιαι β 30 ἐκβληθεῖσαι β

prison from which there was no escaping, yet enjoying a life of luxury and living as free men.

THE SEA BATTLE OF THE GIANTS

This was our life for a year and eight months. But on the fifth day of the ninth month, (**40**) around the second opening of the mouth—here I must explain that the monster opened his mouth once every hour, so we could tell the time of day by calculating the intervals between the openings. As I was saying, it was about the hour of the second opening when we suddenly heard loud shouting, it seemed, of people calling out orders and the sound of the plash of oars. We were shaken by this commotion and crept up to the mouth of the creature. Standing just inside its teeth I witnessed the strangest sight that I ever saw: huge men, about half a stade in size, sailing towards us on vast islands as if they were triremes. I know what I will now relate, although it should be credible, is unbelievable so far as the skeptics are concerned. But, nonetheless, I will report what I saw. The islands were rectangular, but not very mountainous, each about one hundred stades in circumference. About 120 of these had giants who were sailing on them. The giants took their positions on each side of the island, one behind the other, and plied cypress trees with their branches attached. They rowed in alternating rhythm. These trees were their oars. To the rear, on the poop deck, a helmsman stood on a high platform with a bronze rudder five stades long. On the prow some forty giants in armour were in the thick of battle. They were just like humans in everything, except their hair. Their hair was fiery and blazed so fiercely that they had no need of helmets. They had no masts on their island ships; instead, the wind blasted the forests, which were very dense on each island, and, as the wind filled the forests, it carried the islands in any direction the steersmen wanted. The boatswain stood over them, and they rowed in unison just as the oarsmen in our long boats.

(**41**) At first, we could see only two or three of these island ships; a little later some six hundred others hove into view. They came into formation and engaged in a battle of ships and marines. Many of the ships collided head-on and broke apart; others had been rammed on their sides and were

διηγωνίζοντο καὶ οὐ ῥᾳδίως ἀπελύοντο· οἱ γὰρ ἐπὶ τῆς πρῴρας τεταγμένοι πᾶσαν ἐπεδείκνυντο προθυμίαν ἐπιβαίνοντες καὶ ἀναιροῦντες· ἐζώγρει δὲ οὐδείς. ἀντὶ δὲ χειρῶν σιδηρῶν πολύποδας μεγάλους ἐκδεδεμένους ἀλλήλοις ἐπερρίπτουν, οἱ δὲ περιπλεκόμενοι τῇ ὕλῃ κατεῖχον τὴν νῆσον. ἔβαλλον μέντοι καὶ ἐτίτρωσκον (42) ὀστρείοις τε ἁμαξοπληθέσι καὶ σπόγγοις πλεθριαίοις. ἡγεῖτο δὲ τῶν μὲν Αἰολοκένταυρος, τῶν δὲ Θαλασσοπότης· καὶ μάχη αὐτοῖς ἐγεγένητο, ὡς ἐδόκει, λείας ἕνεκα· ἐλέγετο γὰρ ὁ Θαλασσοπότης πολλὰς ἀγέλας δελφίνων τοῦ Αἰολοκενταύρου ἐληλακέναι, ὡς ἦν ἀκούειν ἐπικαλούντων ἀλλήλοις καὶ τὰ ὀνόματα τῶν βασιλέων ἐπιβοωμένων. τέλος δὲ νικῶσιν οἱ τοῦ Αἰολοκενταύρου καὶ νήσους τῶν πολεμίων καταδύουσιν ἀμφὶ τὰς πεντήκοντα καὶ ἑκατόν· καὶ ἄλλας τρεῖς λαμβάνουσιν αὐτοῖς ἀνδράσιν· αἱ δὲ λοιπαὶ πρύμναν κρουσάμεναι ἔφευγον. οἱ δὲ μέχρι τινὸς διώξαντες, ἐπειδὴ ἑσπέρα ἦν, τραπόμενοι πρὸς τὰ ναυάγια τῶν πλείστων ἐπεκράτησαν καὶ τὰ ἑαυτῶν ἀνείλοντο· καὶ γὰρ ἐκείνων κατέδυσαν νῆσοι οὐκ ἐλάττους τῶν ὀγδοήκοντα. ἔστησαν δὲ καὶ τρόπαιον τῆς νησομαχίας ἐπὶ τῇ κεφαλῇ τοῦ κήτους μίαν τῶν πολεμίων νῆσον ἀνασταυρώσαντες. ἐκείνην μὲν οὖν τὴν νύκτα περὶ τὸ θηρίον ηὐλίσαντο ἐξάψαντες αὐτοῦ τὰ ἀπόγεια καὶ ἐπ᾽ ἀγκυρῶν πλησίον ὁρμισάμενοι· καὶ γὰρ ἀγκύραις ἐχρῶντο μεγάλαις ὑαλίναις καρτεραῖς. τῇ ὑστεραίᾳ δὲ θύσαντες ἐπὶ τοῦ κήτους καὶ τοὺς οἰκείους θάψαντες ἐπ᾽ αὐτοῦ ἀπέπλεον ἡδόμενοι καὶ ὥσπερ παιᾶνας ᾄδοντες. ταῦτα μὲν τὰ κατὰ τὴν νησομαχίαν γενόμενα.

2 παρατεταγμένοι Γ[1] ἐπεμβαίνοντες β **4** ἀλλήλων P **6** ὀστρέοις γ **7, 8–9** θαλασσοπώτης β **12** νήσους γ : νήσους τε β **19** νήσων ΩSN **20** ἀπόγαια β **22** ὑαλιναῖς γ : ξυλίναις β Subscriptio in Γ : διώρθωσα ἐγὼ αλέξανδρος επίσκοπος νικαίας τῆς κατα βιθυνιαν μετα ιακώβου τοῦ φιλτάτου αδελφοῦ καὶ μητροπολιτου λαρίσσης subscripsit Γ[a] (sic)

foundering. Other ships stood side by side and engaged in hand-to-hand combat. They only disengaged with difficulty, for the marines stationed on the prows boarded the enemy islands with great courage. They locked in hand-to-hand combat and, filled with martial valor, they slaughtered the enemy. Instead of iron grappling hooks they threw giant octopuses plaited to one another; these attached themselves to the trees of the woods and held fast to the opposing island. They hurled oysters to wound their opponents; these were the size of a wagon. And they threw sponges 100 feet long as missiles.

(**42**) The general of one army was Aiolocentaurus, or Darting Centaur; of the other Brinedrinker. They went to war, it seems, because of rustling. It was said that Brinedrinker had driven off many herds of Aiolocentaurus' dolphins. We learned this as they exchanged mutual recriminations and roared out the names of each of their kings. Finally, the forces of Aiolocentaurus prevailed and they sank about 150 of the enemy islands. Three other islands they captured with the crew aboard them. The rest of Brinedrinker's forces took flight with a damaged prow. They pursued for a time, but, when dusk fell, they returned to the wrecked islands, managed to take most in tow and recovered their own dead. Of their own island fleet, no less than eighty had been scuttled. They erected a trophy of their victory at sea on the whale's head. The trophy was one of the enemy island ships that they fixed on a stake. They attached ropes to the creature and spent the night riding at anchor alongside. Their anchors were of unbreakable glass. The next day, they offered sacrifice on the whale and, when they had buried their own dead upon it, they sailed off content and sang a kind of victory paean. This is the history of the great battle at sea.

ΑΛΗΘΩΝ ΔΙΗΓΗΜΑΤΩΝ Β

Τὸ δὲ ἀπὸ τούτου μηκέτι φέρων ἐγὼ τὴν ἐν τῷ κήτει δίαιταν (1) ἀχθόμενός τε τῇ μονῇ μηχανήν τινα ἐζήτουν, δι᾽ ἧς ἂν ἐξελθεῖν γένοιτο· καὶ τὸ μὲν πρῶτον ἔδοξεν ἡμῖν διορύξασι κατὰ τὸν δεξιὸν τοῖχον ἀποδρᾶναι, καὶ ἀρξάμενοι διεκόπτομεν· ἐπειδὴ δὲ προελθόντες ὅσον πέντε σταδίους οὐδὲν ἠνύομεν, τοῦ μὲν ὀρύγματος ἐπαυσάμεθα, τὴν δὲ ὕλην καῦσαι διέγνωμεν· οὕτω γὰρ ἂν τὸ κῆτος ἀποθανεῖν· εἰ δὲ τοῦτο γένοιτο, ῥᾳδία ἔμελλεν ἡμῖν ἔσεσθαι ἡ ἔξοδος. ἀρξάμενοι οὖν ἀπὸ τῶν οὐραίων ἐκαίομεν, καὶ ἡμέρας μὲν ἑπτὰ καὶ ἴσας νύκτας ἀναισθήτως εἶχε τοῦ καύματος, ὀγδόῃ δὲ καὶ ἐνάτῃ συνίεμεν αὐτοῦ νοσοῦντος· ἀργότερον γοῦν ἀνέχασκεν καὶ εἴ ποτε ἀναχάνοι ταχὺ συνέμνεν. δεκάτῃ δὲ καὶ ἑνδεκάτῃ τέλεον ἀπενεκροῦτο καὶ δυσῶδες ἦν· τῇ δωδεκάτῃ δὲ μόλις ἐνενοήσαμεν ὡς, εἰ μή τις χανόντος αὐτοῦ ὑποστηρίξειεν τοὺς γομφίους, ὥστε μηκέτι συγκλεῖσαι, κινδυνεύσομεν κατακλεισθέντες ἐν νεκρῷ αὐτῷ ἀπολέσθαι. οὕτω δὴ μεγάλοις δοκοῖς τὸ στόμα διερείσαντες τὴν ναῦν ἐπεσκευάζομεν ὕδωρ τε ὡς ἔνι πλεῖστον ἐμβαλλόμενοι καὶ τἄλλα ἐπιτήδεια· κυβερνήσειν δὲ ἔμελλεν ὁ Σκίνθαρος.

Τῇ δὲ ἐπιούσῃ τὸ μὲν ἤδη τεθνήκει, ἡμεῖς δὲ ἀνελκύσαντες τὸ (2) πλοῖον καὶ διὰ τῶν ἀραιωμάτων διαγαγόντες καὶ ἐκ τῶν ὀδόντων ἐξάψαντες ἠρέμα καθήκαμεν ἐς τὴν θάλατταν· ἐπαναβάντες δὲ ἐπὶ τὰ νῶτα καὶ θύσαντες τῷ Ποσειδῶνι αὐτοῦ παρὰ τὸ τρόπαιον ἡμέρας τε τρεῖς ἐπαυλισάμενοι—νηνεμία γὰρ ἦν—τῇ τετάρτῃ

ΓΩ = γ ; ZP = β ; v. p. 82 Titulus ἀληθῶν (ἀληθινῶν Ω) διηγημάτων β̄γ : ἀληθοῦς ἱστορίας λόγος δεύτερος β **2** τινα om. Ω **7** ἡμῖν ἔμελλεν ΩP **8** οὐραίων Γ^{a}β : θυραιῶν Ω^{1} : θυρεῶν ? Γ^{1} **11** ἑνδεκάτῃ β : τῇ ἑνδεκάτῃ γ **12** ἀπενενέκρωτο γ **13** ἐνοήσαμεν β **14** γομφίους Γ^{a}β : γομφούς γ, fort. recte, cf. Hesych. **15–16** τὸ στόμα ante μεγάλοις trs. **16** ἔνι γ : ὅτι β **17** ἐμβαλόμενοι β κυβερνᾶν γ **19** ἐτεθνήκει recc. **20** καὶ ἐκ γ : ἐκ β **21** ἐπιβάντες β **23** τε om. β

Book 2

THE AUTHOR RELATES HOW HE AND HIS COMPANIONS MANAGED TO ESCAPE FROM THE BELLY OF THE WHALE

(1) After this fright, I could no longer endure life in the whale and, terribly miserable in my isolation, I tried to contrive a means of escape. At first, we decided to escape by excavating a tunnel through the right side of the whale and began work hacking through it. But, once we had tunneled into it for about five stades, we could make no further progress. We gave up on the tunnel and decided to burn the forest, thinking that, if we did, the whale would die. If it died, our escape would be all the easier. Beginning with the area of the tail we started the fire. For seven days and seven nights the whale was oblivious to the burning. But on the eighth and ninth day we could tell that he was ill. He would open his mouth less frequently and would quickly close it. Finally on the tenth and eleventh day he was dying. On the twelfth day we realized that if we did not put a prop between his jaws as he was opening his mouth to prevent his closing them, we were in danger of being entombed in the body of the beast and perishing. So it was that we propped his mouth open with strong tall stakes. We got the ship ready and stored in it as much water as we could along with all our other provisions. Scintharus was ready to serve as our helmsman.

HOW LUCIAN AND HIS COMPANIONS ARE FROZEN FAST IN A GREAT SEA OF ICE

(2) By the next day, the monster was already dead. We drew our ship up through the gaps in his teeth and, attaching it to his teeth with cables, we gently lowered it into the sea. We then climbed up onto the back of the whale, and, after we had made sacrifices to Poseidon, we camped on it for

ἀπεπλεύσαμεν. ἔνθα δὴ πολλοῖς τῶν ἐκ τῆς ναυμαχίας νεκροῖς ἀπηντῶμεν καὶ προσωκέλλομεν, καὶ τὰ σώματα καταμετροῦντες ἐθαυμάζομεν. καὶ ἡμέρας μέν τινας ἐπλέομεν εὐκράτῳ ἀέρι χρώμενοι, ἔπειτα βορέου σφοδροῦ πνεύσαντος μέγα κρύος ἐγένετο, καὶ ἀπ᾽ αὐτοῦ πᾶν ἐπάγη τὸ πέλαγος, οὐκ ἐπιπολῆς μόνον, ἀλλὰ καὶ ἐς βάθος ὅσον ἐπὶ τριακοσίας ὀργυιάς, ὥστε καὶ ἀποβάντας διαθεῖν ἐπὶ τοῦ κρυστάλλου. ἐπιμένοντος δὲ τοῦ πνεύματος φέρειν οὐ δυνάμενοι τοιόνδε τι ἐπενοήσαμεν—ὁ δὲ τὴν γνώμην ἀποφηνάμενος ἦν ὁ Σκίνθαρος—σκάψαντες γὰρ ἐν τῷ ὕδατι σπήλαιον μέγιστον ἐν τούτῳ ἐμείναμεν ἡμέρας τριάκοντα, πῦρ ἀνακαίοντες καὶ σιτούμενοι τοὺς ἰχθῦς· εὑρίσκομεν δὲ αὐτοὺς ἀνορύττοντες. ἐπεὶ δὲ ἤδη ἐπέλειπε τὰ ἐπιτήδεια, προελθόντες καὶ τὴν ναῦν πεπηγυῖαν ἀνασπάσαντες καὶ πετάσαντες τὴν ὀθόνην ἐσυρόμεθα ὥσπερ πλέοντες λείως καὶ προσηνῶς ἐπὶ τοῦ πάγους διολισθάνοντες. ἡμέρᾳ δὲ πέμπτῃ ἀλέα τε ἦν ἤδη καὶ ὁ πάγος ἐλύετο καὶ ὕδωρ πάντα αὖθις ἐγίνετο.

(3) Πλεύσαντες οὖν ὅσον τριακοσίους σταδίους νήσῳ μικρᾷ καὶ ἐρήμῃ προσηνέχθημεν, ἀφ᾽ ἧς ὕδωρ λαβόντες—ἐπελελοίπει γὰρ ἤδη—καὶ δύο ταύρους ἀγρίους κατατοξεύσαντες ἀπεπλεύσαμεν. οἱ δὲ ταῦροι οὗτοι τὰ κέρατα οὐκ ἐπὶ τῆς κεφαλῆς εἶχον, ἀλλ᾽ ὑπὸ τοῖς ὀφθαλμοῖς, ὥσπερ ὁ Μῶμος ἠξίου. μετ᾽ οὐ πολὺ δὲ εἰς πέλαγος ἐνεβαίνομεν, οὐχ ὕδατος, ἀλλὰ γάλακτος· καὶ νῆσος ἐν αὐτῷ ἐφαίνετο λευκὴ πλήρης ἀμπέλων. ἦν δὲ ἡ νῆσος τυρὸς μέγιστος συμπεπηγώς, ὡς ὕστερον ἐμφαγόντες ἐμάθομεν, σταδίων εἴκοσι πέντε τὸ περίμετρον· αἱ δὲ ἄμπελοι βοτρύων πλήρεις, οὐ μέντοι οἶνον, ἀλλὰ γάλα ἐξ αὐτῶν ἀποθλίβοντες ἐπίνομεν. ἱερὸν δὲ ἐν μέσῃ τῇ νήσῳ ἀνῳκοδόμητο Γαλατείας τῆς Νηρηΐδος, ὡς ἐδήλου τὸ ἐπίγραμμα. ὅσον οὖν χρόνον ἐκεῖ ἐμείναμεν, ὄψον

1 νησομαχίας Bekker **5** ἀπ᾽ β : ὑπ᾽ γ ἐπιπολῆς γ : ἐξ ἐπιπολῆς β; cf. 8.35, 18.5, 80.9.2, Phryn. 104 etc. **6** ἐπὶ τριακοσίας γ : ἐς τετρακοσίας β : ἐς ϛʹ (ἕξ) E. Schwartz ἀποβάντες γ **7** διαθέειν Γ^{a}β δὲ τοῦ γ : οὖν τοῦ β **8** ἐποιήσαμεν γ **11** ἰχθύας β **12** ἐπεὶ β : ἐπειδὴ γ ἐπέλιπε Ω προσελθόντες β **14** πάγου β **14–15** διολισθαίνοντες Ωβ; cf. 10.12 **15** ἤδη om. β **17** οὖν γ : δὲ β **18** ἐπιλελοίπει SP **20** ὑπὸ β : ἐπὶ γ; cf. 8.32, 70.20 **22** ἐμβαίνομεν β **23–4** τυρὸς μέγιστος γ : τυρῶν μέγιστος πάνυ β **25** περίμετρον γ : μέγεθος β **26** ἀποθλίβοντες ἐπίνομεν γ : ἀπεθλίβομεν β **28** οὖν β : δ᾽ οὖν γ

three days next to the trophy, for now the sea was calm. On the fourth day we sailed away from the whale. On the sea we encountered many bodies of the giants killed in the battle at sea and, as we came up alongside them, we measured them and were astonished by their size. Then for some days we sailed on with a moderate breeze. But then a violent blast of wind from the north swept down upon us and froze us. From this point, the entire sea froze solid, not only on its surface, but to a depth of some 1,800 feet. The ice was so solid that when we disembarked we could skate over it.

Since the wind did not let up and we could not stand the cold, we thought of a solution: it was Scintharus who made the proposal. We excavated a huge cave in the frozen sea and stayed in it for thirty days, kindling fires and eating fish; we discovered the fish as we excavated into the ice. But, as our provisions had begun to give out, we went out to our frozen ship and broke it free from the ice. Hoisting sail, we scudded over the ice as if we were sailing over a smooth, calm sea. On the fifth day it began to warm up, the ice began to melt, and the frozen sea turned to water once again.

(3) After we had sailed for about three hundred stades, we landed on a small, uninhabited island on which we took on a supply of water—ours had already run out. Once we had killed two wild oxen with our arrows, we sailed off again. These wild oxen did not have horns on their heads, but under their eyes, as the god of blame, Momos, recommended. In a short time we entered an open sea, a sea not of water but of milk, and a white island, covered in vines, came into sight. It was a huge lump of cheese, as we discovered when we ate some of it. The island was twenty-five stades in circumference. The vines on it were heavy with grapes. But when we pressed them, we did not drink wine, we drank milk. Built in the middle of the island was the sanctuary of the Nereid Galatea, as we learned from an inscription. We spent some time on the island. The cheese that was its earth

μὲν ἡμῖν καὶ σιτίον ἡ γῆ ὑπῆρχεν, ποτὸν δὲ τὸ γάλα τὸ ἐκ τῶν βοτρύων. βασιλεύειν δὲ τῶν χωρίων τούτων ἐλέγετο Τυρὼ ἡ Σαλμωνέως, μετὰ τὴν ἐντεῦθεν ἀπαλλαγὴν ταύτην παρὰ τοῦ Ποσειδῶνος λαβοῦσα τὴν τιμήν.

Μείναντες δὲ ἡμέρας ἐν τῇ νήσῳ πέντε, τῇ ἕκτῃ ἐξωρμήσαμεν, (4) αὔρας μέν τινος παραπεμπούσης, λειοκύμονος δὲ οὔσης τῆς θαλάττης· ὀγδόῃ δὲ ἡμέρᾳ πλέοντες οὐκέτι διὰ τοῦ γάλακτος, ἀλλ᾽ ἤδη ἐν ἁλμυρῷ καὶ κυανέῳ ὕδατι, καθορῶμεν ἀνθρώπους πολλοὺς ἐπὶ τοῦ πελάγους διαθέοντας, ἅπαντα ἡμῖν προσεοικότας, καὶ τὰ σώματα καὶ τὰ μεγέθη, πλὴν τῶν ποδῶν μόνων· ταῦτα γὰρ φέλλινα εἶχον, ἀφ᾽ οὗ δή, οἶμαι, καὶ ἐκαλοῦντο Φελλόποδες. ἐθαυμάσαμεν οὖν ἰδόντες οὐ βαπτιζομένους, ἀλλὰ ὑπερέχοντας τῶν κυμάτων καὶ ἀδεῶς ὁδοιποροῦντας. οἱ δὲ καὶ προσῄεσαν καὶ ἠσπάζοντο ἡμᾶς Ἑλληνικῇ φωνῇ· ἔλεγον δὲ εἰς Φελλὼ τὴν αὑτῶν πατρίδα ἐπείγεσθαι. μέχρι μὲν οὖν τινος συνωδοιπόρουν ἡμῖν παραθέοντες, εἶτα ἀποτραπόμενοι τῆς ὁδοῦ ἐβάδιζον εὔπλοιαν ἡμῖν ἐπευξάμενοι.

Μετ᾽ ὀλίγον δὲ πολλαὶ νῆσοι ἐφαίνοντο, πλησίον μὲν ἐξ ἀριστερῶν ἡ Φελλώ, ἐς ἣν ἐκεῖνοι ἔσπευδον, πόλις ἐπὶ μεγάλου καὶ στρογγύλου φελλοῦ κατοικουμένη· πόρρωθεν δὲ καὶ μᾶλλον ἐν δεξιᾷ πέντε μέγισται καὶ ὑψηλόταται, καὶ πῦρ πολὺ ἀπ᾽ αὐτῶν ἀνεκαίετο, κατὰ δὲ τὴν πρῷραν μία πλατεῖα καὶ ταπεινή, σταδίους ἀπέχουσα οὐκ ἐλάττους πεντακοσίων. ἤδη δὲ πλησίον ἦμεν, καὶ (5) θαυμαστή τις αὔρα περιέπνευσεν ἡμᾶς, ἡδεῖα καὶ εὐώδης, οἵαν φησὶν ὁ συγγραφεὺς Ἡρόδοτος ἀπόζειν τῆς εὐδαίμονος Ἀραβίας. οἷον γὰρ ἀπὸ ῥόδων καὶ ναρκίσσων καὶ ὑακίνθων καὶ κρίνων καὶ ἴων, ἔτι δὲ μυρρίνης καὶ δάφνης καὶ ἀμπελάνθης, τοιοῦτον ἡμῖν τὸ ἡδὺ προσέβαλλεν. ἡσθέντες δὲ τῇ ὀσμῇ καὶ χρηστὰ ἐκ μακρῶν πόνων ἐλπίσαντες κατ᾽ ὀλίγον ἤδη πλησίον τῆς νήσου ἐγινόμεθα.

1 μὲν γ : τε β τὸ ἐκ γ : ἐκ β **2** τούτων τῶν χωρίων β **7** τῇ ὀγδόῃ δὲ β **8** κυανέῳ γ : κυανῷ Γ^{a}β **10** μόνων τῶν ποδῶν β **12** ἐθαυμάζομεν β **14** δὲ εἰς ΩS : τε εἰς β : δὲ καὶ εἰς Γ ἑαυτῶν Ω **15** οὖν γ : δὴ β **20** καὶ στρογγύλου Γ : om. Ωβ **21** ἀπ᾽ om. β **23** ἦμεν γ : τε ἦμεν β **24** οἵαν Ωβ : οἷον Γ^{1} **25** Hdt. 3. 113 **26** ῥόδου καὶ ναρκίσσου καὶ ὑακίνθου β **27** μυρσίνης β **28** ὀδμῇ β **29** ἐγινόμεθα Γ : ἐγενόμεθα Ω : γινόμεθα β

provided us with our meat and grain and the milk from its vines provided us with drink. It was said that Tyro, the daughter of Salmoneus, had been queen of the island, and that, after she had left our world, she received this honour from Poseidon.

ON PAST THE ISLAND OF CORK

(4) After we had stayed on this island for five days, we set out from it on the sixth, with a breeze to send us on our way over a smooth sea. On the eighth day we were no longer sailing on a sea of milk but on briny, deep blue waters. We sighted many men racing over the surface of the sea. They were like us in all ways, both in their bodies and their size; only their feet were different. These were of cork and, I think, this feature gave them their name, cork-feet. We were amazed as we watched them moving along. They did not get wet but skimmed over the waves with no fear as they sped across the sea. They came up to us and greeted us in Greek. They told us that they were in a great hurry to get to their home, the Island of Cork. They kept us company for a certain distance as they ran alongside our ship. Then they wished us a prosperous voyage and headed in another direction.

Before long, numerous islands came into sight. Nearby to port was the Island of Cork, Phello, the destination of the cork-feet. On it was a city built on top of a huge, round cork. Far ahead of us and slightly to the starboard were five great and enormously mountainous islands. They were flaming with an intense blaze. Just before our prow was a single flat and low-lying island at a distance of no less than five hundred stades. (5) We had already drawn near it when an amazing breeze enveloped us. It was sweet and fragrant, like the breeze the writer Herodotus says emanates from the coast of Arabia Felix.[4] It seemed to waft the scent of roses, narcissi, hyacinths, lilies, violets, myrrh, flowering laurel, and tender vine leaves. We were enchanted by the fragrance and had begun to hope that we had exchanged toil and trouble for prosperity.

[4] Hdt. 3.113.

ἔνθα δὴ καὶ καθεωρῶμεν λιμένας τε πολλοὺς περὶ πᾶσαν ἀκλύστους καὶ μεγάλους, ποταμούς τε διαυγεῖς ἐξιέντας ἠρέμα εἰς τὴν θάλατταν, ἔτι δὲ λειμῶνας καὶ ὕλας καὶ ὄρνεα μουσικά, τὰ μὲν ἐπὶ τῶν ἠϊόνων ᾄδοντα, πολλὰ δὲ καὶ ἐπὶ τῶν κλάδων· ἀήρ τε κοῦφος καὶ εὔπνους περιεκέχυτο τὴν χώραν· καὶ αὖραι δέ τινες ἡδεῖαι πνέουσαι ἠρέμα τὴν ὕλην διεσάλευον, ὥστε καὶ ἀπὸ τῶν κλάδων κινουμένων τερπνὰ καὶ συνεχῆ μέλη ἀπεσυρίζετο, ἐοικότα τοῖς ἐπ᾽ ἐρημίας αὐλήμασι τῶν πλαγίων αὐλῶν. καὶ μὴν καὶ βοὴ σύμμικτος ἠκούετο ἄθρους, οὐ θορυβώδης, ἀλλ᾽ οἵα γένοιτ᾽ ἂν ἐν συμποσίῳ, τῶν μὲν αὐλούντων, τῶν δὲ ἐπαινούντων, ἐνίων δὲ (6) κροτούντων πρὸς αὐλὸν ἢ κιθάραν. τούτοις ἅπασι κηλούμενοι κατήχθημεν, ὁρμίσαντες δὲ τὴν ναῦν ἀπεβαίνομεν, τὸν Σκίνθαρον ἐν αὐτῇ καὶ δύο τῶν ἑταίρων ἀπολιπόντες. προϊόντες δὲ διὰ λειμῶνος εὐανθοῦς ἐντυγχάνομεν τοῖς φρουροῖς καὶ περιπόλοις, οἱ δὲ δήσαντες ἡμᾶς ῥοδίνοις στεφάνοις—οὗτος γὰρ μέγιστος παρ᾽ αὐτοῖς δεσμός ἐστιν—ἀνῆγον ὡς τὸν ἄρχοντα, παρ᾽ ὧν δὴ καὶ καθ᾽ ὁδὸν ἠκούσαμεν ὡς ἡ μὲν νῆσος εἴη τῶν Μακάρων προσαγορευομένη, ἄρχοι δὲ ὁ Κρὴς Ῥαδάμανθυς. καὶ δὴ ἀναχθέντες ὡς αὐτὸν (7) ἐν τάξει τῶν δικαζομένων ἔστημεν τέταρτοι. ἦν δὲ ἡ μὲν πρώτη δίκη περὶ Αἴαντος τοῦ Τελαμῶνος, εἴτε χρὴ αὐτὸν συνεῖναι τοῖς ἥρωσιν εἴτε καὶ μή· κατηγορεῖτο δὲ αὐτοῦ ὅτι μεμήνοι καὶ ἑαυτὸν ἀπεκτόνοι. τέλος δὲ πολλῶν ῥηθέντων ἔγνω ὁ Ῥαδάμανθυς, νῦν μὲν αὐτὸν πιόμενον τοῦ ἐλλεβόρου παραδοθῆναι Ἱπποκράτει τῷ Κῴῳ ἰατρῷ, ὕστερον δὲ σωφρονήσαντα μετέχειν τοῦ συμποσίου. (8) δευτέρα δὲ ἦν κρίσις ἐρωτική, Θησέως καὶ Μενελάου περὶ τῆς Ἑλένης διαγωνιζομένων, ποτέρῳ χρὴ αὐτὴν συνοικεῖν. καὶ ὁ Ῥαδάμανθυς ἐδίκασε Μενελάῳ συνεῖναι αὐτὴν ἅτε καὶ τοσαῦτα πονήσαντι καὶ κινδυνεύσαντι τοῦ γάμου ἕνεκα· καὶ γὰρ αὖ τῷ

1 περὶ πᾶσαν] παντάπασιν E. Schwartz **2** ἐξιόντας β **3** τὰ γ : ὅτε β **4** τε γ : δὲ β **6** διαπνέουσαι β **9** ἠκούετο] ἐφέρετο Thom. Mag. ἄθρους γ, Thom. Mag. : om. β οἷα γ **10** τῶν δὲ γ : ἄλλων δὲ β ἐπαινούντων] ἐπᾳδόντων Rohde **14** εὐανθοῦντος Ωβ ἐτυγχάνομεν Γ **16** δὴ καὶ γ : δὴ β **17–18** προσαγορευομένη γZ : προσαγορευομένων PN **18** ἄρχει β **21** εἴτε μή β αὑτὸν β **22** ἀποκτάνοι γ ἔγνω ὁ Ῥαδάμανθυς γ : ὁ Ῥαδάμανθυς ἀπεφαίνετο β **23** παραδοθῆναι Γ[a]β : παραδοῦναι γ **26** αὐτὴν χρὴ β **27** ἅτε καὶ] ἅτε Ω **28** ποιήσαντι Z αὖ τῷ Fritzsche : αὐτῷ codd.

THE AUTHOR AND HIS COMPANY COME TO THE ISLAND OF THE BLEST

Gradually we drew closer to the island. Around it we could see many large, protected harbors and translucent rivers flowing gently into the sea. We could also see meadows and woods and songbirds. Some were singing on the capes of the island; many of them were perched on the tops of the trees. The entire island was enveloped with a still and gentle atmosphere. The sweet and steady breath of breezes made the leaves quiver so that from the stirring branches sweet, unbroken melodies warbled like the music of cross-flutes played in country solitude. And a medley of murmuring sounds could be heard as well. It was not raucous, but like the confused sounds one hears at a symposium, as some play the wooden flute, others cry out "Bravo," and some beat out a rhythm on a flute or cithara. (**6**) Captivated by the enchantment of the place, we cast anchor and disembarked, leaving Scintharus and two of our companions with the ship. As we made our way through a meadow lush with flowers, we encountered the guards of the island on patrol. They bound us with wreaths of roses—these were the sturdiest restraints on the island—and they took us to their leader. On our way, we learned from our captors that the island was called the Island of the Blest and that its ruler was the Cretan, Rhadamanthus. Once we had been brought to him, we took our place as fourth in the docket that listed those awaiting judgment.

The first case concerned Ajax, the son of Telamon. The question was whether he should join the heroes. The charges brought against him were madness and suicide. Rhadamanthus decreed that for the present he should drink a dose of hellebore and be committed to the care of the doctor, Hippocrates of Cos, for therapy; then, when he had returned to his senses, he could participate in the symposium. (**8**) The second case involved passion. Theseus and Menelaus were in a dispute about which of the two of them Helen should live with. Rhadamanthus' decision was that she should

Θησεῖ καὶ ἄλλας εἶναι γυναῖκας, τήν τε Ἀμαζόνα καὶ τὰς τοῦ
Μίνωος θυγατέρας. τρίτη δ᾽ ἐδικάσθη περὶ προεδρίας Ἀλεξάνδρῳ (9)
τε τῷ Φιλίππου καὶ Ἀννίβᾳ τῷ Καρχηδονίῳ, καὶ ἔδοξε προέχειν
ὁ Ἀλέξανδρος, καὶ θρόνος αὐτῷ ἐτέθη παρὰ Κῦρον τὸν Πέρσην
τὸν πρότερον. τέταρτοι δὲ ἡμεῖς προσήχθημεν· καὶ ὁ μὲν ἤρετο τί (10)
παθόντες ἔτι ζῶντες ἱεροῦ χωρίου ἐπιβαίημεν· ἡμεῖς δὲ πάντα ἑξῆς
διηγησάμεθα. οὕτω δὴ μεταστησάμενος ἡμᾶς ἐπὶ πολὺν χρόνον
ἐσκέπτετο καὶ τοῖς συνέδροις ἐκοινοῦτο περὶ ἡμῶν. συνήδρευον δὲ
ἄλλοι τε πολλοὶ καὶ Ἀριστείδης ὁ δίκαιος ὁ Ἀθηναῖος. ὡς δὲ ἔδοξεν
αὐτῷ, ἀπεφήναντο, τῆς μὲν φιλοπραγμοσύνης καὶ τῆς ἀποδημίας,
ἐπειδὰν ἀποθάνωμεν, δοῦναι τὰς εὐθύνας, τὸ δὲ νῦν ῥητὸν χρόνον
μείναντας ἐν τῇ νήσῳ καὶ συνδιαιτηθέντας τοῖς ἥρωσιν ἀπελθεῖν.
ἔταξαν δὲ καὶ τὴν προθεσμίαν τῆς ἐπιδημίας μὴ πλέον μηνῶν ἑπτά.

Τοὐντεῦθεν αὐτομάτων ἡμῖν τῶν στεφάνων περιρρυέντων (11)
ἐλελύμεθα καὶ εἰς τὴν πόλιν ἠγόμεθα καὶ εἰς τὸ τῶν Μακάρων
συμπόσιον. αὐτὴ μὲν οὖν ἡ πόλις πᾶσα χρυσῆ, τὸ δὲ τεῖχος περίκειται
σμαράγδινον· πύλαι δέ εἰσιν ἑπτά, πᾶσαι μονόξυλοι κινναμώμινοι·
τὸ μέντοι ἔδαφος τῆς πόλεως καὶ ἡ ἐντὸς τοῦ τείχους γῆ ἐλεφαντίνη·
ναοὶ δὲ πάντων θεῶν βηρύλλου λίθου ᾠκοδομημένοι, καὶ
βωμοὶ ἐν αὐτοῖς μέγιστοι μονόλιθοι ἀμεθύστινοι, ἐφ᾽ ὧν ποιοῦσι
τὰς ἑκατόμβας. περὶ δὲ τὴν πόλιν ῥεῖ ποταμὸς μύρου τοῦ
καλλίστου, τὸ πλάτος πήχεων ἑκατὸν βασιλικῶν, βάθος δὲ <πέντε>
ὥστε νεῖν εὐμαρῶς. λουτρὰ δέ ἐστιν αὐτοῖς οἶκοι μεγάλοι ὑάλινοι,
τῷ κινναμώμῳ ἐγκαιόμενοι· ἀντὶ μέντοι τοῦ ὕδατος ἐν ταῖς
πυέλοις δρόσος θερμὴ ἔστιν. ἐσθῆτι δὲ χρῶνται ἀραχνίοις λεπτοῖς, (12)
πορφυροῖς. αὐτοὶ δὲ σώματα μὲν οὐκ ἔχουσιν, ἀλλ᾽ ἀναφεῖς
καὶ ἄσαρκοί εἰσιν, μορφὴν δὲ καὶ ἰδέαν μόνην ἐμφαίνουσιν, καὶ

c. 9 cf. 77.25 **3** ἀνίβᾳ β **6** ἱεροῦ χωρίου Γ^{a}β : ἱερῷ χωρίῳ γ ἑξῆς om. β 7 οὕτω δὴ γ : οὗτος δὲ β **9** ὁ (ante Ἀθηναῖος) om. β **10** ἀπεφήνατο codd. : corr. E. Schwartz πολυπραγμοσύνης β ἐπιδημίας Z; sed cf. Plat. *Phd.* 61 e **11** νυνὶ β **13** ἔταξε β ἀποδημίας γ πλεῖον β **16** seq. cf. N.T. Apoc. 21.18 seq. **16** αὐτὴ Γ^{a}β : αὕτη γ περικεῖται Γ^{a}β : παρακεῖται γ **18** τῆς γ : τὸ τῆς β τοῦ om. ZN **21** τοῦ om. β **22** ε′ (= πέντε) suppl. E. Schwartz **23** ὥστ᾽ ἐννεῖν Herwerden ὑέλινοι β **26** ἀναφεῖς Γ^{a}βΩ : ἀφανεῖς Γ : ἀσαφεῖς Γ^{x} : διαφανεῖς Rohde **27** μόνον Γ^{a}β ἐμφαίνουσιν β : ἔχουσι(ν) καὶ ἐμφαίνουσιν γ

live with Menelaus, considering that he had gone through so much suffering and danger for the sake of his marriage. In any case, Theseus had many other wives, the Amazon and the daughters of Minos. (9) The third case involved the claims on precedence between Alexander, son of Philip, and Hannibal of Carthage. Alexander was judged as having the superior claim and a ceremonial throne was set up for him next to Cyrus the Elder, king of Persia.

(10) We were then brought forward as the fourth case on the docket. Rhadamanthus asked what had possessed us, when we were still alive, to set foot on this sacred soil. We told him our whole story. Afterwards he removed us from his chambers, reflected on the matter for some time, and consulted some of the judges on the bench about our case. Many judges were seated with him, among them the Athenian Aristides the Just. And thus it was decided that for our intrusiveness and travels we should, on our deaths, pay the penalty. For a stipulated period of time we could also stay on the island and associate with the heroes. But then we had to leave. They fixed the limit of our stay at seven months and no more.

(11) At just that moment our flower fetters slipped from us of their own accord and we were free men. We were led up to the city and to the banquet of the blest. The interior of the city was of solid gold, the walls surrounding it of emerald. Seven gates, all of solid cinnamon wood, provided entrance to the city, and the pavement and the interior of the walls were ivory. The temples of all the gods were made of precious beryl and the huge altars within were made of solid blocks of amethyst. The heroes perform their hecatombs on these altars. A river of the finest and most fragrant myrrh encircles the city; it is 100 royal cubits wide and five deep, perfect for swimming. Their baths are large glass houses heated by sticks of cinnamon. Instead of water the pipes conduct heated dew. They wear clothes of subtle spider webs of purple hue. (12) They have no bodies, but are intangible and fleshless. They reveal to the eye only a shape and a form. And, even though they are in their

ἀσώματοι ὄντες ὅμως συνεστᾶσιν καὶ κινοῦνται καὶ φρονοῦσι καὶ φωνὴν ἀφιᾶσιν, καὶ ὅλως ἔοικε γυμνή τις ἡ ψυχὴ αὐτῶν περιπολεῖν τὴν τοῦ σώματος ὁμοιότητα περικειμένη· εἰ γοῦν μὴ ἅψαιτό τις, οὐκ ἂν ἐξελέγξειε μὴ εἶναι σῶμα τὸ ὁρώμενον· εἰσὶ γὰρ ὥσπερ σκιαὶ ὀρθαί, οὐ μέλαιναι. γηράσκει δὲ οὐδείς, ἀλλ᾽ ἐφ᾽ ἧς ἂν ἡλικίας ἔλθῃ παραμένει. οὐ μὴν οὐδὲ νὺξ παρ᾽ αὐτοῖς γίνεται, οὐδὲ ἡμέρα πάνυ λαμπρά· καθάπερ δὲ τὸ λυκαυγὲς ἤδη πρὸς ἕω, μηδέπω ἀνατείλαντος ἡλίου, τοιοῦτο φῶς ἐπέχει τὴν γῆν. καὶ μέντοι καὶ ὥραν μίαν ἴσασιν τοῦ ἔτους· αἰεὶ γὰρ παρ᾽ (13) αὐτοῖς ἔαρ ἐστὶ καὶ εἷς ἄνεμος πνεῖ παρ᾽ αὐτοῖς ὁ ζέφυρος. ἡ δὲ χώρα πᾶσι μὲν ἄνθεσιν, πᾶσι δὲ φυτοῖς ἡμέροις τε καὶ σκιεροῖς τέθηλεν· αἱ μὲν γὰρ ἄμπελοι δωδεκάφοροί εἰσιν καὶ κατὰ μῆνα ἕκαστον καρποφοροῦσιν· τὰς δὲ ῥοιὰς καὶ τὰς μηλέας καὶ τὴν ἄλλην ὀπώραν ἔλεγον εἶναι τρισκαιδεκάφορον· ἑνὸς γὰρ μηνὸς τοῦ παρ᾽ αὐτοῖς Μινῴου δὶς καρποφορεῖν· ἀντὶ δὲ πυροῦ οἱ στάχυες ἄρτον ἕτοιμον ἐπ᾽ ἄκρων φύουσιν ὥσπερ μύκητας. πηγαὶ δὲ περὶ τὴν πόλιν ὕδατος μὲν πέντε καὶ ἑξήκοντα καὶ τριακόσιαι, μέλιτος δὲ ἄλλαι τοσαῦται, μύρου δὲ πεντακόσιαι, μικρότεραι μέντοι αὗται, καὶ ποταμοὶ γάλακτος ἑπτὰ καὶ οἴνου ὀκτώ.

(14) Τὸ δὲ συμπόσιον ἔξω τῆς πόλεως πεποίηνται ἐν τῷ Ἠλυσίῳ καλουμένῳ πεδίῳ· λειμὼν δέ ἐστιν κάλλιστος καὶ περὶ αὐτὸν ὕλη παντοία πυκνή, ἐπισκιάζουσα τοὺς κατακειμένους. καὶ στρωμνὴν μὲν ἐκ τῶν ἀνθῶν ὑποβέβληνται, διακονοῦνται δὲ καὶ παραφέρουσιν ἕκαστα οἱ ἄνεμοι πλήν γε τοῦ οἰνοχοεῖν· τούτου γὰρ οὐδὲν δέονται, ἀλλ᾽ ἔστι δένδρα περὶ τὸ συμπόσιον ὑάλινα μεγάλα τῆς διαυγεστάτης ὑάλου, καὶ καρπός ἐστι τῶν δένδρων τούτων ποτήρια παντοῖα καὶ τὰς κατασκευὰς καὶ τὰ μεγέθη. ἐπειδὰν οὖν παρίῃ τις ἐς τὸ συμπόσιον, τρυγήσας ἓν ἢ καὶ δύο τῶν ἐκπωμάτων παρατίθεται, τὰ δὲ αὐτίκα οἴνου πλήρη γίνεται. οὕτω μὲν

1 συνεστᾶσιν γ : οὖν ἑστᾶσι β **4** ἐλέγξειε β **6** οὐδὲ μὴν οὐδὲ β **7** καθάπερ δὲ γ : ἀλλὰ καθάπερ β **8** τοιοῦτο φῶς γ : τοιοῦτον β **9** ὡρῶν β **10** παρ᾽ αὐτοῖς om. β c. 13 cf. *Od.* 7.114 seq., Diod. 2.56.7 **14** ἔλεγον μὲν εἶναι β **15** Μινῴου om. β καρποφορεῖ γ **16** ἄρτους ἑτοίμους β ἄκρων Ω : ἄκρῳ Γ : ἄκρου $Γ^{a}$β **20** πεποίηται γ **21** καλουμένῳ om. Ω **23** ἀνθέων SPN **23–4** διαφέρουσιν β **25** οὐδὲν $Γ^{a}$β : οὐδὲ γ **26** καὶ καρπός γ : ὁ καρπὸς δέ β **28** παρείῃ ΓΖ **29** τὰ δὲ… γίνεται Γ et (om. οἴνου) Ω : om. β

nature incorporeal, they can move about and think and talk. All in all, they resemble fluid wisps of humans moving about and enveloped with the appearance of a body. And if you did not touch one you could never be sure that what you saw before you was not a body. The dead are like upright shadows, but not as dark. None ever grows old, but they remain at the age they were when they arrived on the island. Nor in this region is there anything like our night nor is the day very bright. The light there is like the first illumination of the sky just before dawn. A faint glimmer envelops the land. And they know only a single season throughout the year. On this island spring is eternal, and the only wind that blows there is the West Wind.

(13) The land is fertile with every variety of cultivated and wild plant. The vines produce grapes twelve times a year, that is, once every month. They say that the pomegranate and apple trees and still other fruit trees bear fruit thirteen times a year. The explanation they give for this is that they have a month of Minos, when there are two crops that ripen. Stalks of wheat produce ready baked bread from their crests, as if the loaves were mushrooms. Three hundred and sixty-five fresh water springs flow around the city, as do an equal number of springs of honey. Of myrrh there are five hundred springs, but these are not abundant. There are seven rivers of milk and eight of wine.

(14) The symposium is held outside the city on what they call the Elysian Fields. There is a meadow of extraordinary beauty fringed by a dense wood of every variety of tree. The trees cast their shade over the reclining shades. As a cushion for their couches they put down a bed of flowers, and the winds wait on them and serve them everything except wine. They have no need of wine servers. Trees of the most transparent glass sprout drinking cups of all shapes and sizes. When a guest arrives at the symposium, he culls one or two of these cups and places them on the table before him. The cups brim up immediately with wine; this is the way they drink. The blest do not

πίνουσιν, ἀντὶ δὲ τῶν στεφάνων αἱ ἀηδόνες καὶ τὰ ἄλλα τὰ μουσικὰ ὄρνεα ἐκ τῶν πλησίον λειμώνων τοῖς στόμασιν ἀνθολογοῦντα κατανίφει αὐτοὺς μετ᾽ ᾠδῆς ὑπερπετόμενα. καὶ μὴν καὶ μυρίζονται ὧδε· νεφέλαι πυκναὶ ἀνασπάσασαι μύρον ἐκ τῶν πηγῶν καὶ τοῦ ποταμοῦ καὶ ἐπιστᾶσαι ὑπὲρ τὸ συμπόσιον ἠρέμα τῶν ἀνέμων ὑποθλιβόντων ὕουσι λεπτὸν ὥσπερ δρόσον.

Ἐπὶ δὲ τῷ δείπνῳ μουσικῇ τε καὶ ᾠδαῖς σχολάζουσιν· ᾄδεται (15) δὲ αὐτοῖς τὰ Ὁμήρου ἔπη μάλιστα· καὶ αὐτὸς δὲ πάρεστι καὶ συνευωχεῖται αὐτοῖς ὑπὲρ τὸν Ὀδυσσέα κατακείμενος. οἱ μὲν οὖν χοροὶ ἐκ παίδων εἰσὶν καὶ παρθένων· ἐξάρχουσι δὲ καὶ συνᾴδουσιν Εὔνομός τε ὁ Λοκρὸς καὶ Ἀρίων ὁ Λέσβιος καὶ Ἀνακρέων καὶ Στησίχορος· καὶ γὰρ τοῦτον παρ᾽ αὐτοῖς ἐθεασάμην, ἤδη τῆς Ἑλένης αὐτῷ διηλλαγμένης. ἐπειδὰν δὲ οὗτοι παύσωνται ᾄδοντες, δεύτερος χορὸς παρέρχεται ἐκ κύκνων καὶ χελιδόνων καὶ ἀηδόνων. ἐπειδὰν δὲ καὶ οὗτοι ᾄσωσιν, τότε ἤδη πᾶσα ἡ ὕλη ἐπαυλεῖ τῶν ἀνέμων καταρχόντων. μέγιστον δὲ δὴ πρὸς (16) εὐφροσύνην ἐκεῖνο ἔχουσιν· πηγαί εἰσι δύο παρὰ τὸ συμπόσιον, ἡ μὲν γέλωτος, ἡ δὲ ἡδονῆς· ἐκ τούτων ἑκατέρας πάντες ἐν ἀρχῇ τῆς εὐωχίας πίνουσιν καὶ τὸ λοιπὸν ἡδόμενοι καὶ γελῶντες διάγουσιν.

Βούλομαι δὲ εἰπεῖν καὶ τῶν ἐπισήμων οὕστινας παρ᾽ αὐτοῖς (17) ἐθεασάμην· πάντας μὲν τοὺς ἡμιθέους καὶ τοὺς ἐπὶ Ἴλιον στρατεύσαντας πλήν γε δὴ τοῦ Λοκροῦ Αἴαντος, ἐκεῖνον δὲ μόνον ἔφασκον ἐν τῷ τῶν ἀσεβῶν χώρῳ κολάζεσθαι, βαρβάρων δὲ Κύρους τε ἀμφοτέρους καὶ τὸν Σκύθην Ἀνάχαρσιν καὶ τὸν Θρᾷκα Ζάμολξιν καὶ Νομᾶν τὸν Ἰταλιώτην, καὶ μὴν καὶ Λυκοῦργον τὸν Λακεδαιμόνιον καὶ Φωκίωνα καὶ Τέλλον τοὺς Ἀθηναίους, καὶ τοὺς σοφοὺς ἄνευ Περιάνδρου. εἶδον δὲ καὶ Σωκράτη τὸν Σωφρονίσκου ἀδολεσχοῦντα μετὰ Νέστορος καὶ Παλαμήδους· περὶ δὲ αὐτὸν ἦσαν Ὑάκινθός τε ὁ Λακεδαιμόνιος καὶ ὁ Θεσπιεὺς Νάρκισσος καὶ Ὕλας καὶ ἄλλοι καλοί. καί μοι ἐδόκει ἐρᾶν τοῦ Ὑακίνθου· τὰ πολλὰ γοῦν ἐκεῖνον διήλεγχεν. ἐλέγετο δὲ χαλεπαίνειν αὐτῷ

2 τοῖς στόμασιν om. β **3** κατανείφει γ ὑπερπετώμενα Γ **4** ὡδί β **6** ἀποθλιβόντων β **8** τὰ τοῦ Ὁμήρου β καὶ αὐτὸς πάρεστι β **13** δὲ καὶ οὗτοι β **15** τότε δὴ β **18** ἑκατέρων γ **22** δὴ om. γ **23** τῶν om. β **27** Σωκράτην β **28** cf. 38.18, 77.6.4, Pl. *Ap.* 41 b **31** γοῦν Γ : δὲ Ω : δ᾽ οὖν β

wear garlands, but nightingales and other song birds from the meadows nearby nip flowers with their beaks and shower the banqueters with a mist of petals as they flutter and warble above them. Now, this is how they anoint themselves with myrrh. Thick clouds draw up myrrh from the springs and river and, as they hover over the symposium, they discharge a fine mist of dew-like myrrh under the pressure of gentle breezes. (15) As they banquet, they entertain themselves with music and song. Homer's epics are their favorite poetry. Indeed, Homer himself was present and he joined in the feasting, reclining on a banqueting couch above Odysseus. Choral dances are performed by young men and young women. Leading the choruses and singing along with them were Eunomus of Locris, Arion of Lesbos, Anacreon, and Stesichorus. Yes, I actually saw Stesichorus in the company; Helen had forgiven him for having insulted her. Then when the choruses have finished performing, a second chorus of swans, swallows, and nightingales makes its appearance and, once they have finished singing, the entire woods pipe like woodwinds as the winds begin to stir. (16) The greatest event of their festivities, which ensures a good time, is this: two springs bubble up along the grounds of the symposium: one flows with Laughter and the other with Mirth. Everyone drinks from them at the beginning of the symposium and they spend their entire time in mirth and laughter.

(17) Now I want to mention who were the important people I saw there among the blest. I saw all of the demigods and the Greeks who fought at Troy, with the exception of Ajax of Locris. People there say that he alone among the heroes was being punished in the Realm of the Impious. Of barbarians I saw the older and the younger Cyrus, Anacharsis the Scythian, Zalmoxis the Thracian, and Numa the Italian. I also saw Lycurgus of Lacedaemon, Phocion and Tellus of Athens, and all the seven sages, except Periander. I saw Socrates too, the son of Sophroniscus, chatting garrulously with Nestor and Palamedes. Standing at his side were Hyacinthus of Lacedaemon, Narcissus of Thespiae, Hylas, and other good-looking young men. I got the impression that he was in love with Hyacinthus—he interrogated him the most. It was reported that Rhadamanthus was very annoyed

ὁ Ῥαδάμανθυς καὶ ἠπειληκέναι πολλάκις ἐκβαλεῖν αὐτὸν ἐκ τῆς νήσου, ἢν φλυαρῇ καὶ μὴ ἐθέλῃ ἀφεὶς τὴν εἰρωνείαν εὐωχεῖσθαι. Πλάτων δὲ μόνος οὐ παρῆν, ἀλλ᾽ ἐλέγετο [καὶ] αὐτὸς ἐν τῇ ἀναπλασθείσῃ ὑπ᾽ αὐτοῦ πόλει οἰκεῖν χρώμενος τῇ πολιτείᾳ καὶ (18) τοῖς νόμοις οἷς συνέγραψεν. οἱ μέντοι ἀμφ᾽ Ἀρίστιππόν τε καὶ Ἐπίκουρον τὰ πρῶτα παρ᾽ αὐτοῖς ἐφέροντο ἡδεῖς τε ὄντες καὶ κεχαρισμένοι καὶ συμποτικώτατοι. παρῆν δὲ καὶ Αἴσωπος ὁ Φρύξ· τούτῳ δὲ ὅσα καὶ γελωτοποιῷ χρῶνται. Διογένης μέν γε ὁ Σινωπεὺς τοσοῦτον μετέβαλεν τοῦ τρόπου, ὥστε γῆμαι μὲν ἑταίραν τὴν Λαΐδα, ὀρχεῖσθαι δὲ πολλάκις ὑπὸ μέθης ἀνιστάμενον καὶ παροινεῖν. τῶν δὲ Στωϊκῶν οὐδεὶς παρῆν· ἔτι γὰρ ἐλέγοντο ἀναβαίνειν τὸν τῆς ἀρετῆς ὄρθιον λόφον. ἠκούομεν δὲ καὶ περὶ Χρυσίππου ὅτι οὐ πρότερον αὐτῷ ἐπιβῆναι τῆς νήσου θέμις, πρὶν τὸ τέταρτον ἑαυτὸν ἐλλεβορίσῃ. τοὺς δὲ Ἀκαδημαϊκοὺς ἔλεγον ἐθέλειν μὲν ἐλθεῖν, ἐπέχειν δὲ ἔτι καὶ διασκέπτεσθαι· μηδὲ γὰρ αὐτὸ τοῦτό πω καταλαμβάνειν, εἰ καὶ νῆσός τις τοιαύτη ἐστίν. ἄλλως τε τὴν ἐπὶ τοῦ Ῥαδαμάνθυος, οἶμαι, κρίσιν ἐδεδοίκεσαν, ἅτε καὶ τὸ κριτήριον αὐτοὶ ἀνῃρηκότες. πολλοὺς δὲ αὐτῶν ἔφασκον ὁρμηθέντας ἀκολουθεῖν τοῖς ἀφικνουμένοις ὑπὸ νωθείας ἀπολείπεσθαι μὴ καταλαμβάνοντας καὶ ἀναστρέφειν ἐκ μέσης τῆς ὁδοῦ.

(19) Οὗτοι μὲν οὖν ἦσαν οἱ ἀξιολογώτατοι τῶν παρόντων. τιμῶσι δὲ μάλιστα τὸν Ἀχιλλέα καὶ μετὰ τοῦτον Θησέα. περὶ δὲ συνουσίας καὶ ἀφροδισίων οὕτω φρονοῦσιν· μίσγονται μὲν ἀναφανδὸν πάντων ὁρώντων καὶ γυναιξὶ καὶ ἄρρεσι, καὶ οὐδαμῶς τοῦτο αὐτοῖς αἰσχρὸν δοκεῖ· μόνος δὲ Σωκράτης διώμνυτο ἦ μὴν καθαρῶς πλησιάζειν τοῖς νέοις· καὶ μέντοι πάντες αὐτοῦ ἐπιορκεῖν κατεγίνωσκον· πολλάκις γοῦν ὁ μὲν Ὑάκινθος ἢ ὁ Νάρκισσος ὡμολόγουν, ἐκεῖνος δὲ ἠρνεῖτο. αἱ δὲ γυναῖκές εἰσι πᾶσι κοιναὶ

3 καὶ del. Sommerbrodt **3–5** ἐν τῇ ὑπ᾽ αὐτοῦ ἀναπλ. πολιτείᾳ καὶ τοῖς νόμοις οἷς ξυνέγραψε πολιτεύεσθαι β **8–9** μέν γε Γβ : μέντοι Ω **9** μὲν om. β **9–10** cf. D.L. 6.29, 54 **10** Λαΐδα τὴν ἑταίραν ὀρχεῖσθαί τε ὑπὸ μέθης πολλάκις β **11–12** cf. Hes. *Op.* 290 **13** πρὶν] πρὶν ἂν recc. **14** ἐλλεβορίσῃ ΓΡ (Z incert.) : ἐλλεβορίσει ΩΝ : ἐλλεβορίσειε Sommerbrodt ἀκαδημιακοὺς Γ (sed -αϊκοὺς schol.) **16** πω β : πῶς γ **17** τε γ : τε καὶ β **18** δὲ αὐτοῖς β **20** δ᾽ ἀπολ. ΩSZ **22** οὖν om. β οἱ om. β ἀξιολογικώτατοι β **25** ἄρσεσι β **25–6** αἰσχρὸν αὐτοῖς β **29** πᾶσαι β

with Socrates and often threatened to exile him from the island, if he insisted on talking and did not give up on his ironical distance and join in the festivities. Only Plato was absent. It was said that he was living in the city that he had invented and lived according to the *Republic* and *Laws* that he had written. (**18**) They indeed crowned the followers of Aristippus and Epicurus for their love of pleasure, their grace and charm, and for being great partygoers. Aesop of Phrygia was also there. He served as their court jester. As for Diogenes of Sinope, he had so changed in character that he had married the courtesan, Lais, and would often leap up from his banqueting couch while under the influence and dance and go on drinking too much. None of the Stoics was there. They were said to be still trudging up the steep path to Virtue. And, as for Chrysippus, we heard that it was not sanctioned for him to set foot on the island until he took a fourth dose of hellebore. They said too that the Academic philosophers wanted to come to the island, but that they were withholding assent from the decision and were still weighing it, for they had not yet arrived at a "clear and distinct" conclusion that such an island exists. And, I think, they would have dreaded the judgment of Rhadamanthus, because they themselves had rejected any sure basis of judgment. They said that some of them had actually begun to join the procession to the island, but out of sheer inertia they could not catch up, fell behind, and turned back half way there.

(**19**) These, then, were the most notable inhabitants of the island. The blest show the greatest deference to Achilles and after him to Theseus. Their wisdom concerning sexual intercourse is this. They have intercourse with partners of both sexes in the open for all to see, without any tinge of embarrassment. It was only Socrates who swore on oath that he did not have sex openly in public. Despite (or because of) his oath everyone condemned him for perjury. On many occasions Hyacinthus and Narcissus agreed with them, but Socrates remained firm in denial. They all have women in common and no one is jealous of his neighbour, and in this they are perfect "Platonists." The boys grant their favors to anyone who wants them and do not protest.

καὶ οὐδεὶς φθονεῖ τῷ πλησίον, ἀλλ᾿ εἰσὶ περὶ τοῦτο μάλιστα Πλατωνικώτατοι· καὶ οἱ παῖδες δὲ παρέχουσι τοῖς βουλομένοις οὐδὲν ἀντιλέγοντες.

Οὔπω δὲ δύο ἢ τρεῖς ἡμέραι διεληλύθεσαν, καὶ προσελθὼν ἐγὼ (20) Ὁμήρῳ τῷ ποιητῇ, σχολῆς οὔσης ἀμφοῖν, τά τε ἄλλα ἐπυνθανόμην καὶ ὅθεν εἴη, λέγων τοῦτο μάλιστα παρ᾿ ἡμῖν εἰσέτι νῦν ζητεῖσθαι. ὁ δὲ οὐδ᾿ αὐτὸς μὲν ἀγνοεῖν ἔφασκεν ὡς οἱ μὲν Χῖον, οἱ δὲ Σμυρναῖον, πολλοὶ δὲ Κολοφώνιον αὐτὸν νομίζουσιν· εἶναι μέντοι γε ἔλεγεν Βαβυλώνιος, καὶ παρά γε τοῖς πολίταις οὐχ Ὅμηρος, ἀλλὰ Τιγράνης καλεῖσθαι· ὕστερον δὲ ὁμηρεύσας παρὰ τοῖς Ἕλλησιν ἀλλάξαι τὴν προσηγορίαν. ἔτι δὲ καὶ περὶ τῶν ἀθετουμένων στίχων ἐπηρώτων, εἰ ὑπ᾿ ἐκείνου εἰσὶ γεγραμμένοι. καὶ ὃς ἔφασκε πάντας αὐτοῦ εἶναι. κατεγίνωσκον οὖν τῶν ἀμφὶ τὸν Ζηνόδοτον καὶ Ἀρίσταρχον γραμματικῶν πολλὴν τὴν ψυχρολογίαν. ἐπεὶ δὲ ταῦτα ἱκανῶς ἀπεκέκριτο, πάλιν αὐτὸν ἠρώτων τί δή ποτε ἀπὸ τῆς μήνιδος τὴν ἀρχὴν ἐποιήσατο· καὶ ὃς εἶπεν οὕτως ἐπελθεῖν αὐτῷ μηδὲν ἐπιτηδεύσαντι. καὶ μὴν κἀκεῖνο ἐπεθύμουν εἰδέναι, εἰ προτέραν ἔγραψεν τὴν Ὀδύσσειαν τῆς Ἰλιάδος, ὡς οἱ πολλοί φασιν· ὁ δὲ ἠρνεῖτο. ὅτι μὲν γὰρ οὐδὲ τυφλὸς ἦν, ὃ καὶ αὐτὸ περὶ αὐτοῦ λέγουσιν, αὐτίκα ἠπιστάμην· ἑώρα γάρ, ὥστε οὐδὲ πυνθάνεσθαι ἐδεόμην. πολλάκις δὲ καὶ ἄλλοτε τοῦτο ἐποίουν, εἴ ποτε αὐτὸν σχολὴν ἄγοντα ἑώρων· προσιὼν γὰρ ἄν τι ἐπυνθανόμην αὐτοῦ, καὶ ὃς προθύμως πάντα ἀπεκρίνετο, καὶ μάλιστα μετὰ τὴν δίκην, ἐπειδὴ ἐκράτησεν· ἦν γάρ τις γραφὴ κατ᾿ αὐτοῦ ἀπενηνεγμένη ὕβρεως ὑπὸ Θερσίτου ἐφ᾿ οἷς αὐτὸν ἐν τῇ ποιήσει ἔσκωψεν, καὶ ἐνίκησεν ὁ Ὅμηρος Ὀδυσσέως συναγορεύοντος.

Κατὰ δὲ τοὺς αὐτοὺς χρόνους ἀφίκετο καὶ Πυθαγόρας ὁ Σάμιος (21) ἑπτάκις ἀλλαγεὶς καὶ ἐν τοσούτοις ζῴοις βιοτεύσας καὶ ἐκτελέσας

1 περὶ om. β **4** οὔπω γ : οὕτω β **6** εἴη λέγων· τοῦτο γὰρ μάλιστα γ **7** οὐδ᾿ om. β ὡς οἱ μὲν γ : οἱ μὲν γὰρ β **9** γε (post μέντοι) om. β πολίταις Γ^{a}β : πλείστοις γ **12** εἰσὶν ἐγγεγραμμένοι Γ : εἶεν γεγραμμένοι Cobet **13** πάντας Γ^{a}β : πάντα γ **15** ἀπεκρίνατο Ω **18** οἱ om. β **20** ἑώρων Cobet **22–3** γὰρ ἄν τι ἐπυνθανόμην Γ^{a}β et (del. τι) Cobet : γάρ τι ἐπυνθανόμην γ : ἀπεπυνθανόμην E. Schwartz, cf. Hdt. 3.154 **23** πάντα β : πάλιν γ **24** μετὰ γ : κατὰ β **25** ἀπενηνεγμένη Γ^{a}β : ἐπενηνεγμένη γ **26** συνηγοροῦντος β **27** χρόνους γ : χρόνους τούτους β **28** καὶ^{2} del. Russell

(20) Not two or three days had gone by when I went to see Homer, since we both had some free time. I had many questions to put to him, but I was mainly interested in knowing where he came from. I informed him that there was still some controversy about his native country among the living. He said that he himself was not unaware that some people thought that he came from Chios, others claimed that he came from Smyrna, and others from Colophon. He said that he actually came from Babylon, and his fellow citizens called him not Homer but Tigranes. It was later in life, when he lived as a hostage in Greece, that he changed his name. I also asked him about the verses in his poems that had been "athetized." "Did you write them?" He said that he wrote them all. So I came to condemn the total lack of taste of the followers of Zenodotus and Aristarchus. When he had answered these questions to my satisfaction, I asked why in the world he began the *Iliad* with "the wrath of Achilles." He replied that the words just came to him at random, with no thought on his part. And I had still another question for him: "Did you write the *Odyssey* before the *Iliad*, as many claim?" This he denied. I could see at first glance that he was also not blind, as people say. He had perfectly good eyesight, so I did not even have to ask. I would often ask him such questions, when I saw that he was free. I would come up to him with some question, and he was happy to answer, especially after his acquittal. A defamation suit had been brought against him by Thersites, who complained of Homer's libel and ridicule of him in his poetry. Odysseus joined Homer as his defense lawyer and the bard was acquitted.

(21) It was about this time that Pythagoras of Samos arrived on the island. He had lived and completed seven lives as he experienced metempsychosis.

τῆς ψυχῆς τὰς περιόδους. ἦν δὲ χρυσοῦς ὅλον τὸ δεξιὸν ἡμίτομον. καὶ ἐκρίθη μὲν συμπολιτεύσασθαι αὐτοῖς, ἐνεδοιάζετο δὲ ἔτι πότερον Πυθαγόραν ἢ Εὔφορβον χρὴ αὐτὸν ὀνομάζειν. ὁ μέντοι Ἐμπεδοκλῆς ἦλθεν μὲν καὶ αὐτός, περίεφθος καὶ τὸ σῶμα ὅλον ὠπτημένος· οὐ μὴν παρεδέχθη καίτοι πολλὰ ἱκετεύων.

(22) Προϊόντος δὲ τοῦ χρόνου ἐνέστη ὁ ἀγὼν ὁ παρ᾽ αὐτοῖς, τὰ Θανατούσια. ἠγωνοθέτει δὲ Ἀχιλλεὺς τὸ πέμπτον καὶ Θησεὺς τὸ ἕβδομον. τὰ μὲν οὖν ἄλλα μακρὸν ἂν εἴη λέγειν· τὰ δὲ κεφάλαια τῶν πραχθέντων διηγήσομαι. πάλην μὲν ἐνίκησεν Κάρανος ὁ ἀφ᾽ Ἡρακλέους Ὀδυσσέα περὶ τοῦ στεφάνου καταγωνισάμενος· πυγμὴ δὲ ἴση ἐγένετο Ἀρείου τοῦ Αἰγυπτίου, ὃς ἐν Κορίνθῳ τέθαπται, καὶ Ἐπειοῦ ἀλλήλοις συνελθόντων. παγκρατίου δὲ οὐ τίθεται ἆθλα παρ᾽ αὐτοῖς. τὸν μέντοι δρόμον οὐκέτι μέμνημαι ὅστις ἐνίκησεν. ποιητῶν δὲ τῇ μὲν ἀληθείᾳ παρὰ πολὺ ἐκράτει Ὅμηρος, ἐνίκησεν δὲ ὅμως Ἡσίοδος. τὰ δὲ ἆθλα ἦν ἅπασι στέφανος πλακεὶς ἐκ πτερῶν ταωνείων.

(23) Ἄρτι δὲ τοῦ ἀγῶνος συντετελεσμένου ἠγγέλλοντο οἱ ἐν τῷ χώρῳ τῶν ἀσεβῶν κολαζόμενοι ἀπορρήξαντες τὰ δεσμὰ καὶ τῆς φρουρᾶς ἐπικρατήσαντες ἐλαύνειν ἐπὶ τὴν νῆσον· ἡγεῖσθαι δὲ αὐτῶν Φάλαρίν τε τὸν Ἀκραγαντῖνον καὶ Βούσιριν τὸν Αἰγύπτιον καὶ Διομήδη τὸν Θρᾷκα καὶ τοὺς περὶ Σκείρωνα καὶ Πιτυοκάμπτην. ὡς δὲ ταῦτα ἤκουσεν ὁ Ῥαδάμανθυς, ἐκτάσσει τοὺς ἥρωας ἐπὶ τῆς ἠϊόνος· ἡγεῖτο δὲ Θησεύς τε καὶ Ἀχιλλεὺς καὶ Αἴας ὁ Τελαμώνιος ἤδη σωφρονῶν· καὶ συμμίξαντες ἐμάχοντο, καὶ ἐνίκησαν οἱ ἥρωες, Ἀχιλλέως τὰ πλεῖστα κατορθώσαντος. ἠρίστευσε δὲ καὶ Σωκράτης ἐπὶ τῷ δεξιῷ ταχθείς, πολὺ μᾶλλον ἢ ὅτε ζῶν ἐπὶ Δηλίῳ ἐμάχετο. προσιόντων γὰρ τεττάρων πολεμίων οὐκ ἔφυγε καὶ τὸ πρόσωπον ἄτρεπτος ἦν· ἐφ᾽ οἷς καὶ ὕστερον ἐξῃρέθη αὐτῷ ἀριστεῖον, καλός τε καὶ μέγας παράδεισος

2 συμπολιτεύεσθαι β **3** αὐτὸν ὀνομάζειν χρή. β **4** καὶ οὗτος β τὸ ὅλον σῶμα Γ[a]β **5** γε (ante καίτοι) add. β **6–7** ὁ ἀγὼν τὰ παρ᾽ αὐτοῖς θανατούσια β **7** τὸ πέμπτον γ : τότε πέμπτον β **9** Κάρανος Gronovius : κάρος Γβ : κῦρος Ω **11** Ἀρείου τε τοῦ Γ[a]β **12** συνεξελθόντον γ **14** ὅστις γ : τίς β **15** cf. Certamen 207 **16** ταΐνων β **19** δὲ β : τε γ **20** τε τὸν… Βούσιριν om. β **21** Διομήδην β **27** ἰόντων β γὰρ Γ : δὲ Ω : τε γὰρ τῶν β **28** ἐφ᾽ β : ἐν γ **29** ἐξήρθη β

His entire left thigh was of gold. It was decided that he could live among the community of the blest, but some doubt lingered whether he should be called Pythagoras or Euphorbus. Empedocles also arrived as no other than himself, singed and baked from head to toe. Even though he begged and entreated them, they would not admit him.

(22) As time went on, a competition arose among the blest, the Olympics of the dead. Achilles served as umpire for the fifth time, and Theseus for the seventh. It would take some time to describe all of the events, but I will describe the highlights. Caranus, a descendant of Heracles, defeated Odysseus in the wrestling match. The boxing match between Areius the Egyptian and Epeius was declared a tie. Areius is buried in Corinth. On the island there is no prize for the pankration. I can no longer recall who was victorious in the footrace. In the poetic contest, Homer was in fact far superior to Hesiod, but, even so, Hesiod won. For the victors the prize was a wreath of plaited peacock feathers.

(23) No sooner had the games finished than reports began to arrive that the criminals being punished in the Land of the Impious had broken their fetters, overpowered their guards, and were on their way to the Island of the Blest. Their leaders were Phalaris of Acragas, the Egyptian Busiris, King Diomedes of Thrace, and the henchmen of Sciron and Sinis, the Pine Bender. As soon as he had received these reports, Rhadamanthus marshalled the heroes on the promontory to face their criminal assault. The commanders of the heroes were Theseus, Achilles, and Ajax, the son of Telamon, who had recovered his sanity. They met the Impious in battle and the heroes were victorious. Achilles won the prize for valor among the heroes. And, on the right flank, Socrates distinguished himself even more conspicuously than when in life he fought at the sanctuary of Apollo in Boeotia. When four enemies encountered him he did not run away but faced them without flinching. For his bravery he was later awarded with a special gift, a lovely

ἐν τῷ προαστείῳ, ἔνθα καὶ συγκαλῶν τοὺς ἑταίρους διελέγετο, Νεκρακαδημίαν τὸν τόπον προσαγορεύσας. συλλαβόντες οὖν τοὺς (24)
νενικημένους καὶ δήσαντες ἀπέπεμψαν ἔτι μᾶλλον κολασθησομένους. ἔγραψεν δὲ καὶ ταύτην τὴν μάχην Ὅμηρος καὶ ἀπιόντι μοι ἔδωκεν τὰ βιβλία κομίζειν τοῖς παρ᾽ ἡμῖν ἀνθρώποις· ἀλλ᾽ ὕστερον καὶ ταῦτα μετὰ τῶν ἄλλων ἀπωλέσαμεν. ἦν δὲ ἡ ἀρχὴ τοῦ ποιήματος αὕτη,

Νῦν δέ μοι ἔννεπε, Μοῦσα, μάχην νεκύων ἡρώων.

τότε δ᾽ οὖν κυάμους ἑψήσαντες, ὥσπερ παρ᾽ αὐτοῖς νόμος ἐπειδὰν τὸν πόλεμον κατορθώσωσιν, εἱστιῶντο τὰ ἐπινίκια καὶ ἑορτὴν μεγάλην ἦγον· μόνος δὲ αὐτῆς οὐ μετεῖχε Πυθαγόρας, ἀλλ᾽ ἄσιτος πόρρω ἐκαθέζετο μυσαττόμενος τὴν κυαμοφαγίαν.

Ἤδη δὲ μηνῶν ἓξ διεληλυθότων περὶ μεσοῦντα τὸν ἕβδομον (25)
νεώτερα συνίστατο πράγματα· Κινύρας ὁ τοῦ Σκινθάρου παῖς, μέγας ὢν καὶ καλός, ἤρα πολὺν ἤδη χρόνον τῆς Ἑλένης, καὶ αὐτὴ δὲ οὐκ ἀφανὴς ἦν ἐπιμανῶς ἀγαπῶσα τὸν νεανίσκον· πολλάκις γοῦν καὶ διένευον ἀλλήλοις ἐν τῷ συμποσίῳ καὶ προὔπινον καὶ μόνοι ἐξανιστάμενοι ἐπλανῶντο περὶ τὴν ὕλην. καὶ δή ποτε ὑπ᾽ ἔρωτος καὶ ἀμηχανίας ἐβουλεύσατο ὁ Κινύρας ἁρπάσας τὴν Ἑλένην—ἐδόκει δὲ κἀκείνῃ ταῦτα—οἴχεσθαι ἀπιόντας ἔς τινα τῶν ἐπικειμένων νήσων, ἤτοι ἐς τὴν Φελλὼ ἢ ἐς τὴν Τυρόεσσαν. συνωμότας δὲ πάλαι προσειλήφεσαν τρεῖς τῶν ἑταίρων τῶν ἐμῶν τοὺς θρασυτάτους. τῷ μέντοι πατρὶ οὐκ ἐμήνυσε ταῦτα· ἠπίστατο γὰρ ὑπ᾽ αὐτοῦ κωλυθησόμενος. ὡς δὲ ἐδόκει αὐτοῖς, ἐτέλουν τὴν ἐπιβουλήν. καὶ ἐπειδὴ νὺξ ἐγένετο—ἐγὼ μὲν οὐ παρήμην· ἐτύγχανον γὰρ ἐν τῷ συμποσίῳ κοιμώμενος—οἱ δὲ λαθόντες τοὺς

1 καὶ (post ἔνθα) om. β **2** δ᾽ οὖν Ω **3** ἀπέπεμψαν γ : αὖθις ἀπέπεμψαν Γ^{a}β **6** ἡ om. γ **8** cf. *Od.* 1.1 **9** τότε βΩ et γρ. mg. Γ : τοὺς Γ **10** τὸν om. β κατορθώσαντες ἑστιῶνται ἐπινίκια β **11** μεγίστην β ταύτης β **14** νεωτέρα…πραγματεία γ Κινύρας ΓΩ^{1} : ὁ add. Γ^{a}Ω^{2} : ὁ Κίνυρος γὰρ β **15** μέγας τε β αὐτὴ S : αὕτη βγ **16** ἐπιμανῶς Γ : ἐπινῶς Ωβ, confirmantibus scholiis et Suda **16–17** πολλάκις γοῦν om. γ **18** ἐξιστάμενοι Ω ποτε om. β **19** ὁ Κίνυρος β **21** Τυρόεσσαν Γ^{a}β : Τυρώ γ **22** προσειλήφεσαν Γ^{a}β : συνειλήφεσαν γ **25** καὶ ἐπεὶ β παρῆν Γ^{a}β **26** κεκοιμημένος β

and large garden in the suburbs. He invited his companions to its grounds and engaged them in dialogue. He named this place *Necracademia*, or the Academy of the Dead. (24) They arrested the enemies they had conquered, put them in fetters, and sent them back to the Land of the Impious for even harsher punishment. Homer wrote an epic poem on this battle and, as I was departing, he gave me the book rolls to bring back to the Land of the Living. But afterwards we lost the manuscript with everything else. But this was the first line of the poem:

Now tell me, Muses, of the battle of the heroic dead.

Then they boiled beans—as was their custom when they are victorious in war—and they held a victory feast and celebrated with a great festival. Only Pythagoras refused to participate in it. He sat far off from the company, since he loathed the eating of beans.

(25) Six months had now passed, and we were in the middle of our seventh month when the island was thrown into a great commotion. Cinyras, Scintharus' son, was a strapping, handsome lad. For a long time now he had conceived a passion for Helen. And Helen did not conceal the fact that she was mad about the young man. They would often make eyes at one another during the symposium and, after toasts to one another, they would rise from the banquet and wander off in the wood. The day came when Cinyras, driven by a passion he could not resist, decided to carry Helen off—Helen being in full agreement—and take her to one of the neighbouring islands, perhaps to the Island of Cork or to Cheese Island. Sometime before this, they enlisted as co-conspirators three of my most reckless companions. To his father Cinyras revealed nothing of his plan. He was sure that his father would prevent him. When they thought that the right moment had arrived, they set their plot into motion. With nightfall—I was not on hand, since, as

(26) ἄλλους ἀναλαβόντες τὴν Ἑλένην ὑπὸ σπουδῆς ἀνήχθησαν. περὶ δὲ τὸ μεσονύκτιον ἀνεγρόμενος ὁ Μενέλαος ἐπεὶ ἔμαθεν τὴν εὐνὴν κενὴν τῆς γυναικός, βοήν τε ἠφίει καὶ τὸν ἀδελφὸν παραλαβὼν ἦλθε πρὸς τὸν βασιλέα τὸν Ῥαδάμανθυν. ἡμέρας δὲ ὑποφαινούσης ἔλεγον οἱ σκοποὶ καθορᾶν τὴν ναῦν πολὺ ἀπέχουσαν· οὕτω δὴ ἐμβιβάσας ὁ Ῥαδάμανθυς πεντήκοντα τῶν ἡρώων εἰς ναῦν μονόξυλον ἀσφοδελίνην παρήγγειλε διώκειν· οἱ δὲ ὑπὸ προθυμίας ἐλαύνοντες περὶ μεσημβρίαν καταλαμβάνουσιν αὐτοὺς ἄρτι ἐς τὸν γαλακτώδη τοῦ ὠκεανοῦ τόπον ἐμβαίνοντας πλησίον τῆς Τυροέσσης· παρὰ τοσοῦτον ἦλθον διαδρᾶναι· καὶ ἀναδησάμενοι τὴν ναῦν ἁλύσει ῥοδίνῃ κατέπλεον. ἡ μὲν οὖν Ἑλένη ἐδάκρυέν τε καὶ ᾐσχύνετο καὶ ἐνεκαλύπτετο, τοὺς δὲ ἀμφὶ τὸν Κινύραν ἀνακρίνας πρότερον ὁ Ῥαδάμανθυς, εἴ τινες καὶ ἄλλοι αὐτοῖς συνίσασιν, ὡς οὐδένα εἶπον, ἐκ τῶν αἰδοίων δήσας ἀπέπεμψεν ἐς τὸν τῶν ἀσεβῶν χῶρον μαλάχῃ πρότερον μαστιγωθέντας. (27) ἐψηφίσαντο δὲ καὶ ἡμᾶς ἐμπροθέσμους ἐκπέμπειν ἐκ τῆς νήσου, τὴν ἐπιοῦσαν ἡμέραν μόνην ἐπιμείναντας.

Ἐνταῦθα δὴ ἐγὼ ἐποτνιώμην τε καὶ ἐδάκρυον οἷα ἔμελλον ἀγαθὰ καταλιπὼν αὖθις πλανήσεσθαι. αὐτοὶ μέντοι παρεμυθοῦντο λέγοντες οὐ πολλῶν ἐτῶν ἀφίξεσθαι πάλιν ὡς αὐτούς, καί μοι ἤδη εἰς τοὐπιὸν θρόνον τε καὶ κλισίαν ἐπεδείκνυσαν πλησίον τῶν ἀρίστων. ἐγὼ δὲ προσελθὼν τῷ Ῥαδαμάνθυι πολλὰ ἱκέτευον εἰπεῖν τὰ μέλλοντα καὶ ὑποδεῖξαί μοι τὸν πλοῦν. ὁ δὲ ἔφασκεν ἀφίξεσθαι μὲν εἰς τὴν πατρίδα πολλὰ πρότερον πλανηθέντα καὶ κινδυνεύσαντα, τὸν δὲ χρόνον οὐκέτι τῆς ἐπανόδου προσθεῖναι ἠθέλησεν· ἀλλὰ δὴ καὶ δεικνὺς τὰς πλησίον νήσους—ἐφαίνοντο δὲ

2 ὁ Μενελέως β **3** βοήν cf. *Il.* 2.408 etc. ἠφίει γ : ἵστη Γ^{a}β, cf. c. 46 **4** ἦλθε γ : ᾔει β πρὸς τὰ βασίλεια τοῦ Ῥαδαμάνθυος β **5** ἔλεγον β : εἶπον γ πολὺ β : οὐ πολὺ γ **6** δὴ Γ^{a}β : δὲ γ **7** παρήγγελλεν γ **9** τοῦ ὠκεανοῦ τόπον γ : ὠκεανὸν β **11** ἀλύσει γ **12** καὶ ἐνεκαλύπτετο N et fort. P : καὶ ἀνεκαλύπτετο Z : καὶ ἀμφεκαλύπτετο γ : κἀνεκαλύπτετο E. Schwartz **13** Κίνυρον β **14–15** ἀπέπεμψεν Γ^{a}β : ἔπεμψεν γ **15** τῶν om. Ω **16** ἐψηφίσατο γ; cf. c. 10 ἐμπροθέσμως S **17** ἀναμείναντας Ω **18** ἔνθα δὴ β ἐποτνιώμην Γ : ἠνιώμην Ωβ et mg. Γ **19** πλανήσεσθαι Γ^{a}β : πλανηθήσεσθαι γ μέντοι γP : μὲν Z **21** εἰς… ἐπεδείκνυσαν γ : θρόνον τε καὶ κλισίαν ἐς τοὐπιὸν παρεδείκνυσαν β **24** πολλὰ δὲ πρότερον β

it happened, I had fallen asleep at the table— (26) they took Helen away without anyone knowing. They put to sea as quickly as they could. Now, Menelaus woke up around midnight and, when he saw that his wife was not with him, he let out a great roar, grabbed his brother, and went to King Rhadamanthus. At daybreak the island scouts reported that they had sighted their ship far in the distance. On this report, Rhadamanthus put fifty of the heroes on a ship constructed of the solid wood of asphodel and ordered them to pursue the ship. They pursued them with all their energy and about midday they caught up with them just as they were about to enter the galactic stretch of the Ocean near Cheese Island. They made their escape this far, but no farther. The heroes secured their ship with a cable of roses and sailed back. Now Helen burst into tears and covered her head out of shame. But Rhadamanthus first interviewed Cinyras' men, asking if others were involved in the plot. When they said that only they were involved, he had them fettered by their genitals and sent them away to the Land of the Impious, after having them flogged with a stalk of mallow.

(27) They also voted to expel us from the island, well before the limit of our stay had expired. We were allowed only one additional day. I broke out in wails of lamentation and tears streamed down my face, as I thought of the paradise I would leave to resume my life of wandering. They, for their part, tried to console me, telling me that, after only a few years, I would return to them and they pointed out to me my future throne and banquet couch near the best of the heroes. I went to Rhadamanthus and implored him to reveal my future and show me the journey of my life. He told me that, after many wanderings and perilous adventures, I would return home, but he was

πέντε τὸν ἀριθμόν, ἄλλη δὲ ἕκτη πόρρωθεν—ταύτας μὲν εἶναι ἔφασκεν τῶν ἀσεβῶν, τὰς πλησίον, Ἀφ᾽ ὧν, ἔφη, ἤδη τὸ πολὺ πῦρ ὁρᾷς καιόμενον, ἕκτη δὲ ἐκείνη τῶν ὀνείρων ἡ πόλις· μετὰ ταύτην δὲ ἡ τῆς Καλυψοῦς νῆσος, ἀλλ᾽ οὐδέπω σοι φαίνεται. ἐπειδὰν δὲ ταύτας παραπλεύσῃς, τότε δὴ ἀφίξῃ εἰς τὴν μεγάλην ἤπειρον τὴν ἐναντίαν τῇ ὑφ᾽ ὑμῶν κατοικουμένῃ· ἐνταῦθα δὴ πολλὰ παθὼν καὶ ποικίλα ἔθνη διελθὼν καὶ ἀνθρώποις ἀμίκτοις ἐπιδημήσας χρόνῳ ποτὲ ἥξεις εἰς τὴν ἑτέραν ἤπειρον.

Τοσαῦτα εἶπεν, καὶ ἀνασπάσας ἀπὸ τῆς γῆς μαλάχης ῥίζαν **(28)**
ὤρεξέν μοι, ταύτῃ κελεύσας ἐν τοῖς μεγίστοις κινδύνοις προσεύχεσθαι· παρῄνεσε δὲ εἰ καί ποτε ἀφικοίμην ἐς τήνδε τὴν γῆν, μήτε πῦρ μαχαίρᾳ σκαλεύειν μήτε θέρμους ἐσθίειν μήτε παιδὶ ὑπὲρ τὰ ὀκτωκαίδεκα ἔτη πλησιάζειν· τούτων γὰρ ἂν μεμνημένον ἐλπίδας ἔχειν τῆς εἰς τὴν νῆσον ἀφίξεως.

Τότε μὲν οὖν τὰ περὶ τὸν πλοῦν παρεσκευασάμην, καὶ ἐπεὶ καιρὸς ἦν, συνειστιώμην αὐτοῖς. τῇ δὲ ἐπιούσῃ ἐλθὼν πρὸς Ὅμηρον τὸν ποιητὴν ἐδεήθην αὐτοῦ ποιῆσαί μοι δίστιχον ἐπίγραμμα· καὶ ἐπειδὴ ἐποίησεν, στήλην βηρύλλου λίθου ἀναστήσας ἐπέγραψα πρὸς τῷ λιμένι. τὸ δὲ ἐπίγραμμα ἦν τοιόνδε·

Λουκιανὸς τάδε πάντα φίλος μακάρεσσι θεοῖσιν
εἶδέ τε καὶ πάλιν ἦλθε φίλην ἐς πατρίδα γαῖαν.

μείνας δὲ κἀκείνην τὴν ἡμέραν, τῇ ἐπιούσῃ ἀνηγόμην τῶν ἡρώων **(29)**
παραπεμπόντων. ἔνθα μοι καὶ Ὀδυσσεὺς προσελθὼν λάθρᾳ τῆς Πηνελόπης δίδωσιν ἐπιστολὴν εἰς Ὠγυγίαν τὴν νῆσον Καλυψοῖ κομίζειν. συνέπεμψε δέ μοι ὁ Ῥαδάμανθυς τὸν πορθμέα Ναύπλιον, ἵν᾽ ἐὰν καταχθείημεν ἐς τὰς νήσους, μηδεὶς ἡμᾶς συλλάβῃ ἅτε κατ᾽ ἄλλην ἐμπορίαν καταπλέοντας.

1 ἄλλη δὲ γ : καὶ ἄλλη β **2** τῶν γ : τὰς τῶν β **2–3** ἀφ᾽ ὧν δὴ ἔφη ὁρᾷς τὸ πολὺ πῦρ β **3–4** μετ᾽ αὐτὴν β **6** ἡμῶν codd. : corr. Du Soul δὴ γ : δὲ β **7** ἔθη β; cf. *Od.* 1.3–4 **10–11** μοι ταύτην, κελεύσας…ταύτῃ προσεύχεσθαι β **11** εἰ καί γ : καὶ εἴ β **12** cf. D.L. 8.17, 19 **13** ἂν om. β μεμνημένος β **15** παρεσκευαζόμην β **16** τῇ ἐπιούσῃ δὲ β **20** cf. *Od.* 1.82 etc. **21** ἦλθε φίλην β : ἤλθεν ἑὴν γ; cf. *Od.* 1.290 etc. **26** ἐὰν καταχθείημεν γ, cf. 28.33, etc. : εἰ καταχθείημεν Γ^{a}β : ἐὰν καταχθῶμεν E. Schwartz ἡμᾶς om. β συλλάβοι β **27** παραπλέοντας β

unwilling to set a date for my return. But he pointed to the neighbouring islands—five were just visible and there was a sixth in the distance. "These," he said, "the five islands nearest us, are the Islands of the Impious. You can see fierce fires burning from them. The sixth island in the far distance is the City of Dreams. Beyond this is Calypso's Island, which is not visible from here. Once you have sailed beyond these islands, you will arrive at the great continent that lies opposite your inhabited world. After experiencing many hardships and having passed through the countries of many different peoples, you will arrive at the other continent." **(28)** This much would he tell me. He then pulled the root of a mallow plant from the ground and handed it to me. He told me to pray to it in my moments of greatest peril. And he gave me this solemn advice: if ever I reached this land, I should never stir a fire with a knife or eat lupines or have sex with a boy over 18. If I followed these instructions, he said that I could hope to return to the island once again.

Well, then I prepared to set out to sea. And, as the opportunity presented itself, I joined the heroes at their banquet. The next day, I approached the poet Homer and asked him to compose a distich. He composed it, and I had it inscribed. This roughly is the text:

> All of this world did Lucian, beloved of the blessed gods,
> observe and then to his beloved fatherland did he return.

(29) I spent the rest of the day on the island. On the next day the heroes saw me off and I set sail. It was at that moment that Odysseus, unknown to Penelope, came up to me and gave me a letter to carry to Calypso on the island of Ogygia. Rhadamanthus sent Nauplius along so that, if we landed on the islands, no one would arrest us, since supposedly we were sailing back on another trading expedition.

Ἐπεὶ δὲ τὸν εὐώδη ἀέρα προϊόντες παρεληλύθειμεν, αὐτίκα ἡμᾶς ὀσμή τε δεινὴ διεδέχετο οἷον ἀσφάλτου καὶ θείου καὶ πίττης ἅμα καιομένων, καὶ κνῖσα δὲ πονηρὰ καὶ ἀφόρητος ὥσπερ ἀνθρώπων ὀπτωμένων, καὶ ὁ ἀὴρ ζοφερὸς καὶ ὁμιχλώδης, καὶ κατέσταζεν ἐξ αὐτοῦ δρόσος πιττίνη· ἠκούομεν δὲ καὶ μαστίγων

(30) ψόφον καὶ οἰμωγὴν ἀνθρώπων πολλῶν. ταῖς μὲν οὖν ἄλλαις οὐ προσέσχομεν, ἧς δὲ ἐπέβημεν, τοιάδε ἦν· κύκλῳ μὲν πᾶσα κρημνώδης καὶ ἀπόξυρος, πέτραις καὶ τράχωσι κατεσκληκυῖα, δένδρον δ᾽ οὐδέν οὐδὲ ὕδωρ ἐνῆν· ἀνερπύσαντες δὲ ὅμως κατὰ τοὺς κρημνοὺς προῄειμεν διά τινος ἀκανθώδους καὶ σκολόπων μεστῆς ἀτραποῦ, πολλὴν ἀμορφίαν τῆς χώρας ἐχούσης. ἐλθόντες δὲ ἐπὶ τὴν εἱρκτὴν καὶ τὸ κολαστήριον, πρῶτα μὲν τὴν φύσιν τοῦ τόπου ἐθαυμάζομεν· τὸ μὲν γὰρ ἔδαφος αὐτὸ μαχαίραις καὶ σκόλοψι πάντῃ ἐξηνθήκει, κύκλῳ δὲ ποταμοὶ περιέρρεον, ὁ μὲν βορβόρου, ὁ δὲ δεύτερος αἵματος, ὁ δὲ ἔνδον πυρός, πάνυ μέγας οὗτος καὶ ἀπέρατος, καὶ ἔρρει ὥσπερ ὕδωρ καὶ ἐκυματοῦτο ὥσπερ θάλαττα, καὶ ἰχθῦς δὲ εἶχεν πολλούς, τοὺς μὲν δαλοῖς προσεοικότας, τοὺς δὲ μικροὺς ἄνθραξι πεπυρωμένοις· ἐκάλουν δὲ αὐτοὺς λυχνίσκους.

(31) εἴσοδος δὲ μία στενὴ διὰ πάντων ἦν, καὶ πυλωρὸς ἐφειστήκει Τίμων ὁ Ἀθηναῖος. παρελθόντες δὲ ὅμως τοῦ Ναυπλίου καθηγουμένου ἑωρῶμεν κολαζομένους πολλοὺς μὲν βασιλέας, πολλοὺς δὲ καὶ ἰδιώτας, ὧν ἐνίους καὶ ἐγνωρίζομεν· εἴδομεν δὲ καὶ τὸν Κινύραν καπνῷ ὑποτυφόμενον ἐκ τῶν αἰδοίων ἀπηρτημένον. προσετίθεσαν δὲ οἱ περιηγηταὶ καὶ τοὺς ἑκάστων βίους καὶ τὰς ἁμαρτίας ἐφ᾽ αἷς κολάζονται· καὶ μεγίστας ἁπασῶν τιμωρίας ὑπέμενον οἱ ψευσάμενοί τι παρὰ τὸν βίον καὶ οἱ μὴ τὰ ἀληθῆ

2 ὀδμή Γ^{a}β διεχέετο Z **3** καὶ κνίσης δὲ πονηρᾶς καὶ ἀφορήτου γ **3–4** ὥσπερ ἀπὸ ἀνθρώπων β **5** κατέσταξεν Z πιττίνη Γ^{a}β : πίττης γ **5–6** ἠκούομεν…οἰμωγὴν γ : καὶ μέντοι καὶ μαστίγων ψόφος ἠκούετο καὶ οἰμωγὴ β **7** ἧς β : ᾗ γ μὲν post κύκλῳ om. Γ **8** πέτραις τραχέσι (om. καὶ) Γ **9** οὐδὲν om. β ἀφερπύσαντες γ **10** προῄειμεν S : προσήειμεν ΓΩ : πρόϊμεν β : προῇμεν Γ^{x} **11** ἐχούσης γ : διελθόντες. (deinde ἐλθ.) β **13** δεύτερος δὲ (om. ὁ) β **16** ἀπέρατος Γ^{a}β : ἄμετρος γ **18** λυχνούχους fort. voluit Γ^{a} **19** ἦν om. β πυλωρὸς γ : τιμωρὸς β **21–2** δὲ καὶ γ : δὲ β **23** Κίνυρον β **24–5** τὰς ἁμαρτίας γ : τὰς αἰτίας Γ^{a}β : del. Lehmann **25** ἐφ᾽ οἷς β Lehmann

HELL ISLAND

Once we had passed beyond the Fragrant Zone, a terrible stench engulfed us. It was as if asphalt, sulfur, and pitch were being burned together. The smoke was vile and unbearable. It smelled like the burning of human flesh. The atmosphere was murky and dense, and beads of pitch oozed down upon us. (**30**) We could hear the crack of whips and the groaning of many men. We did not land on all of the islands, but I will describe the island we did land on: it was surrounded by a sheer cliff sculpted of dry rocks. No tree grew on it and there was not a drop of water on it. Even so, we scaled the cliffs and made our way on a small path overgrown with acanthus and thorns. The landscape was bleak and desolate. When we came to the Pen of Punishment, we were struck by amazement at the nature of the place. The ground was spiked with knives and stakes. Rivers flowed around it, one of mud, another of blood. The innermost river was of fire. It was wide and could not be forded. The fire flowed like molten water and it crested in waves like the sea. Many fish swam in it. Some resembled torches; the smaller fry were incandescent like burning coal. They called these "lampries."

(**31**) Through this there was a single entrance. Timon of Athens stood there as guard. We got past him, with Nauplius as our guide, and could see the people being punished there. Many were kings, many just ordinary people; some we even knew. We saw Cinyras there, smoldering and suspended by his genitals. The official guides introduced each of the Damned and gave an account of their lives and the crimes for which they were being punished. Those who awaited the greatest punishments had told lies in the

συγγεγραφότες, ἐν οἷς καὶ Κτησίας ὁ Κνίδιος ἦν καὶ Ἡρόδοτος καὶ ἄλλοι πολλοί. τούτους οὖν ὁρῶν ἐγὼ χρηστὰς εἶχον εἰς τοὐπιὸν τὰς ἐλπίδας· οὐδὲν γὰρ ἐμαυτῷ ψεῦδος εἰπόντι συνηπιστάμην. ταχέως δ᾿ οὖν ἀναστρέψας ἐπὶ τὴν ναῦν—οὐδὲ γὰρ ἠδυνάμην φέρειν (32) τὴν ὄψιν—ἀσπασάμενος τὸν Ναύπλιον ἀπέπλευσα.

Καὶ μετ᾿ ὀλίγον ἐφαίνετο πλησίον ἡ τῶν ὀνείρων νῆσος, ἀμυδρὰ καὶ ἀσαφὴς ἰδεῖν· ἔπασχε δὲ καὶ αὐτή τι τοῖς ὀνείροις παραπλήσιον· ὑπεχώρει γὰρ προσιόντων ἡμῶν καὶ ὑπέφευγε καὶ πορρωτέρω ὑπέβαινε. καταλαβόντες δὲ ποτε αὐτὴν καὶ εἰσπλεύσαντες εἰς τὸν Ὕπνον λιμένα προσαγορευόμενον πλησίον τῶν πυλῶν τῶν ἐλεφαντίνων, ᾗ τὸ τοῦ Ἀλεκτρυόνος ἱερόν ἐστιν, περὶ δείλην ὀψίαν ἀπεβαίνομεν· παρελθόντες δὲ ἐς τὴν πόλιν πολλοὺς ὀνείρους καὶ ποικίλους ἑωρῶμεν. πρῶτον δὲ βούλομαι περὶ τῆς πόλεως εἰπεῖν, ἐπεὶ μηδέ ἄλλῳ τινὶ γέγραπται περὶ αὐτῆς, ὃς δὲ καὶ μόνος ἐπεμνήσθη Ὅμηρος, οὐ πάνυ ἀκριβῶς συνέγραψεν. κύκλῳ μὲν περὶ πᾶσαν αὐτὴν ὕλη ἀνέστηκεν, τὰ δένδρα δέ ἐστι (33) μήκωνες ὑψηλαὶ καὶ μανδραγόραι καὶ ἐπ᾿ αὐτῶν πολύ τι πλῆθος νυκτερίδων· τοῦτο γὰρ μόνον ἐν τῇ νήσῳ γίνεται ὄρνεον. ποταμὸς δὲ παραρρέει πλησίον ὁ ὑπ᾿ αὐτῶν καλούμενος Νυκτιπόρος, καὶ πηγαὶ δύο παρὰ τὰς πύλας· ὀνόματα καὶ ταύταις, τῇ μὲν Νήγρετος, τῇ δὲ Παννυχία. ὁ περίβολος δὲ τῆς πόλεως ὑψηλός τε καὶ ποικίλος, ἴριδι τὴν χρόαν ὁμοιότατος· πύλαι μέντοι ἔπεισιν οὐ δύο, καθάπερ Ὅμηρος εἴρηκεν, ἀλλὰ τέσσαρες, δύο μὲν πρὸς τὸ τῆς Βλακείας πεδίον ἀποβλέπουσαι, ἡ μὲν σιδηρᾶ, ἡ δὲ κεράμου πεποιημένη, καθ᾿ ἃς ἐλέγοντο ἀποδημεῖν αὐτῶν οἵ τε φοβεροὶ καὶ φονικοὶ καὶ ἀπηνεῖς, δύο δὲ πρὸς τὸν λιμένα καὶ τὴν θάλατταν, ἡ μὲν κερατίνη, ἡ δὲ καθ᾿ ἣν ἡμεῖς παρήλθομεν ἐλεφαντίνη. εἰσιόντι δὲ εἰς τὴν πόλιν ἐν δεξιᾷ μέν ἐστι τὸ Νυκτῷον—σέβουσι γὰρ θεῶν

3 τὰς om. Γ 4 δ᾿ οὖν Γ : οὖν Ωβ ἐπὶ ναῦν β; cf. c. 37 init. οὐ γὰρ ἐδυνάμην β 5 ἀπέπεμψα Γ^{a}β 7 ἔπασχε β : εἶχε γ αὔτη γ τι τοῖς ὀνείρους Ω : τοῖς ὀνείροις Γ : τοῖς ὀνείροις τι β 8 προσιοῦσιν ἡμῖν β 11 cf. *Od.* 19.563 12 ἀπεβαίνομεν Γ^{a}S : ἐπιβαίνομεν γ : ἀποβαίνομεν ZP πόλιν γ : πύλην Γ^{a}β 15 cf. *Od.* 19.560 seq., 24.12 16 τὰ Γ^{a}β : om. γ 19 παραρρέει β : παρέρρει γ : παραρρεῖ S ὁ om. β ννκτίπορος γ 21 νήγερτος γ ὁ δὲ περίβολος β 22 χροιὰν β 24 κεράμου β : ἐκ κεράμου γ 25 ἔλεγον β 26–7 αἱ μὲν κερατίναι, αἱ δὲ καθ᾿ ἃς…ἐλεψάντιναι β 27 εἰσιόντων β 28 θεὸν S^{i}Γ^{d}

course of their lives or had written fiction. Among them were Ctesias of Cnidus, Herodotus, and many others. As I contemplated these, I was flooded with good hope for what I would encounter in the afterlife. My conscience was clear; I had never told a lie. (32) I could not endure the sight of this Hell, so I returned quickly back to the ship and embraced Nauplius to say a fond farewell and sailed away.

THE CITY OF DREAMS

After we had sailed on for a short time, the Island of Dreams appeared vague and indistinct in the haze. The island itself hovered in a kind of dreamlike state. The closer we came to it, the more it eluded us and retreated into the distance. But, in time, we managed to catch up with it and, once we had entered the harbor, Sleep, as it was called, we sailed by the Gates of Ivory, where there is a sanctuary of the Cock, and disembarked late in the day. As we passed on to the city we could see dreams of many kinds. But, before I describe these, I want to say something about the City of Dreams, since no author has described it. The only author who has mentioned it is Homer and his account is not quite accurate. A wood surrounds the city on all sides. The trees are tall mushrooms and mandrake plants; nesting on their branches is a cloud of bats. This is the only species of flying creatures to be found on the island. A river they call Nightford flows nearby. It is fed by two springs that arise at the foot of the Gates of Ivory. They are called Insomnia and Nocturn. The wall around the city is tall and variegated. In colour it is just like a rainbow. It does not have two doors, as Homer said, but four. Two of these face the Plain of Stupor; one is of iron, the other of terra cotta. These were the exits for the blood-curdling nightmares of the City of Dreams. The other two gates faced the harbor and the sea. One was the Gate of Horn; the other, through which we entered the city, the Gate of Ivory.

As you enter the city to the right you will find the sanctuary of Night. They are especially devoted to this goddess and to the Cock. His sanctuary is near the harbor. (33) To the left is the Palace of Sleep. Sleep is the potentate, and he has appointed two satraps over them—Panic, the son of Skitterish, and Devil Fame, the son of Apparition. In the middle of the agora

ταύτην μάλιστα καὶ τὸν Ἀλεκτρυόνα· ἐκείνῳ δὲ πλησίον τοῦ λιμένος τὸ ἱερὸν πεποίηται—ἐν ἀριστερᾷ δὲ τὰ τοῦ Ὕπνου βασίλεια. οὗτος γὰρ δὴ ἄρχει παρ' αὐτοῖς σατράπας δύο καὶ ὑπάρχους πεποιημένος, Ταραξίωνά τε τὸν Ματαιογένους καὶ Πλουτοκλέα τὸν Φαντασίωνος. ἐν μέσῃ δὲ τῇ ἀγορᾷ πηγή τίς ἐστιν, ἣν καλοῦσι Καρεῶτιν· καὶ πλησίον ναοὶ δύο, Ἀπάτης καὶ Ἀληθείας· ἔνθα καὶ τὸ ἄδυτόν ἐστιν αὐτοῖς καὶ τὸ μαντεῖαν, οὗ προεστήκει προφητεύων Ἀντιφῶν ὁ τῶν ὀνείρων ὑποκριτής, (34) ταύτης παρὰ τοῦ Ὕπνου λαχὼν τῆς τιμῆς. αὐτῶν μέντοι τῶν ὀνείρων οὔτε φύσις οὔτε ἰδέα ἡ ἀντή, ἀλλ' οἱ μὲν μακροὶ ἦσαν καὶ καλοὶ καὶ εὐειδεῖς, οἱ δὲ μικροὶ καὶ ἄμορφοι, καὶ οἱ μὲν χρύσεοι, ὡς ἐδόκουν, οἱ δὲ ταπεινοί τε καὶ εὐτελεῖς. ἦσαν δ' ἐν αὐτοῖς καὶ πτερωτοί τινες καὶ τερατώδεις, καὶ ἄλλοι καθάπερ ἐς πομπὴν διεακευασμένοι, οἱ μὲν ἐς βασιλέας, οἱ δὲ ἐς θεούς, οἱ δὲ εἰς ἄλλα τοιαῦτα κεκοσμημένοι. πολλοὺς δὲ αὐτῶν καὶ ἐγνωρίσαμεν, πάλαι παρ' ἡμῖν ἑωρακότες, οἳ δὴ καὶ προσῄεσαν καὶ ἠσπάζοντο ὡς ἂν καὶ συνήθεις ὑπάρχοντες, καὶ παραλαβόντες ἡμᾶς καὶ κατακοιμίσαντες πάνυ λαμπρῶς καὶ δεξιῶς ἐξένιζον, τήν τε ἄλλην ὑποδοχὴν μεγαλοπρεπῆ παρασκευάσαντες καὶ ὑπισχνούμενοι βασιλέας τε ποιήσειν καὶ σατράπας. ἔνιοι δὲ καὶ ἀπῆγον ἡμᾶς εἰς τὰς πατρίδας καὶ τοὺς οἰκείους ἐπεδείκνυον καὶ αὐθημερὸν (35) ἐπανῆγον. ἡμέρας μὲν οὖν τριάκοντα καὶ ἴσας νύκτας παρ' αὐτοῖς ἐμείναμεν καθεύδοντες εὐωχούμενοι. ἔπειτα δὲ ἄφνω βροντῆς μεγάλης καταρραγείσης ἀνεγρόμενοι καὶ ἀναθορόντες ἀνήχθημεν ἐπισιτισάμενοι.

Τριταῖοι δ' ἐκεῖθεν τῇ Ὠγυγίᾳ νήσῳ προσσχόντες ἀπεβαίνομεν. πρότερον δ' ἐγὼ λύσας τὴν ἐπιστολὴν ἀνεγίνωσκον τά γεγραμμένα. ἦν δὲ τοιάδε· Ὀδυσσεὺς Καλυψοῖ χαίρειν.

Ἴσθι με, ὡς τὰ πρῶτα ἐξέπλευσα παρὰ σοῦ τὴν σχεδίαν κατασκευασάμενος, ναυαγίᾳ

5 Πλουτοκλέα Γ[a]β : Πλουτοκέα γ τίς om. β **8** προειστήκει β **10** μακροί τε ἦσαν β **11** εὐειδεῖς γ : ἠδεῖς β **14** οἱ δέ καὶ εἰς θεούς Ω **15** κεκοσμημένοι γ : διεσκευασμένοι β **16** οἳ δὴ Γ[a]β : οἱ δέ γ **17** ὑπάρχοντας Z παραλαβόντες Γ[a]β : παραλαμβάνοντες β **18** κατακοιμήσαντες γ **18–19** (τὴν τε αὐτῶν?) παρασκευὴν μεγαλοπρεπ(ῆ παρα?) σκευάσαντες add. in mg. Γ[a] **24** ἐγρόμενοι β **26** προσχόντες codd. : corr. Lehmann ἀπεβαίνομεν SΓ[a] : ἀποβαίνομεν ZPN : ἐπεβαίνομεν γ

is a spring they call Slumberwell. Nearby are two temples, the temple of Deceit and the temple of Verity. Both have an inner sanctum and an oracle. Antiphon, the dream interpreter, is the prophet in charge of these temples. He has received this high position from Sleep.

(34) In their physical features these dreams are very different. Some are tall, noble, and good-looking, others squat and ugly. Some strike the viewer as golden, others as cheap and commonplace. Among them some were winged and monstrous dreams; some seemed appareled for a great procession, dressed as kings and gods and other kinds of characters. We could even recognize some of them, since we had seen them back home. They actually came up to us and greeted us as long-lost friends. They took us and put us to sleep and treated us to their hospitality, with great elegance and expertise. They were lavish in their entertainment and promised to make us kings and satraps. Some dreams even conveyed us back home and pointed out to us family and friends and then returned us to the City of Dreams that same day. We passed thirty days and thirty nights in the Kingdom of Sleep, feasting and sound asleep. (35) But then we were awakened suddenly by a terrible clap of thunder. We sprang to our feet, put provisions on our ship, and sailed away.

ON CALYPSO'S ISLAND

On the third day after leaving the Island of Dreams we reached the island of Ogygia and disembarked. The first thing I did was to unfold Odysseus' letter and read it. It went like this: "To Calypso Odysseus sends his greetings. You should be aware that, after I had constructed the raft and sailed away from

χρησάμενον μόλις ὑπὸ Λευκοθέας διασωθῆναι εἰς τὴν τῶν Φαιάκων χώραν, ὑφ᾽ ὧν ἐς τὴν οἰκείαν ἀποπεμφθεὶς κατέλαβον πολλούς τῆς γυναικὸς μνηστῆρας ἐν τοῖς ἡμετέροις τρυφῶντας· ἀποκτείνας δὲ ἅπαντας ὑπὸ Τηλεγόνου ὕστερον τοῦ ἐκ Κίρκης μοι γενομένου ἀνῃρέθην, καὶ νῦν εἰμι ἐν τῇ Μακάρων νήσῳ πάνυ μετανοῶν ἐπὶ τῷ καταλιπεῖν τὴν παρά σοὶ δίαιταν καὶ τὴν ὑπὸ σοῦ προτεινομένην ἀθανασίαν. ἢν οὖν καιροῦ λάβωμαι, ἀποδρὰς ἀφίξομαι πρὸς σέ. ταῦτα μὲν ἐδήλου ἡ ἐπιστολή, καὶ περὶ ἡμῶν, ὅπως ξενισθῶμεν. ἐγὼ δὲ προελθὼν ὀλίγον ἀπὸ τῆς θαλάττης (36) εὗρον τὸ σπήλαιον τοιοῦτον οἷον Ὅμηρος εἶπεν, καὶ αὐτὴν ταλασιουργοῦσαν. ὡς δὲ τὴν ἐπιστολὴν ἔλαβεν καὶ ἐπελέξατο, πρῶτα μὲν ἐπὶ πολὺ ἐδάκρυεν, ἔπειτα δὲ παρεκάλει ἡμᾶς ἐπὶ ξένια καὶ εἱστία λαμπρῶς καὶ περὶ τοῦ Ὀδυσσέως ἐπυνθάνετο καὶ περὶ τῆς Πηνελόπης, ὁποία τε εἴη τὴν ὄψιν καὶ εἰ σωφρονοίη, καθάπερ Ὀδυσσεὺς πάλαι περὶ αὐτῆς ἐκόμπαζεν· καὶ ἡμεῖς τοιαῦτα ἀπεκρινάμεθα, ἐξ ὧν εἰκάζομεν εὐφρανεῖσθαι ἀυτήν.

Τότε μὲν οὖν ἀπελθόντες ἐπὶ ναῦν πλησίον ἐπὶ τῆς ᾐόνος ἐκοιμήθημεν. ἕωθεν δὲ ἀνηγόμεθα σφοδρότερον κατιόντος τοῦ (37) πνεύματος· καὶ δὴ χειμασθέντες ἡμέρας δύο τῇ τρίτῃ περιπίπτομεν τοῖς Κολοκυνθοπειραταῖς. ἄνθρωποι δὲ εἰσιν οὗτοι ἄγριοι ἐκ τῶν πλησίον νήσων λῃστεύοντες τοὺς παραπλέοντας. τά πλοῖα δὲ ἔχουσι μεγάλα κολοκύνθινα τὸ μῆκος πήχεων ἑξήκοντα· ἐπειδὰν γὰρ ξηράνωσι τὴν κολόκυνθαν, κοιλάναντες αὐτὴν καὶ ἐξελόντες τὴν ἐντεριώνην ἐμπλέουσιν, ἱστοῖς μὲν χρώμενοι καλαμίνοις, ἀντὶ δὲ τῆς ὀθόνης τῷ φύλλῳ τῆς κολοκύνθης. προσβαλόντες οὖν ἡμῖν ἀπὸ δύο πληρωμάτων ἐμάχοντο καὶ πολλοὺς κατετραυμάτιζον βάλλοντες τῷ σπέρματι τῶν κολοκυνθῶν. ἀγχωμάλως δὲ ἐπὶ πολὺ ναυμαχοῦντες περὶ μεσημβρίαν εἴδομεν κατόπιν τῶν

1 χρησάμενον καὶ μόλις…διασωθένπα β 2 ὑφ᾽ β : ἐφ᾽ γ 4 δὲ ὅμως ἅπαντας Γ[a]β ὕστερον ὑπὸ Τηλεγόνου β 6 παρὰ σοῦ γ δίαιταν γ : δαῖτα β 9 ξενισθείημεν β τῆς om. β 10 *Od.* 5.55 seq. 11 ἐπελέξατο Γ[a]β : ὑπεδέξατο γ 13 ξένια Belin : ξενία vel ξενίαι codd.; cf. 13.29 14 σωφρονοίη Γ[a]β : σώφρων γ 15 πάλαι om. γ 16 ἀπεκρινόμεθα β 21 πλησίων Z τά om. β 22 μεγάλα γ : μέγιστα β 23 ξηράνωσι τὴν κολόκυνθαν γ : ξηρανθῶσι β 24 μὲν γ : μέντοι β 27 βάλλοντες γ : βάλλοντες ἀντί λίθων Γ[a]β

your island, I was shipwrecked and was saved by Leucothea at the very last moment and carried to the land of the Phaeacians. They sent me home, where I discovered many suitors, who were living a life of luxury in our palace, vying for my wife. I killed them all and was then later killed by Telegonus, the son I had by Circe. Now I am on the Island of the Blest, where I repine that I ever left you and that I rejected your offer of immortality. If I can find the opportunity, I will escape and come to you." This was pretty much the content of the letter. It also contained instructions that we should be treated to her hospitality. **(36)** I advanced inland a short distance from the sea and I came upon a cave. It was just as Homer described it.[5] I found Calypso working at her loom. When she had taken the letter from me and read it, at first she wept for a long time, but then invited us to her table and a magnificent meal. She asked us about Odysseus and Penelope. How did Penelope look? Was she as intelligent as Odysseus boasted that she was long ago? We gave her the diplomatic answers that we thought would please her.

FURTHER ADVENTURES AT SEA

Well, we returned to our ship and then slept on the cape. **(37)** At dawn we set sail with a freshening breeze and, enduring heavy weather for two days, we came upon the pumpkin-pirates. These pirates are savages who plundered the ships that reached their coast from the other islands. Their vessels are huge pumpkins, some 120 feet wide. They fashion these vessels by drying the pumpkin, removing the "meat," and then hollowing them out. For actual sailing, they use the pumpkin stem for masts and for sails its flower. They attacked us in two manned pumpkins and injured many of us by pelting us with pumpkin seeds. For a long time this naval battle hung in the balance, but around midday we sighted to the rear of the pumpkin-pirates

[5] *Od.* 5.55–281.

Κολοκυνθοπειρατῶν προσπλέοντας τοὺς Καρυοναύτας. πολέμιοι δὲ ἦσαν ἀλλήλοις, ὡς ἔδειξαν· ἐπεὶ γὰρ κἀκεῖνοι ᾔσθοντο αὐτοὺς ἐπιόντας, ἡμῶν μὲν ὠλιγώρησαν, τραπόμενοι δὲ ἐπ᾽ ἐκείνους (38) ἐναυμάχουν. ἡμεῖς δὲ ἐν τοσούτῳ ἐπάραντες τὴν ὀθόνην ἐφεύγομεν ἀπολιπόντες αὐτοὺς μαχομένους, καὶ δῆλοι ἦσαν κρατήσοντες οἱ Καρυοναῦται ἅτε καὶ πλείους—πέντε γὰρ εἶχον πληρώματα—καὶ ἀπὸ ἰσχυροτέρων νεῶν μαχόμενοι· τὰ γὰρ πλοῖα ἦν αὐτοῖς κελύφανα καρύων ἡμίτομα, κεκενωμένα, μέγεθος δὲ ἑκάστου ἡμιτομίου εἰς μῆκος ὀργυιαὶ πεντεκαίδεκα.

Ἐπεὶ δὲ ἀπεκρύψαμεν αὐτούς, ἰώμεθα τοὺς τραυματίας, καὶ τὸ λοιπὸν ἐν τοῖς ὅπλοις ὡς ἐπίπαν ἦμεν, ἀεί τινας ἐπιβουλὰς (39) προσδεχόμενοι· οὐ μάτην. οὔπω γοῦν ἐδεδύκει ὁ ἥλιος, καὶ ἀπό τινος ἐρήμου νήσου προσήλαυνον ἡμῖν ὅσον εἴκοσι ἄνδρες ἐπὶ δελφίνων μεγάλων ὀχούμενοι, λῃσταὶ καὶ οὗτοι· καὶ οἱ δελφῖνες αὐτοὺς ἔφερον ἀσφαλῶς, καὶ ἀναπηδῶντες ἐχρεμέτιζον ὥσπερ ἵπποι. ἐπεὶ δὲ πλησίον ἦσαν, διαστάντες οἱ μὲν ἔνθεν, οἱ δὲ ἔνθεν ἔβαλλον ἡμᾶς σηπίαις ξηραῖς καὶ ὀφθαλμοῖς καρκίνων. τοξευόντων δὲ ἡμῶν καὶ ἀκοντιζόντων οὐκέτι ὑπέμενον, ἀλλὰ τρωθέντες οἱ πολλοὶ αὐτῶν πρὸς τὴν νῆσον κατέφυγον.

(40) Περὶ δὲ τὸ μεσονύκτιον γαλήνης οὔσης ἐλάθομεν προσοκείλαντες ἀλκυόνος καλιᾷ παμμεγέθει· σταδίων γοῦν ἦν αὕτη ἑξήκοντα τὸ περίμετρον. ἐπέπλεεν δὲ ἡ ἀλκυὼν τὰ ᾠὰ θάλπουσα οὐ πολὺ μείων τῆς καλιᾶς. καὶ δὴ ἀναπταμένη μικροῦ μὲν κατέδυσε τὴν ναῦν τῷ ἀνέμῳ τῶν πτερῶν, ᾤχετο δ᾽ οὖν φεύγουσα γοεράν τινα φωνὴν προϊεμένη. ἐπιβάντες δὲ ἡμεῖς ἡμέρας ἤδη ὑποφαινούσης ἐθεώμεθα τὴν καλιὰν σχεδίᾳ μεγάλῃ προσεοικυῖαν ἐκ δένδρων μεγάλων συμπεφορημένην· ἐπῆν δὲ καὶ ᾠὰ πεντακόσια, ἕκαστον αὐτῶν Χίου πίθου περιπληθέστερον. ἤδη μέντοι καὶ οἱ νεοττοὶ ἔνδοθεν ἐφαίνοντο καὶ ἔκρωζον. πελέκεσιν γοῦν διακόψαντες ἓν τῶν ᾠῶν νεοττὸν ἄπτερον ἐξεκολάψαμεν εἴκοσι γυπῶν ἁδρότερον.

2 ἐπεὶ γ᾽ : ἐπειδή β **5** αὐτοὺς γ : τοὺς Z : τούτους P κρατήσαντες Ω **7** νηῶν Ω **8** κελύφανα Ω : καλύφανα Z^1P^1 : κελύφη Γ δὲ om. β **9** ἡμιτόμου β **10** ἰώμεθά τε τοὺς β **13** ἐρήμης β νήσου... εἴκοσι om. ZP **16** οἱ ἵπποι β ἐπεὶ δὲ γ : ἐπειδὴ β **18** ἡμῶν καὶ γ : καὶ ἡμῶν καὶ β ὑπέμειναν β **21** γοῦν ἦν αὕτη ἑξήκοντα γ : που ἑξήκοντα ἦν αὐτῇ β **22** ἐπέπλει β ἡ om. γ **25** ἐσβάντες Ω **27** μεγάλων om. β ἐνῆν E. Schwartz **29** ἔκραζον βΩ

the nut-marines sailing towards them. As they demonstrated, they were their enemies. When the pumpkin-pirates saw the nut-mariners bearing down upon them, they forgot all about us and turned to confront these new enemies and joined battle with them. (**38**) At this juncture we hoisted sail and made our escape, leaving them locked in battle. It was evident that the nut-mariners were getting the better of the pumpkin-pirates. They were more numerous—there were five contingents of them—and they fought on stronger ships. Their ships were the halves of walnut shells that had been hollowed out. In size, each half nut reached a length of 30 yards.

When we had managed to pull out of sight, we took care of our wounded and for the rest of the day we remained ready for battle, since we continued to expect an attack. (**39**) And for good reason. The Sun had not yet set when as many as twenty men mounted on dolphins came out against us from an uninhabited island. These too were pirates. The dolphins carried them securely on their backs and, as they leapt up from the water, they would whiney like horses. Once they had come within range, they took up their positions on each side of the ship and began to pelt us with dry cuttlefish and crab eyes. But, when we responded by shooting arrows and throwing spears at them, they gave up and fled back to the island. Most of them had been wounded.

(**40**) Around midnight on a calm sea we landed on an enormous halcyon nest. We did not realize that it was there. It must have been 6,000 feet round. The mother bird floated on it brooding on her eggs. She was not much smaller than her nest. When she took flight, she very nearly sank our ship with the draft of her wings. She flew off screeching with a terrible, melancholy wail. At first light, we boarded the nest and observed it; it looked like a huge raft constructed out of tall trees. In it were five hundred eggs, each of them somewhat larger than a Chian amphora. Some of the young hatchlings were visible inside and they began to caw. We took some hatchets and broke an egg. Out came a still featherless chick bigger than twenty buzzards.

Ἐπεὶ δὲ πλέοντες ἀπείχομεν τῆς καλιᾶς ὅσον σταδίους διακοσίους, τέρατα ἡμῖν μεγάλα καὶ θαυμαστὰ ἐπεσήμανεν· ὅ τε γὰρ ἐν τῇ πρύμνῃ χηνίσκος ἄφνω ἐπτερύξατο καὶ ἀνεβόησεν, καὶ ὁ κυβερνήτης ὁ Σκίνθαρος φαλακρὸς ἤδη ὢν ἀνεκόμησεν, καὶ τὸ πάντων δὴ παραδοξότατον, ὁ γὰρ ἱστὸς τῆς νεὼς ἐξεβλάστησεν καὶ κλάδους ἀνέφυσεν καὶ ἐπὶ τῷ ἄκρῳ ἐκαρποφόρησεν, ὁ δὲ καρπὸς ἦν σῦκα καὶ σταφυλὴ μέλαινα, οὔπω πέπειρος. ταῦτα ἰδόντες ὡς εἰκὸς ἐταράχθημεν καὶ ηὐχόμεθα τοῖς θεοῖς διὰ τὸ ἀλλόκοτου τοῦ φαντάσματος. οὔπω δὲ πεντακοσίους σταδίους (42) διελθόντες εἴδομεν ὕλην μεγίστην καὶ λάσιον πιτύων καὶ κυπαρίττων. καὶ ἡμεῖς μὲν εἰκάσαμεν ἤπειρον εἶναι· τὸ δ᾽ ἦν πέλαγος ἄβυσσον ἀρρίζοις δένδροις καταπεφυτευμένον· είστήκει δὲ τὰ δένδρα ὅμως ἀκίνητα, ὀρθὰ καθάπερ ἐπιπλέοντα. πλησιάσαντες δ᾽ οὖν καὶ τὸ πᾶν κατανοήσαντες ἐν ἀπόρῳ εἰχόμεθα τί χρὴ δρᾶν· οὔτε γὰρ διὰ τῶν δένδρων πλεῖν δυνατὸν ἦν—πυκνὰ γὰρ καὶ προσεχῆ ὑπῆρχεν—οὔτε ἀναστρέφειν ἐδόκει ῥᾴδιον· ἐγὼ δὲ ἀνελθὼν ἐπὶ τὸ μέγιστον δένδρου ἐπεσκόπουν τὰ ἐπέκεινα ὅπως ἔχοι, καὶ ἑώρων ἐπὶ σταδίους μὲν πεντήκοντα ἢ ὀλίγῳ πλείους τὴν ὕλην οὖσαν, ἔπειτα δὲ αὖθις ἕτερον ὠκεανὸν ἐκδεχόμενον. καὶ δὴ ἐδόκει ἡμῖν ἀναθεμένους τὴν ναῦν ἐπὶ τὴν κόμην τῶν δένδρων—πυκνὴ δὲ ἦν—ὑπερβιβάσαι, εἰ δυναίμεθα, εἰς τὴν θάλατταν τὴν ἑτέραν· καὶ οὕτως ἐποιοῦμεν. ἐκδήσαντες γὰρ αὐτὴν κάλῳ μεγάλῳ καὶ ἀνελθόντες ἐπὶ τὰ δένδρα μόλις ἀνιμησάμεθα, καὶ θέντες ἐπὶ τῶν κλάδων, πετάσαντες τὰ ἱστία καθάπερ ἐν θαλάττῃ ἐπλέομεν τοῦ ἀνέμου προωθοῦντος ἐπισυρόμενοι· ἔνθα δὴ καὶ τὸ Ἀντιμάχου τοῦ ποιητοῦ ἔπος ἐπεισῆλθέ με—φησὶν γάρ που κἀκεῖνος·

Τοῖσιν δ᾽ ὑλήεντα διὰ πλόον ἐρχομένοισιν.

1 ἀπέσχομεν Γ^{a}β 2 θαυμάσια ἐπεσήμαινεν β 3 ἄφνω γ : ἄνω β 5 ἐξεβλάστα Ωβ 6 ἀνέφυσε β : ἀπέφυσεν Γ^{1} : ἀπέφυε Ω ἐπ᾽ ἄκρῳ β 7 σταφυλαὶ μέλαιναι οὔπω πέπειροι β 8 ὡς τὸ εἰκὸς β διὰ γ : ἀποστρέψαι ZP et γρ. mg. Γ vel Γ^{s} : ἀποτρέψαι γρ. S 9 φάσματος β 12 καταφυτευόμενον β 14 δ᾽ οὖν β : γοῦν γ : οὖν E. Schwartz 16 ῥᾴδιον ἐδόκει β 17 ἐπεσκόπουν Γ : ἀπεσκόπουν β : ἐσκόπουν Ω ἔχει β 21 πυκνὴ γὰρ ἦν β δυνάμεθα β 21–2 ἐς τὴν ἑτέραν θάλατταν β 22 κάλῳ (καλάμῳ Ω) μεγάλῳ γ : κάλων μεγάλων Γ^{a}β 24 πετάσαντές τε τὰ β 25 προσωθοῦντος γ ἔνθα δὴ γ : ἔνθα με β καὶ τὸ τοῦ Ω 26 εἰσῆλθε β 27 Fr. 62, Kinkel, *EGF*

(41) We sailed on, but when we were about two hundred stades from the halcyon nest, uncanny and ominous things began to occur. First, the wooden gooseneck finial at the end of the prow of our ship suddenly sprouted wings and began to honk. At the same time our pilot, Scintharus, who was bald, grew a new head of hair, and, strangest of all, the ship's mast came back to life and sprouted new branches and fruit on its top. There were figs and hard unripe black grapes. When we witnessed these strange and incredible phenomena we were understandably thrown into a panic and prayed to the gods. (42) We hadn't sailed on for five hundred stades when we sighted an immense forest dense with pine and cypress. We supposed that we had reached the mainland, but, in fact, we had come upon an unfathomable sea with rootless trees growing upon it. Yet the trees stood straight upright and motionless, as if they were floating on the sea. When we drew nearer and studied the situation, we had no idea what to do. It was impossible to sail through the forest—it was dense and had no clearings—and it was not easy to turn back either. I then climbed to the top of the tallest tree to see what was on the other side of the forest. I could see that the forest stretched out for 30,000 feet—perhaps a little more—and then another ocean appeared on the other side. It then occurred to us that, if we hoisted our ship up onto the foliage of the trees, which was very thick, we could manage, if we had the strength, to draw our ship across the forest to the sea beyond. This is what we did. We attached the ship to a long cable and, climbing up the trees, we hoisted it up to the trees with great effort and we set it upon the branches. Unfurling our sails we began to sail as if we were on the surface of the sea and glided along with the wind to our backs. I was reminded of the verse of the poet Antimachus. It went something like this:

> For those making their way through the sylvan sailing....

(43) Βιασάμενοι δὲ ὅμως τὴν ὕλην ἀφικόμεθα ἐς τὸ ὕδωρ, καὶ πάλιν ὁμοίως καθέντες τὴν ναῦν ἐπλέομεν διὰ καθαροῦ καὶ διαυγοῦς ὕδατος, ἄχρι δὴ ἐπέστημεν χάσματι μεγάλῳ ἐκ τοῦ ὕδατος διεστῶτος γεγενημένῳ, καθάπερ ἐν τῇ γῇ πολλάκις ὁρῶμεν ὑπὸ σεισμῶν γενόμενα διαχωρίσματα. ἡ μὲν οὖν ναῦς καθελόντων ἡμῶν τὰ ἱστία οὐ ῥᾳδίως ἔστη παρ᾽ ὀλίγον ἐλθοῦσα κατενεχθῆναι. ὑπερκύψαντες δὲ ἡμεῖς ἑωρῶμεν βάθος ὅσον σταδίων χιλίων μάλα φοβερὸν καὶ παράδοξον· εἱστήκει γὰρ τὸ ὕδωρ ὥσπερ μεμερισμένον· περιβλέποντες δὲ ὁρῶμεν κατὰ δεξιὰ οὐ πάνυ πόρρωθεν γέφυραν ἐπεζευγμένην ὕδατος συνάπτοντος τὰ πελάγη κατὰ τὴν ἐπιφάνειαν, ἐκ τῆς ἑτέρας θαλάττης εἰς τὴν ἑτέραν διαρρέοντος. προσελάσαντες οὖν ταῖς κώπαις κατ᾽ ἐκεῖνο παρεδράμομεν καὶ μετὰ πολλῆς ἀγωνίας ἐπεράσαμεν οὔποτε προσδοκήσαντες.

(44) Ἐντεῦθεν ἡμᾶς ὑπεδέχετο πέλαγος προσηνὲς καὶ νῆσος οὐ μεγάλη, εὐπρόσιτος, συνοικουμένη· ἐνέμοντο δὲ αὐτὴν ἄνθρωποι ἄγριοι, Βουκέφαλοι, κέρατα ἔχοντες, οἷον παρ᾽ ἡμῖν τὸν Μινώταυρον ἀναπλάττουσιν. ἀποβάντες δὲ προῄειμεν ὑδρευσόμενοι καὶ σιτία ληψόμενοι, εἴ ποθεν δυνηθείημεν· οὐκέτι γὰρ εἴχομεν. καὶ ὕδωρ μὲν αὐτοῦ πλησίον εὕρομεν, ἄλλο δὲ οὐδὲν ἐφαίνετο, πλὴν μυκηθμὸς πολὺς οὐ πόρρωθεν ἠκούετο. δόξαντες οὖν ἀγέλην εἶναι βοῶν, κατ᾽ ὀλίγον προχωροῦντες ἐπέστημεν τοῖς ἀνθρώποις. οἱ δὲ ἰδόντες ἡμᾶς ἐδίωκον, καὶ τρεῖς μὲν τῶν ἑταίρων λαμβάνουσιν, οἱ δὲ λοιποὶ πρὸς τὴν θάλατταν καταφεύγομεν. εἶτα μέντοι πάντες ὁπλισάμενοι—οὐ γὰρ ἐδόκει ἡμῖν ἀτιμωρήτους περιιδεῖν τοὺς φίλους—ἐμπίπτομεν τοῖς Βουκεφάλοις τὰ κρέα τῶν ἀνῃρημένων διαιρουμένοις· φοβήσαντες δὲ πάντας διώκομεν, καὶ

1 βιασάμενοι γ : διελθόντες β et γρ. mg. Γ vel Γ^{s} ἐς γ : πρὸς β 2 καταθέντες codd. : corr. Cobet 4 ἑωρῶμεν β 5 γενόμενα Γ : γινόμενα Ω : γιγνόμενα β διαχωρίσματα recc. et Γ^{2} vel Γ^{x} : διαχωρήματα Γ^{1} et cett. codd. καθελκόντων N 6 οὐ ῥᾳδίως recc. : ῥᾳδίως cett. 9 ὁρῶμεν κατὰ δεξιὰ γ : καὶ τὰ δεξιὰ ἑωρῶμεν β οὐ πάνυ om. β 10 ὑπεζευγμένην Ω 11 ἐκ γ : κἀκ β 15 τοὐντεῦθεν β πέλαγός τε προσηνὲς Γ^{a}β 16 εὐπροσίτως β 18 προσήειμεν β 19 καὶ σιτία γ : καί τι καὶ σιτίον β οὐκέτι γὰρ εἴχομεν om. β 24 κατεφεύγομεν γ 27 φοβήσαντες δὲ πάντας Γ^{a}β : βοήσαντες δὲ πάντες γ διώκομεν E. Schwartz : ἐδιώκομεν codd. : ἐκδιώκομεν conieci

Despite the difficulty, we made our way through the forest and arrived at open water. Just as we had hoisted our ship up into the trees, we lowered it and sailed through a crystal-clear sea until we came upon a vast chasm produced by the parting of the water. It was very much like the deep fissures we often see on land that are produced by earthquakes. We lowered our sails and the ship was brought to a halt; it came within a hair of being carried down into the chasm. We peered over the edge and could look down to a depth of perhaps a thousand stades. It was a strange and terrifying sight! The water was sheered off, as if it had been cut by a knife. Looking about, we sighted a bridge of water that spanned the two seas on their surface. It flowed from one sea to the other. We rowed up to it, made a run over it and, with great effort and anguish, we made the passage beyond all expectation.

AN ADVENTURE AMONG THE BULL-HEADS

(**44**) From there a smooth sea and a small island awaited us. Its approach was easy and it was inhabited. Savages lived on the island, the Boukephali, or bull-heads. They had horns and were like artists' representations of the Minotaur. We disembarked and went inland to see if we could find provisions and water. And, indeed, we soon found fresh water on the island, but nothing else came to light, except that we could hear the loud sound of mooing not far off. Thinking that it came from a herd of cattle, we made our way gradually towards the source of the noise and came upon—not cows—the men I described. When they laid eyes upon us, they began to pursue us and they captured three of our companions. The rest of us managed to escape to the sea. Despite the threat, we all put on our armour—we did not think that it was right to leave our friends unavenged—and attacked the bull-heads who were dividing the flesh of the three men they had killed. They panicked and we pursued them all; we killed about fifty of them and took two alive. Then we turned back to the ship with the two captives. In the end, we could find no provisions on the island. My crew urged me to slaughter the captives. I did not approve, however, but had them tied up and put under guard. And in time an embassy from the bull-heads appeared asking

κτείνομέν γε ὅσον πεντήκοντα καὶ ζῶντας αὐτῶν δύο λαμβάνομεν, καὶ αὖθις ὀπίσω ἀναστρέφομεν τοὺς αἰχμαλώτους ἔχοντες. σιτίον μέντοι οὐδὲν εὕρομεν. οἱ μὲν οὖν ἄλλοι παρῄνουν ἀποαφάττειν τοὺς εἰλημμένους, ἐγὼ δὲ οὐκ ἐδοκίμαζον, ἀλλὰ δήσας ἐφύλαττον αὐτούς, ἄχρι δὴ ἀφίκοντο παρὰ τῶν Βουκεφάλων πρέσβεις ἀπαιτοῦντες ἐπὶ λύτροις τοὺς συνειλημμένους· συνίεμεν γὰρ αὐτῶν διανευόντων καὶ γοερόν τι μυκωμένων ὥσπερ ἱκετευόντων. τὰ λύτρα δὲ ἦν τυροὶ πολλοὶ καὶ ἰχθύες ξηροὶ καὶ κρόμμυα καὶ ἔλαφοι τέτταρες, τρεῖς ἑκάστη πόδας ἔχουσα, δύο μὲν τοὺς ὄπισθεν, οἱ δὲ πρόσω ἐς ἕνα συμπεφύκεσαν. ἐπὶ τούτοις ἀποδόντες τοὺς συνειλημμένους καὶ μίαν ἡμέραν ἐπιμείναντες ἀνήχθημεν.

Ἤδη δὲ ἰχθύες τε ἡμῖν ἐφαίνοντο καὶ ὄρνεα παρεπέτετο καὶ (45) ἄλλ᾽ ὁπόσα γῆς πλησίον οὔσης σημεῖα προφαίνεται. μετ᾽ ὀλίγον δὲ καὶ ἄνδρας εἴδομεν καινῷ τῳ τρόπῳ ναυτιλίας χρωμένους· αὐτοὶ γὰρ καὶ ναῦται καὶ νῆες ἦσαν. λέξω δὲ τοῦ πλοῦ τὸν τρόπον· ὕπτιοι κείμενοι ἐπὶ τοῦ ὕδατος ὀρθώσαντες τὰ αἰδοῖα—μεγάλα δὲ φέρουσιν—ἐξ αὐτῶν ὀθόνην πετάσαντες καὶ ταῖς χερσὶν τοὺς ποδεῶνας κατέχοντες ἐμπίπτοντος τοῦ ἀνέμου ἔπλεον. ἄλλοι δὲ μετὰ τούτους ἐπὶ φελλῶν καθήμενοι ζεύξαντες δύο δελφῖνας ἤλαυνόν τε καὶ ἡνιόχουν· οἱ δὲ προϊόντες ἐπεσύροντο τοὺς φελλούς. οὗτοι ἡμᾶς οὔτε ἠδίκουν οὔτε ἔφευγον, ἀλλ᾽ ἤλαυνον ἀδεῶς τε καὶ εἰρηνικῶς τὸ εἶδος τοῦ ἡμετέρου πλοίου θαυμάζοντες καὶ πάντοθεν περισκοποῦντες.

Ἑσπέρας δὲ ἤδη προσήχθημεν νήσῳ οὐ μεγάλῃ· κατῳκεῖτο δὲ (46) ὑπὸ γυναικῶν, ὡς ἐνομίζομεν, Ἑλλάδα φωνὴν προϊεμένων· προσῄεσαν γὰρ καὶ ἐδεξιοῦντο καὶ ἠσπάζοντο, πάνυ ἑταιρικῶς κεκοσμημέναι καὶ καλαὶ πᾶσαι καὶ νεάνιδες, ποδήρεις τοὺς χιτῶνας ἐπισυρόμεναι. ἡ μὲν οὖν νῆσος ἐκαλεῖτο Κοβαλοῦσα, ἡ δὲ

2 ἀνεστρέψαμεν γ **4** παρειλημμένους β **6** αἰτοῦντες γ **8** ἰχθῦς β πολλοὶ καὶ ante ξηροὶ iterat γ **10** ὀπίσω γ πρόσω συνεπεφύκεσαν γ **13** παρεπέτατο β **15** καινῷ τῳ Herwerden : καινῷ τῷ γ : καινῷ β : καινοτάτῳ Nilén **18** ἐξ Γ^{a}βΩ : ἐπ᾽ Γ **21** ἡνιόχευον β ἐπεσύροντο Γ^{a}β : ἐπεφέροντο γ **25** κατῴκητο β δὲ γ : δὲ αὕτη Γ^{a}β **28** καὶ καλαὶ γ : καλαὶ β **29** Κοβαλοῦσα vel Κοβαλόεσσα Guyet : καβαλλοῦσα Γ^{a}β : καβαλοῦσα Ω : ἐκβαλοῦσα Γ : Καββαλοῦσα corrector in cod. recc. : Κοβαλοῦσσα E. Schwartz

to ransom our captives. We caught their drift as they nodded their heads and mooed most mournfully, as if they were suppliants. The ransom consisted of many heads of cheese, dried fish, onions, and four deer, each of which had only three legs—two hind legs and two legs in front that were fused together. We returned the hostages in exchange for this ransom, stayed on the island for a day, and sailed off.

OUR AUTHOR ENCOUNTERS NEW AND WONDEROUS FORMS OF SEAFARING, AS WELL AS A FEW MORE ODYSSEAN ADVENTURES

(45) Fish now began to appear in the water, birds flew about us, and there were many other indications that we were approaching land. Soon we could see men navigating in a very strange fashion. They were at once sailors and ships. I will describe how they sailed. They were stretched out on their backs on the surface of the sea with their penis erect—they had very big penises—and they unfurled a sail from these and controlled the sheets with their hands. As the wind caught their sails, they scudded along. After these we saw others seated on corks and driving a yoke of dolphins, as if they were charioteers. As they cut through the sea the dolphins drew the corks behind them. These sailors neither did us any harm nor fled from us, but fearlessly and peaceably they went on their way as they marveled at our fashion of sailing, examining our ship from all sides.

(46) At dusk we drew near a small island. It was inhabited by women—at least we thought—who spoke Greek. They came up to us, greeted us, and hugged us. They were all dolled up like prostitutes and they were all young and beautiful. Their dresses trailed at their feet. Now the name of the island is Kobalousa and its city Hydramargia. Each of these ladies received one of us by lot and made him her personal guest. But I kept my distance, for I had a foreboding of trouble to come. As I looked about me with greater

πόλις αὐτὴ Ὑδαμαργία. λαχοῦσαι δ᾽ οὖν ἡμᾶς αἱ γυναῖκες ἑκάστη πρὸς ἑαυτὴν ἀπῆγεν καὶ ξένον ἐποιεῖτο. ἐγὼ δὲ μικρὸν ἀποστὰς—οὐ γὰρ χρηστὰ ἐμαντευόμην—ἀκριβέστερόν τε περιβλέπων ὁρῶ πολλῶν ἀνθρώπων ὀστᾶ καὶ κρανία κείμενα. καὶ τὸ μὲν βοὴν ἱστάναι καὶ τοὺς ἑταίρους συγκαλεῖν καὶ ἐς τὰ ὅπλα χωρεῖν οὐκ ἐδοκίμαζον. προχειρισάμενος δὲ τὴν μαλάχην πολλὰ ηὐχόμην αὐτῇ διαφυγεῖν ἐκ τῶν παρόντων κακῶν· μετ᾽ ὀλίγον δὲ τῆς ξένης διακονουμένης εἶδον τὰ σκέλη οὐ γυναικός, ἀλλ᾽ ὄνου ὁπλάς· καὶ δὴ σπασάμενος τὸ ξίφος συλλαμβάνω τε αὐτὴν καὶ δήσας περὶ τῶν ὅλων ἀνέκρινον. ἡ δέ, ἄκουσα μέν, εἶπεν δὲ ὅμως, αὐτὰς μὲν εἶναι θαλαττίους γυναῖκας Ὀνοσκελέας προσαγορευομένας, τροφὴν δὲ ποιεῖσθαι τοὺς ἐπιδημοῦντας ξένους. ἐπειδὰν γάρ, ἔφη, μεθύσωμεν αὐτούς, συνευνηθεῖσαι κοιμωμένοις ἐπιχειροῦμεν. ἀκούσας δὲ ταῦτα ἐκείνην μὲν αὐτοῦ κατέλιπον δεδεμένην, αὐτὸς δὲ ἀνελθὼν ἐπὶ τὸ τέγος ἐβόων τε καὶ τοὺς ἑταίρους συνεκάλουν. ἐπεὶ δὲ συνῆλθον, τὰ πάντα ἐμήνυον αὐτοῖς καὶ τά γε ὀστᾶ ἐδείκνυον καὶ ἦγον ἔσω πρὸς τὴν δεδεμένην· ἡ δὲ αὐτίκα ὕδωρ ἐγένετο καὶ ἀφανὴς ἦν. ὅμως δὲ τὸ ξίφος εἰς τὸ ὕδωρ καθῆκα πειρώμενος· τὸ δὲ αἷμα ἐγένετο.

(47) Ταχέως οὖν ἐπὶ ναῦν κατελθόντες ἀπεπλεύσαμεν. καὶ ἐπεὶ ἡμέρα ὑπηύγαζεν, ἤδη τὴν ἤπειρον ἀπεβλέπομεν εἰκάζομέν τε εἶναι τὴν ἀντιπέρας τῇ ὑφ᾽ ἡμῶν οἰκουμένῃ κειμένην. προσκυνήσαντες δ᾽ οὖν καὶ προσευξάμενοι περὶ τῶν μελλόντων ἐσκοποῦμεν, καὶ τοῖς μὲν ἐδόκει ἐπιβᾶσιν μόνον αὖθις ὀπίσω ἀναστρέφειν, τοῖς δὲ τὸ μὲν πλοῖον αὐτοῦ καταλιπεῖν, ἀνελθόντας δὲ ἐς τὴν μεσόγαιαν πειραθῆναι τῶν ἐνοικούντων. ἐν ὅσῳ δὲ ταῦτα ἐλογιζόμεθα, χειμὼν σφοδρὸς ἐπιπεσὼν καὶ προσαράξας τὸ σκάφος τῷ αἰγιαλῷ

1 αὐτὴ β : αὔτη γ Ὑδαμαργία. λαχοῦσαι Mras : Ὑδαμαρδία. λαβοῦσαι γ : Ὑδαμή Γ[a] (Οὐδαμῇ vel Οὐδαμῶν Z? P vix legi potest). διαλαχοῦσαι β : Ὑδαμαυρία. λαβοῦσαι Gesner : Ὑδαταρδία (vel Ὑδαταιμία) . . . temptavi δ᾽ οὖν γ : γοῦν β **2** ἀποστὰς S : ὑποστὰς cett. : ὑπεκστὰς Mras **4** κείμενα om. β **8–9** καὶ διασπασάμενος γ **9** αὐτὴν Γ[a]β : ταύτην γ **13** συνευνασθεῖσαι β **15** στέγος γ **16** τά τε γ **17** ἔξω γ **18** τε ἐγέν. β **21** ὑπηύγαζε β : ἐπηύγαζεν Γ : ἀπηύγαζεν Ω ἤδη τὴν ἤπειρον ἀπεβλέπομεν εἰκάζομέν τε β : τήν τε ἤπειρον ἀποβλεπόμενοι (ἀποβλέπομεν ἣν E. Schwartz) εἰκάζομεν γ : aliquid excidisse putat Nilén
22 ἀντιπέραν Ω **23** δ᾽ οὖν γ : δὲ β ἐσκοπούμεθα β

attention, I could see the bones and skulls of many men scattered about. But I did not think that it was the best idea to shout and summon my companions and make for our weapons. I pulled the sacred mallow out and prayed to it: "Let us escape from these dangers." After a little while, I saw that the legs of the woman who was taking care of me were not a woman's but the those of an ass. I drew my sword, took hold of her, and bound her entire body tight. I interrogated her. In response to my questions, she said that these ladies were mermaids called ass-shanks. They ate the strangers who visited their island. "Once," she said, "we get them drunk, they go to bed with us and we attack them in their sleep." When I heard this, I left her bound up on the spot and went to the rooftop and shouted out to summon my companions. When they had gathered around me, I revealed our situation to them, pointed to the bones, and led them inside my shelter to the woman I had tied up. She immediately dissolved into water and vanished from sight. Nevertheless, I plunged my sword into the water as an experiment. It turned to blood.

THE RETURN TO EARTH AND THE ANTIPODAL WORLD

(47) We ran down to our ship and sailed off. And, when dawn was just breaking on the horizon, we saw the mainland in the distance and conjectured that it must be the continent opposite our own inhabited world. We bent down and kissed the earth and prayed for prosperity. Some of us thought that we should land but immediately turn back and sail away. Others thought that we should leave the ship and go up to the inland plain to determine what kind of people lived there. While we were discussing our options, a terrible storm fell upon us and drove and shattered our ship upon

διέλυσεν. ἡμεῖς δὲ μόλις ἐξενηξάμεθα τὰ ὅπλα ἕκαστος καὶ εἴ τι ἄλλο οἷός τε ἦν ἁρπασάμενοι.

Ταῦτα μὲν οὖν τὰ μέχρι τῆς ἑτέρας γῆς συνενεχθέντα μοι ἐν τῇ θαλάττῃ καὶ παρὰ τὸν πλοῦν ἐν ταῖς νήσοις καὶ ἐν τῷ ἀέρι καὶ μετὰ ταῦτα ἐν τῷ κήτει καὶ ἐπεὶ ἐξήλθομεν, παρά τε τοῖς ἥρωσι καὶ τοῖς ὀνείροις καὶ τὰ τελευταῖα παρὰ τοῖς Βουκεφάλοις καὶ ταῖς Ὀνοσκελέαις, τὰ δὲ ἐπὶ τῆς γῆς εν ταῖς ἑξῆς βίβλοις διηγήσομαι.

2 ἁρπασάμενος β et fort. Γ[a] **5** μετ᾿ αὐτὰ γ Subscriptio in Γ : διώρθωσα εγὼ αλεξανδρος επισκοπος νικαίας τῆς κατα βιθυνίαν μετα τοῦ οικειου αδελψοῦ ιακιωβου τοῦ μητροπολίτου λαρίσσης subscr. mg. Γ[a]

the shore. One by one, we managed with great difficulty to recover our weapons and anything else we could save.

Until that moment in which I reached the other world on the sea, this has been the story of my adventures, namely of my voyage among the islands and in the air, of the events in the belly of the whale, of our stay among the heroes and dreams, after our escape from the beast, and finally of our encounter with the bull-heads and ass-shanks. In the books that follow I will tell of my adventures in this new land.

COMMENTARY

Book 1

The Episodes of *True History* Book 1

1.1–4 The opening
1.5–9 The voyage to the Western Island
1.9–12 Violent ascent to the Moon and the kingdom of Endymion
1.13–18 The defeat of the Selenitai in the war between Endymion and Phaethon
1.18–20 The capture of Lucian and his crew and a treaty of peace
1.21–6 The Selenitai described
1.27–9 Descent down to the Ocean, arrival at the island of Lychnopolis, and the trip past Cloudcuckooland
1.30–42 In the belly of the whale (continued in *VH* 2.1–2)

1.1–4 The opening

Our author introduces his first-person narrative by an elaborate comparison between the entertainment he will offer his reader and the periods of relaxation that are an integral part of athletic training (ὥσπερ…οὕτω). In his studied rhetorical and antithetical style he promises not only recreation (ἀνέσεως) for the reader wearied by serious reading (the equivalent of physical training), but also the charm of novelty, philosophical vistas, and the parody of earlier writers. In his confession that what he has written is a lie, the author parts company with liars like Homer's Odysseus, Ctesias of Cnidus, Herodotus, and Iambulus. This confession thus immediately stands out as a parody of the kind of introduction that one finds in historiography (see Introduction 1.3). Lucian also addresses a reader never named and never recognized again, not even in the conclusion to Book 2.

That the *VH* was preceded by a short introductory piece (*prolalia*) is conjectural and a matter of scholarly debate. Lucian's *Dionysus* and *Heracles* have been suggested; on this matter and whether or not Book 2 even had an introductory piece, see GL.

ληтικοῖς: with the verbal -το- plus adjectival suffix -ικο- (Smyth §858), the word essentially means "capable" or "suitable" for combat/contest. With the definite article the adjective is substantivized, and Lucian seems to use it in order to cast a wide net, i.e. inclusive of all those involved in hard physical training, whether games or actual combat. There is freedom in translation here, as evident in Fowlers's (1905) "Athletes and physical trainers...," Harmon's (1913) "Men interested in athletics...," and Paul Turner's (1961) "If you were training to be an athlete...." ἀθλητικοῖς also supplies the implied antecedent of ὑπολαμβάνουσιν in the parenthetical clause marked by the postpositive particle γοῦν. On Matteuzzi's suggestion that ἀθλητικοῖς is a gloss (an intrusion into the manuscripts from marginal comments), see the comprehensive discussion by Möllendorff, who also considers the text uncertain and thus marks τοῖς ἀθλητικοῖς καὶ as corrupt (†).

GL notes the common analogy between athletic training and the training of the soul in philosophical works. The depth to which Lucian engages in actual philosophy is a topic that continually arises in Lucianic scholarship, even though the consensus typically leans toward Lucian as a writer that simply uses philosophy and philosophers as satiric or comic fodder. In a philosophical context, Laird (2003) goes further and explores the relationship between philosophy and fiction (see also Introduction 2.3), namely arguing that *True History* uses the *Republic* as an important model and is a response to Plato; while ἄνεσις is an important part of physical training (Philostr. *De gymn.* 47), this kind of relaxation certainly has intellectual, educational, and philosophical situations (Cic. *De off.* 1.29; Sen. *De tranq. an.* 17.5–8). But as Kidd (2017, 360) notes, even Aristotle's use of ἄνεσις is in fact close to Lucian's—it may even be on Lucian's mind here—in that it is because of and in preparation for work, i.e. the serious work to which one will return.

τοὺς λόγους...τὴν πολλὴν τῶν σπουδαιοτέρων ἀνάγνωσιν: the reading from which to take a break. GL notes both that λόγοι can suggest philosophy and that, in connection with τῶν σπουδαιοτέρων, there might be a juxtaposition of serious writings and serious readers. While both words have their philosophical contexts, they are sufficiently generic to allow multiple inferences, e.g. λόγος is also simply a tale, story, or legend, even in Plato (see LSJ). Lucian's ambiguity makes this kind of reading inclusive of anything requiring great attention and study.

ἡγοῦμαι: governs προσήκειν...ἀνιέναι τε...καὶ...παρασκευάζειν.

1.2 ἐμμελὴς ἡ ἀνάπαυσις: ἐμμελής derives from ἐν μέλει, "in tune." ἀνάπαυσις often describes the relaxation associated with festivals or poetry (Hes. *Th.* 55; Thuc. 2.38; Plat. *Phlb.* 30e; Luc. *Nigr.* 18).

ψιλὴν…ψυχαγωγίαν…θεωρίαν οὐκ ἄμουσον ἐπιδείξεται: Jerram's "bare enticement to the mind," which indicates amusement both by the marvelous and the parodic engagement with Greek literature. LSJ documents the sense of "amusement" or "entertainment" for ψυχαγωγία, as opposed to instruction (διδασκαλία), as found in Strabo (Erotasth. in St. 1.1.10 = F 1 A 20 Berger; cf. also Philod. *Mus.* Page 86 K), whom Lucian may indeed have in mind here (see Möllendorff ad loc.). Laird (2003) again suggests philosophical undertones, noting the use of the term in philosophical discussions in the context of the transporting effect of speech and poetry (cf. Plat. *Phdr.* 261a, 271c). He even translates ψυχαγωγία as the "sheer flight of the mind." With ψιλός, this can perhaps be further qualified. λόγος in the sense of reading, and thus text, just appeared a few lines above in 1.1 (see note above). Lucian might be playing with the common idiom of λόγος ψιλός, i.e. prose, and with θεωρίαν οὐκ ἄμουσον ἐπιδείξεται a larger picture is being framed. First, with οὐκ ἄμουσον (common litotes of negative οὐκ with alpha privative (Smyth §3032), e.g. "a spectacle not unrefined") in the second half of the balanced μὴ μόνον/ἀλλὰ…καί clauses, Lucian might possibly even be obliquely referencing his parodic absorption of poetry within his prose. Second, although Laird chooses to give his translation of θεωρίαν an intellectual or philosophical patina ("contemplation"), with ἐπιδείξεται, which recalls the rhetorical term ἐπίδειξις, a performance meant to display an orator's skill outside of the courts or political assemblies, the theatrical context of this term might be more appropriate. In this bigger picture, Lucian thus seems to construct an elaborate way of describing a dramatic prose spectacle that does not lack its poetic charm, even if there is no music. The use of the vocabulary of the theater is also common in Lucian; human life as a "theater" goes back to Plato and is a common trope in literature of the imperial period (see Abdel Wahab 1988).

οἷόν τι…φρονήσειν ὑπολαμβάνω: οἷόν τι "something of the kind." The neuter singular refers back to the entire relative μὴ μόνον/ἀλλά…καὶ construction. The phrase lacks a subject accusative to govern φρονήσειν because it must be supplied from the dative pronoun, referencing the reader who has been engaged in serious reading at the beginning of the sentence (γένοιτο δ' ἂν ἐμμελὴς ἡ ἀνάπαυσις αὐτοῖς); see also Möllendorff. Schwartz's supplement of αὐτούς is superfluous and is essentially a *lectio* *facilior* (an easier reading, something often introduced into manuscripts, either in the margin or directly in the text, to ensure reading comprehension). This abridged form of expression is an example of a brachylogy (Smyth §3017).

τὸ ξένον τῆς ὑποθέσεως οὐδὲ τὸ χαρίεν τῆς προαιρέσεως ἐπαγωγὸν ἔσται: technical terminology critical to how Lucian expresses himself and his unique brand. ὑπόθεσις, which here is "foreign," is a topic or subject, often of a poem or treatise. But it also has theatrical uses, indicating an actor's role or even a type of play. τὸ χαρίεν, the neuter adjective from χαρίεις used as a substantive, is commonly used in terms of literary grace or even cleverness. While προαίρεσις can simply be rendered as a "purpose" or "plan," we should note the term also conveys a sect or school of philosophy or music; Lucian uses this term in the context of philosophical schools in his *Demonax* (4).

ποικίλα: Lucian's "varied lies" that are plausible (πιθανῶς). Herodotus, Plato, and Demosthenes are cited by Dionysius of Halicarnassus (*Comp.* 19) as the greatest practitioners of variety. In the bigger picture of Lucian and his literary relationship and engagement with Plato, one should not overlook the significance of this literary technical term. It appears in early discussions on Plato and the very development of the dialogue form (see *P.Oxy.* XLV 3219 = *FGrHist* 1134). The mixing of styles, at which Lucian is so clearly an innovative expert, was a topic of theory and applied teaching in the study of Plato in late antiquity (cf. the sixth-century CE *Prolegomena to Plato* 17.2–18 and Hunter (2012: 154)); definitions of varied styles include digressions, varied figures, and the so-called "powerful" (ἁδρός) and "plain" (ἰσχνός) styles. For a list of parallels on passages that use ποικιλία in literary critical discussions of character design and development, see Haslam (1972: 26); cf. also Grand-Clément (2015). Yet the term also appears in a philosophical context. It typically refers to Plato's offering of different explanations or arguments for the same philosophical thesis (cf. Attic. F 7.9.1 DES PLACES). The term's position here straddles, as it does in Plato, literature and philosophy. Lucian's lies are plausible because of his style that invokes the genre of dialogue. But as we will see, one of the jokes, one of the problems, concerning philosophy and philosophers is the multiple explanations and arguments used—by multiple and opposing philosophical schools—to answer a simple question; the most important being what is, or how does one find, a happy life.

ἐξενηνόχαμεν: second perfect active of ἐκφέρω. It is not uncommon for Greek poets to employ the first-person plural for the first-person singular, the so-called "poetic we," though the introduction of the phenomenon is more likely due to the conventions of Greek meter than anything else. Although GL suggests this may be used to convey "the collective experience of all the travellers," this perhaps is more indicative of the reading experience Lucian offers, the one not lacking the refined entertainment associated mostly with poetry and the music (οὐκ ἄμουσον) that often accompanied it. In using the form, Lucian is, in a way, being poetic.

οὐκ ἀκωμῳδήτως ᾔνικται: perfect passive of αἰνίσσομαι, "to hint at," "to speak indirectly," or "to speak in riddles" (αἰνίγματα). Lucian further qualifies this action with the adverb "not without comedy"; the adverb is only found here. Attic Old Comedy, especially Aristophanes and Eupolis, is an important model for Lucian's comic dialogue (see especially *Double Indictment*) both in terms of language and the art of Athenian comedy.

πρός τινας τῶν παλαιῶν... τεράστια καὶ μυθώδη: the pejorative sense of μυθώδη is already evident in Thucydides' reference to Herodotus (Thuc. 1.22). The root of τεράστια is τέρας, a portent, omen, or, in this case, a wonder, the likes of which would be found in works of paradoxography, such as the aptly titled Ἄπιστα of Isigonus of Nicaea (*PGR* XI) and Phlegon of Tralles' Περὶ θαυμασίων (*FGrHist / BNJ* 257/257a). These poets, historians, and philosophers are also qualified as παλαιῶν to mark them as ancient or "classical."

οὓς... ἂν ἔγραφον, εἰ μὴ καὶ αὐτῷ σοι... φανεῖσθαι ἔμελλον: a condition ("if... were (now),... would"), in which the imperfects refer to present time (Smyth §2304). As for σοι, the addressee of this narrative is never identified, unlike, for example, the Celsus of Lucian's *Alexander*; nor is the addressee referred to again. The gesture is obviously meant for Lucian's reader, i.e. *you*.

1.3 ἔμελλον ⟨ὧν⟩ Κτησίας ὁ Κτησιόχου ὁ Κνίδιος: A lacuna has been conjectured before Κτησίας, and thus Macleod places the relative pronoun in angle brackets to correct the text. To place a full stop after ἔμελλον, one must, like Jerram, follow MS β, which omits ὅς before συνέγραψεν and establishes the aorist as the main verb of the sentence. If not, something is needed to link this lingering clause to the main sentence. Bekker suggested either ὧν or οἷον.

Ctesias, son of Ctesiochus, of Cnidus, was a doctor in the court of the Persian king Artaxerxes II (405–398/7 BCE) and the author of a *Persica* and

Indica, both of which were summarized by Photius in his *Bibliotheca* (*Pers.* 35b35–45a21; *Ind.* 45a21–50a3). The fragments are collected in Jacoby (*FGrHist* 688). Strabo (2.2.9) notably considered all writers on India as ψευδολόγοι, and both Aristotle (*HA* 606a) and Plutarch (*Art.* 1.4) considered Ctesias untrustworthy. In *VH* 2.31 Lucian places him on the Island of the Impious, and it comes as no surprise to find him in Lucian's *The Lover of Lies* (2).

Ἰαμβοῦλος: for Iambulus we rely solely on the summary of his travel narrative by Diodorus Siculus (2.55–60); Diodorus gives a long and somewhat confusing paraphrase of his description of the Islands of the Sun, a description reflected perhaps in *VH* 1.22–6. The conclusion of Iambulus' narrative in Diodorus Siculus (60.2) is perhaps the model for the conclusion to Lucian's *True History* (*VH* 2.47).

μήτε: οὔτε, as Jerram notes, might be expected to express the fact that Ctesias writes about things of which he does not know. Smyth (§2689 c) specifically notes Lucian as an example of later Greek in which "μή has encroached on οὐ," i.e. there is no longer much of a distinction between the two.

ἐν τῇ μεγάλῃ θαλάττῃ: Lucian must mean the Indian Ocean, as at Str. 15.2.8.

ὡς δή . . . ἱστοροῦντες: GP notes the essential meaning of δή as "verily" and "actually," and thus true. Jerram is indeed correct to observe both Lucian's irony in ὡς δή and that, although Herodotus called his work ἱστορία, since the term originally had the meaning of inquiry or research, Lucian's use of ἱστοροῦντες is indicative of narrating or telling a story; cf. Thuc. 1.1 where his work of history is described as a συγγραφή.

βωμολοχίας: buffoonery and coarse jesting (Plat. *R.* 606c). The physical action of the term has its origin in its literal meaning, "crowding altars," to pick up scraps of roasted meat from sacrifices. In the context of literary criticism in the second century, the term is used to describe Old Comedy and Old Comic poets; Aspasius, in his commentary on Aristotle's *Nicomachean Ethics*, does not simply recount Aristotle's damaging portrayal of Old Comedy as foul-mouthed (τὸ αἰσχρολογεῖν) and the entertainment of the uneducated, but considers the Old Comic poets themselves to be buffoons (βωμολόχος; in *EN* 125.18–22).

τοῖς περὶ τὸν Ἀλκίνουν . . . ἐτερατεύσατο: as for Homer's Odysseus, the marvels he told (ἐτερατεύσατο) in the court of Alcinous on the island of

Scheria were notorious in Greco-Roman antiquity and gained the opprobrious label "the stories Odysseus told Alcinous" (Ἀλκίνου ἀπόλογον; Plat. *R.* 10.614b). Famous episodes of the *Odyssey* are referred to: the winds tied by King Aeolus in a bag (*Od.* 10.1–79); the one-eyed Cyclopes (*Od.* 9.105–542); Scylla and Charybdis (*Od.* 12.201–59); the island of Circe (*Od.* 10.133–74). The phrase Ἀλκίνου ἀπόλογον, as a scholiast on Plato observes, became proverbial for a long and tedious tale (*Scholia Platonica* 276 Greene). In Plato it introduces Socrates' myth of Er and indicates the narrative of *Odyssey* 9–12, which includes Odysseus' account of his visit to the World of the Dead and his meeting with the shade of Teiresias (*Od.* 11.13–635).

πρὸς ἰδιώτας ἀνθρώπους: the "simple-minded" or "idiots," here specifically referring to the Phaeacians. Yet the term is very much at home in Second Sophistic discourse on the uneducated vs. the educated, e.g. the ἰδιώταις τε καὶ πεπαιδευμένοις ἀνδράσιν (a distinction Lucian notes at *The Hall* 2–3). The educated, of course, would never believe such stories to be true.

1.4 καὶ τοῖς φιλοσοφεῖν ὑπισχνουμένοις: καί is adverbial, "even in the case of those who profess to be philosophers." A scholion (*sch. in Luc.* 4 p. 18 Rabe) concludes that this is a direct attack on Plato's *Republic* and the myth of Er. Considering that Lucian may indeed be playing with the paradox of the noble lie associated with Platonic myth (see Introduction 2.3), this may be an accurate reading. Be that as it may, the deceitful and phony who profess to be intellectuals and wise men pervade Lucian's work, especially in the guise of philosophers.

τῆς ἐν τῷ μυθολογεῖν ἐλευθερίας: on not wanting to be excluded from mythological license, see the Introduction 2.2. The word μῦθος has long lost its general meaning of "something said" or a "narrative story," as found in Homer (*Od.* 3.94), at which point the term does not convey an exact distinction between true and false content. In Plato μῦθος is indicative of something fabricated, and, within a philosophical context, whether or not it can convey truth is a subject of great interest (see Introduction 2.3); a negative connotation is ultimately evident. Aristotle too treats it as a fabrication but in a positive sense: "The devotee of myth is in a way a philosopher, for myth is made up of things that cause wonder" (*Metaph.* 1.986b18–19). By Lucian's time μῦθος and μυθολογέω are indicative of fiction, and unless the occasion or context is explicit, it can carry a pejorative connotation, as we see in Strabo (see Introduction 2.2).

οὐδὲν γὰρ ἐπεπόνθειν: the pluperfect is usually avoided in classical Attic, yet that does not mean it will unequivocally be avoided by later Atticists; the pluperfect ἐδεδοίκεσαν in *VH* 2.18 is justified because the perfect δέδοικα has a present sense: "I am afraid." Jerram notes in his commentary on the pluperfect πεπονθείμεν at *VH* 1.33, "Lucian's frequent use of pluperfects is a mark of his later style." By "later" he means later than the pure Attic of Xenophon and Demosthenes. Yet the issue rests with the model itself. ἐπεπόνθειν, in particular, appears three times in Demosthenes (21.25 and 51; 24.8). And as a canonical author and model of the grand periodic style in Lucian's time and beyond, a use by Demosthenes would technically make a pluperfect form permissible—even if not advisable.

κἂν...ἀληθεύσω: κἂν = καὶ ἄν. ἄν with the future indicative appears in early poetry, including Homer. It is, however, rare in classical Attic, and the construction has been subject to emendation, thus reducing the number of instances. When accepted, the contingency of the expression is usually enforced; see Goodwin §196 and 197. Keeping in mind Lucian's most important models, there is an instance in Plato (*R*. 615d).

μήτε τὴν ἀρχήν: adverbial accusative (Smyth §1606–11). Common with a negative it means "not at all," or here even in the common intensive sense of "not at all whatsoever."

γράφω τοίνυν περὶ ὧν μήτε εἶδον μήτε...μήτε...μήτε...μήτε: again we have μήτε instead of οὔτε. Either another example of a lack of distinction between οὐ and μή in later Greek, or perhaps a clever manipulation of this now lax rule employed by an expert in Attic Greek. This is the critical moment in which Lucian admits that he does not know anything about what he writes, and so his work is a lie; as noted, this is largely a parody of the common introductions found in works of historiography (see Introduction 1.3). οὐ would make this a negative of fact. μή, if understood according to the standards of classical Attic, would make this a negative of thought or a simple generality (see Smyth §2688).

1.5–9 The voyage to the Western Island

Lucian's trip beyond the Pillars of Heracles takes him out into the Western Ocean. The Pillars of Heracles, or Straits of Gibraltar, long stood as the limits of the inhabited world to the West (cf. Pind. *I*. 4.12 and Str. 3.5.5). In

Plato's *Phaedo* (109a) they represent the extreme West just as the river Phasis that feeds into the Black Sea from the East represents the extreme East. The chorus of Euripides' *Hippolytus* describes the Pillars of Heracles as guarded by an "Old Man" who allows no one to pass further, thus confirming the "holy boundary of the sky held up by Atlas" (741–51; cf. Hes. *Th.* 517–18). From Herodotus' descriptions of the voyages of Neko and Sataspes (4.42–3) it is clear that, despite the proverbial status of the Pillars of Heracles, the world outside the Mediterranean and the west coast of Africa had become known long before Lucian wrote. This is also clear in Plutarch's *Sertorius* (8.2–3 and from an echo of an original source in Horace *Epode* 16). In Lusitania (now Portugal) Sertorius heard reports that the Islands of the Blest (Madeira and Porto Santo perhaps) were located far out into the Atlantic. Moreover, the voyage of Pytheas of Massalia—well before Lucian's time, in the fourth century BCE—proceeded north up the English Channel, and he may have even reached the North Sea.

On Lucian's journey into the Atlantic he and his crew are driven onto a mountainous island where they discover two single footprints: one of Heracles and the other of Dionysus. Here they encounter vine-maidens who become entangled with two of them. These men become rooted to their partners and cannot return to their ship. Here Lucian recognizes and yet skirts the plot line of the *Odyssey* and the enchantment of the Sirens (as he will again in *VH* 2.46). In this episode of his wanderings Lucian begins to lose his companions; however, unlike Odysseus, Lucian will not lose all his companions on his voyage.

1.5 ἀπὸ Ἡρακλείων στηλῶν: the so-called Pillars of Heracles are the mountain mass of Gibraltar and "Apes' Hill" near Tangier (Hdt. 2.33 and 4.8; Pind. *I.* 4.12). Of all Greek heroes it was only Heracles who managed to penetrate the Western Ocean beyond the columns named after him, as is already attested in Hesiod (*Th.* 289–94).

ἀφεὶς εἰς τὸν ἑσπέριον ὠκεανὸν οὐρίῳ ἀνέμῳ τὸν πλοῦν ἐποιούμην: ἀφείς, aorist participle of ἀφίημι, "to loose or release a ship," i.e. "set sail," as found at Hdt. 5.42. For πλόον with ποιεῖσθαι, as at Soph. *Aj.* 552, the middle verb plus the direct object is a periphrasis (Symth §1722), equivalent to πλέειν. For the rhetorical meaning of "setting sail" in the context of telling a story, i.e. a long story adrift and without trajectory, see Plu. *De garr.* 507a–b.

περιεργία: Lucian's "curiosity" has its parallel in the Lucianic *Lucius or the Ass* (39.15) and the *curiositas improspera* of Lucius in Apuleius'

Metamorphoses (11.15). In Lucian the word generally has a negative connotation, as GL notes with a list of examples; though they do note both a positive and negative sense in *D. deor.* 11.4, where Hermes' motivation for going to Hades is explained. Using "curiosity" is indeed fine in translation, but current usage may not carry that negative connotation it once did (e.g. "curiosity killed the cat"). One should remain aware of the other second-century usages documented in LSJ, where the notion of "futility," "needlessness," and "over-elaboration" are listed. Jerram translates as "impatience."

κυβερνήτην τὸν ἄριστον μισθῷ μεγάλῳ πείσας: only the helmsman must be persuaded by payment. This is possibly a quick and—from Lucian—expected insult aimed at philosophers and sophists. While the helmsman is a common symbol or metaphor in philosophical works, Lucian (*Herm.* 29) particularly notes that one needs a good helmsman on the voyage to obtaining philosophical knowledge. Lucian and his crew are all of like mind (περιεργία) in their rationale for making the journey. Yet the helmsman here, like all philosophers and sophists in exchange for their services, must be paid.

ἄκατος: a light vessel, therefore it required reinforcement. ἄκατος can simply mean "boat," referencing a variety of small crafts. It was oar driven and, depending on the size, required thirty or even fifty rowers (Lucian may be the only evidence for fifty); there was also a small mast, sail, and sailyard. As proof that such a light vessel could be outfitted for combat, we find *actuaria* outfitted with rams in *B. Alex.* 44.3 (see Casson (1971) and Morrison and Williams (1968)). Including narrator and helmsman, the total number is fifty-two, i.e. the same number Alcinous proposes to accompany Odysseus (*Od.* 8.35). The ἄκατος is also associated with the Eleusinian Mysteries; *IG* 1.313, ll. 149 and 160.

1.6 ἀνηγόμεθα: imperfect middle of ἀνάγω. Greek mariners sailing on the open sea imagined that they were moving up on its back, as it appeared on the horizon. The reckoning of the time it took Lucian to reach the Island of the Vine-Maidens might reflect the reckoning of the time it took Iambulus and his companion to reach the Islands of the Sun (Diod. 2.55.6), as Macleod notes in his apparatus.

ὡς ἄν: elliptical, i.e. without a verb (Smyth §1766; Goodwin §227); Jerram's suggestion of "as you might expect" accurately fits the context.

1.7 ἀμυδροῖς δὲ καὶ ἐκτετριμμένοις: *hysteron proteron* (Smyth §3030), the reversal of natural order; i.e. the adjective, which conveys the result, is actually placed before the perfect passive participle of ἐκτρίβω.

ἦν δὲ καὶ ἴχνη δύο πλησίον ἐπὶ πέτρας, τὸ μὲν πλεθριαῖον, τὸ δὲ ἔλαττον—ἐμοὶ δοκεῖν, τὸ μὲν τοῦ Διονύσου, τὸ μικρότερον, θάτερον δὲ Ἡρακλέους: on the Island of the Vine-Maidens the footprint of Heracles is gigantic; a πλέθρον is a measure of length, corresponding to 100 feet. The smaller footprint of Dionysus is merely huge. Lucian has in his sights Herodotus' report of a footprint of Heracles by the river Tyres in Scythia, which is two cubits long (4.82 τὸ μέγαθος δίπηχυς). A cubit is just short of a foot long, and so Lucian is clearly exaggerating for effect. ní Mheallaigh notes that footprints are also common metaphors for literary *mimesis* (2014, 209).

These figures are markers of the extreme West and East, as GL observes. While they form a pair in that context, exemplars of far-reaching voyages, Megasthenes also claims (Diod. 2.38.3–6) that Heracles and Dionysus ruled India together. As noted above, the tradition of Heracles has him penetrate the limits of the known world. But so do the traditions surrounding Dionysus. In the tradition recited in Euripides' *Bacchae*, the god starts his westward migration from Lydia and Phrygia to reach Thebes in Boeotia (*Ba.* 13, 55, 86). In Lucian's *The Goddess of Syria* Dionysus penetrates south into Ethiopia and east into Syria (16); in Syria Dionysus leaves colossal phalluses, which are a part of the *propylaea* (or entrance gate) of the temple of Adonis, to commemorate his arrival. In Nonnus of Panopolis in Egypt, Dionysus goes to India and wages war with an Indian king (Deriades), as did Alexander of Macedon when he confronted the Indian king Porus. In his own *Dionysus* Lucian also takes Dionysus to India. Like the Pillars of Heracles marking his journey west, Dionysus' "Pillars" were established on the high mountains of India to mark the extreme eastern boundary of the inhabited world (Dion. Per. 620–6 Bernhardy). See also the treatment by Möllendorff ad loc.

GL also notes that both figures made successful trips to the underworld, and this may be Lucian's purpose in pairing the two together. But we should further qualify this idea of the footprints as possible markers of entry into the world of the dead. After all, Lucian and his crew may indeed encounter the dead on the Island of the Blest, but before that they must travel to the Moon and get stuck in the belly of a whale; in the whale the living and the dead are distinguished by the graves dug by Scintharus and his son for their deceased crew. Heracles had monuments (markers) in the West. Dionysus left monuments (markers) in the East. Both indicate the extreme points in the construction of the known world. It thus seems rather pointed that Lucian takes the extreme points of West and East and places them side by side, as if he could fold time and space and pull the two together. In coming upon and crossing these footprints, which are in effect a limit or boundary, Lucian and his crew eventually find the world of the dead, and, as Lye (2016, 3) observes, time-space dislocation or disorientation are typical attributes of underworld chronotopes in Greek literature (a literary configuration of time and space). But this boundary, or Lucian's chronotope, seems to mark a general entry into the unknown and strange, comprising of everything beyond the limits of knowledge and imagination, including the underworld. Specifically, notions of geography—East and West—are now even irrelevant.

ἐμοὶ δοκεῖν: a very common colloquial expression, "in my opinion," in which ὡς (ὡς ἐμοὶ δοκεῖν) in the ὡς + infinitive construction is omitted; this is an example of the absolute infinitive (Smyth §2012 d).

προσκυνήσαντες: while the term can convey prostration before a divinity, it is also well known in the context of eastern and non-Greek prostration before a king (a human). GL suggests the eastern connotation may be at play, if we see an allusion to Dionysus' eastern origins. The same exact form also appears at *VH* 2.47, and commentators are right to see this as a ring composition. As prostration marks the true beginning of their journey here, so it marks the end of their journey and the return to the real or recognizable world. But we should note that the final act of prostration, accompanied by prayers (προσευξάμενοι), is before nothing except the "world opposite the one which we inhabit." The usage seems more in tune with showing reverence to sacred places (cf. Soph. *El.* 1374). But LSJ documents papyri evidence indicating that the term also has a more general meaning of "to welcome with respect"; one fragment in particular (*P.Oxy.* 237) is of the second century CE.

ποταμῷ οἶνον ῥέοντι: rivers of wine or rivers that taste like wine are not uncommon in the imagination of Greek and Latin authors; see especially Plin. *HN* 2.230–1, Athen. 42e, Vitruv. 8.3, Dio Chrys. 35.18, Str. 15.1.64, Nonn. *Dion.* 40.238. Ctesias also mentions a fountain of wine on Naxos (*FGrHist* 688 F 45). Rivers that flow with wine in Lucian's *Saturnalia* (20) are particularly indicative of the Golden Age of Cronus.

οἶνον . . . ὁ Χῖός: the wine produced on the island of Chios. The son of Dionysus, properly named Oinopion (from οἰνώψ, wine-coloured, or with a face flushed with wine, an epithet for Dionysus), is said to have been the first human to begin the cultivation of the vine on Chios. The wines of Chios and Lesbos were famous, and that fame seems to go all the way back to their initial production; even Callimachus sang their praises at *Anthologia*

Palatina 13.9 = Gow-Page LXVIII; cf. also Dionysius 1454n and Hedylus 1855 in the *Anthologia Graeca*, Ath. 1.32e (or 167e), Str. 14.637, *RE* 3.2291, Plin. *HN* 14.73. Due to the fact that the expression οἴνοπα πόντον is common in Homer and that the bard is linked with Chios as a place of origin, an allusive nod to Homer here is possible (see ní Mheallaigh 2014, 210).

ὁμοιότατον μάλιστα: an intensified superlative (Smyth §1090), or "double superlative" according to Jerram.

δόξαν δέ μοι: "since I decided to," accusative absolute of the aorist active participle (Smyth §2059 b and §2076).

ἐμφαγόντες ἐμεθύσθημεν: both participle and the main verb are in the aorist tense, and this is a typical combination; the aorist participle does not have to refer to past time, though one action more often clearly precedes the other. One could easily translate "having eaten the fish, we got drunk," or even "we got drunk, eating the fish." Lucian is certainly not the first to have "edible" wine. οἰνοῦττα is a type of cake made with wine in Aristophanes (*Plut.* 1121), and Aristotle uses the same word for an intoxicating plant (F 107 Rose). As for fish that can make one drunk, Pliny mentions a fish called the "Bacchus" (*HN* 9.61; 32.102; 145).

ἀμέλει: "of course," properly the imperative of ἀμέλεω, but used adverbially.

παραμιγνύντες ἐκεράννυμεν: Greek wine was mixed with water, and this was considered an act of proper decorum (cf. Hom. *Il.* 3.269 and *Od.* 1.110); among the many reasons the Greeks regarded the Macedonians to the north as barbarians was the fact that they did not dilute their wine with water. The mixture of water and wine-fish explains the Lucianic invention of the word οἰνοφαγία.

1.8 τὸ δὲ ἄνω γυναῖκες ἦσαν, ὅσον ἐκ τῶν λαγόνων: these vine-maidens resemble other Greek composite creatures such as Centaurs, Tritons, Sirens (Mermaids), and the snake-woman Heracles is said to have mated with to produce the three tribes of Scythia. The description of Echidna in Herodotus (4.9.1–2) makes Lucian's reference clear (τῆς τὰ μὲν ἄνω ἀπὸ τῶν γλουτῶν εἶναι γυναικός, τὰ δὲ ἔνερθε ὄφιος). His vine-maidens are normal women from the "flanks" up and they manage to have sex with two of Lucian's crew. Herodotus' Echidna is a woman from her buttocks up. In the context of sex, the anatomy of Herodotus' snake woman seems straightforward, but Lucian's use of λαγόνων might require more clarification. This is mainly due to translation. "Flanks"—a word without much currency these days in terms of the body—is not appropriate, as Bulloch (1985) observes in his comment on line 88 of Callimachus' *Fifth Hymn*. In noting the lack of sexual significance conveyed by "flank," Bulloch says, "In fact, λαγών, when used with precision, denotes that part of the body which extends from the hallow between the ribs and the hip down the side of the abdomen as far as the groin...." On the Greek notion that humans become less human and especially more like animals as one travels further from the Mediterranean core, see Romm (1992, 46–9); Duris of Samos (*FGrHist / BNJ* 76; Plin. *HN* 7.30) also claimed that Indians have sex with animals and the resulting offspring are hybrids. On metaliterary symbolism and the vine-women, see ní Mhealleigh (2014, 208–16).

τοιαύτην παρ' ἡμῖν τὴν Δάφνην γράφουσιν...ἀποδενδρουμένην: the passive participle is present, meaning "as she is being transformed into a tree" (Apollo's laurel). Representations of Daphne being transformed into a tree at the touch of Apollo are not as common in ancient art—that is, based on the remaining data, since wall art is not well preserved—as in the history of Apollo and Daphne in European art, and perhaps most well known in Bernini's Apollo and Daphne in the Villa Borghese in Rome (cf. *LIMC* III 1 344–8 Olga Palagia); though that is likely due to the influence of Ovid and his treatment of this scene in his *Metamorphoses*. Women changing into trees to escape men intent on rape are found elsewhere; cf. *Paradox. Vatic.* 15 in *PGR* 336 and Nonn. *Dion.* 21.17–169.

αἱ μὲν Λύδιον, αἱ δ' Ἰνδικήν, αἱ πλεῖσται δὲ τὴν Ἑλλάδα φωνὴν προϊέμεναι: common use of the definite article in a μέν/δέ balance, i.e. "some...others." The languages of India and Lydia are perhaps not unexpected, since both Dionysus and Heracles are associated with these lands. Dionysus and his Lydian origins, and thus a blend of East/West, are commemorated in Eur. *Ba.* 13, 55, and 86. For talking plants we should note that trees speak the Indian language in the *Alexander Romance* (3.17) and that in Philostratus (*VA* 6.10) a tree speaks with a female voice. Ἑλλάδα is adjectival: "Greek," not "Greece," as in *VH* 2.46.

ἀλλ' ἤλγουν καὶ ἐβόων ἀποσπωμένου: Jerram notes the possible allusion to the story of Polydorus and the groaning cornel-tree in Vergil (*A.* 3.22–46). The question regarding Lucian's exact proficiency in Latin and knowledge of Latin literature remains a matter of debate. That he worked in Gaul as a teacher suggests some familiarity with Latin.

καὶ μίγνυσθαι: καί is adverbial ("even"). μίγνυσθαι is a common euphemism for sex (cf. *VH* 2.19). The euphemism continues in the word ἀμπελομιξίαν, which is a *hapax legomenon* (the word is attested only here in Greek) meaning "intercourse with vines."

δύο τινὲς τῶν ἑταίρων πλησιάσαντες: πλησιάζω, "to approach," "to draw near," "to consort with," is another euphemism for sex.

οὐκέτι ἀπελύοντο: the imperfect tense here denotes attempted action (Goodwin §36) and should be translated as "they could not manage to get free."

ὅσον οὐδέπω: an adverbial expression, "only so far as to not yet...," which is equivalent to the English adverbial "about," in the sense of motion or action and thus "they were about to bear grapes themselves." Lucian seems to be playing with Homer's description of the transformation of Odysseus' men into animals at the house of Circe (*Od.* 10.229–43). Yet Odysseus' men are returned to their human form thanks to the μῶλυ revealed to him by Hermes (*Od.* 10.305).

1.9 Περὶ μεσημβρίαν δὲ οὐκέτι τῆς νήσου φαινομένης ἄφνω τυφὼν ἐπιγενόμενος καὶ περιδινήσας τὴν ναῦν καὶ μετεωρίσας ὅσον ἐπὶ σταδίους τριακοσίους οὐκέτι καθῆκεν εἰς τὸ πέλαγος, ἀλλ᾽ ἄνω μετέωρον ἐξηρτημένην ἄνεμος ἐμπεσὼν τοῖς ἱστίοις ἔφερεν κολπώσας τὴν ὀθόνην: Lucian seems to produce a deliberate parody of the hypotactic style. In this long sentence describing the typhoon and the wind that carried his ship up to the Moon there are seven participles. The first functions in a genitive absolute construction; the others are subordinate to the two main verbs of the sentence (καθῆκεν and ἔφερεν). The syntax can be described as periodic and suspended.

1.9–12 Lucian arrives on the Moon and describes Endymion's preparations for war with the Sun and its king, Phaethon

As noted in the Introduction 3.3.1., the war between Endymion and Phaethon is typically seen as a hyperbolic and parodic war between philosophical schools. Behind the composite creatures and nearly every event scholars have suggested covert references to Stoics, Cynics, Epicureans, etc. The commentary in GL is particularly comprehensive in its coverage of possible links or references to the various philosophical schools; one should also consult Möllendorff ad loc.

τυφών: GL notes two things of which we should be aware: (1) Lucian quite possibly reverses the function of Charybdis in the *Odyssey* (12.101–4), i.e. a whirlwind that carries things up instead of a whirlpool that sucks everything down; (2) the connection between the Moon and sea (tides) is found in Greco-Roman antiquity (especially Sext. Emp. *Math.* 9.78–9 (= *SVF* 2.1013)), and this relationship may be the root cause of Lucian's journey to the Moon itself. One should also recall that in order for Odysseus to find entry into the underworld Circe advises him to disregard his lack of a pilot and simply allow the winds to take him there (*Od.* 10.504–7).

μετεωρίσας...μετέωρον: recalling the use of ἀνάγω above (1.6) to convey ships riding on the "back" of the sea, the verb here has both the nautical context of "rising up" on the sea and simply "lifting up," keeping in mind τυφών is the subject and the ship (τὴν ναῦν) is the object. But μετέωρος, which can also be used of a ship afloat, has a very pointed and comic meaning. In Aristophanes (*Av.* 690) the study and pursuit of τὰ μετέωρα is an attribute of philosophers; this is the study of both the heavenly bodies and meteorological phenomena. But the contempt is clear. Dunbar (1995) on Aristoph. *Av.* 60 explains that this kind of study is both a waste of time and likely goes against the divinely influenced world to which the majority of the population prescribed. In Aristophanes' *Clouds* we also find μετεωροφένακες (333) and μετεωροσοφισταί (360). And since Socrates says (*Nu.* 360) that he can better study τὰ μετέωρα πράγματα in the air, the joke of useless philosophy as "up in the air"—useless in the sense of application to everyday life—is evident. So too Lucian and his crew are now up in the air in this unbelievable true tale, and perhaps heading toward the proper home of philosophy and philosophers, i.e. not on firm ground.

1.10 ἀεροδρομήσαντες: another *hapax*, "coursed through the air." Bearing in mind the influence of Plato and Aristophanes on Lucian's prose, cf. ἀεροβατέω at Aristoph. *Nu.* 225 and 1503; Plat. *Ap.* 19c.

λαμπρὰν καὶ σφαιροειδῆ καὶ φωτὶ μεγάλῳ καταλαμπομένην: the Sun, Moon, and stars are typically described as fiery stones due to their brightness (Anaxag. DK 59 A 42 (6)). In Plutarch (*De gen.* 590c) the stars are described as islands on a sea illuminated by fire.

προσενεχθέντες: the aorist passive participle of προσφέρω, which is a common verb to describe ships putting into harbor (usually in the middle voice). Notice how the language of seafaring does not change, even though Lucian's ship and crew are flying.

τὴν χώραν εὑρίσκομεν οἰκουμένην: the Greeks long believed the Moon was inhabited, going back at least to Anaxagoras (DK 59 A 77); see the Introduction 3.3.1. The topic is also notably treated by Plato (*Tim.* 42d) and Plutarch (*De Is. et Os.* 367c–d and *De fac.* 937d–940f), who also mentions human-like creatures. For an extensive list of sources, see GL ad loc. In Lucian's *Icaromenippus* (20) the Moon (Selene) mentions the belief of earth-bound men that she is inhabited.

τὴν καθ' ἡμᾶς οἰκουμένην εἰκάζομεν: "our inhabited world." The preposition κατά with the accusative here seems to fall under what Smyth labels "conformity" (Smyth §1690 2c), i.e. Lucian and his crew are not making a comparison between the world below and the Moon, but simply note that what they see below is "according to" our world. Still, we must remember Jerram's observation that καθ' ἡμᾶς here is equivalent to a possessive pronoun, as is typical in the Koine Greek of the New Testament.

1.11 εἴ τις εὑρεθείη ξένος: the aorist passive optative signals a past general condition, "if…were" (Smyth §2291). The protasis is without an apodosis, and this is most likely due to its parenthetical nature (Smyth §2352 c).

καὶ ὅς: relative with a demonstrative force, a use as old as Homer, and here simply translated as "he" (Smyth §1114).

Ἐνδυμίων: Endymion, the king of the Moon (Selene). In Greek legend Selene was said to have fallen in love with Endymion as she gazed down on him. She then descended to take him to the Latmian Cave in Caria where he slept eternally. In Plutarch (*De fac.* 945b) it is Endymion's soul that is asleep on the Moon. On the symbolism of sleep, the soul, and the Moon see the comment in GL ad loc. Although Lucian is not interested in explaining how Endymion was taken up to the Moon, it is likely that he was taken up by Selene. Sappho seems to recognize the myth (Sappho F 168 B Voigt), as does Apollonius of Rhodes (4.57–8). The myth is noted in *Dialogue of the Gods* (11), and Lucian gives his own version of it in his *In Praise of the Fly* (10).

πάντα γὰρ ἡμῖν παρέσεσθαι ὧν δεόμεθα: the so-called act of reporting vividly; while the optative would be appropriate in an oblique statement, according to the rules of sequence, we find the present indicative δεόμεθα in the dependent clause.

1.12 ἐκφέρω: commonly used in the language of war, meaning to bring troops beyond one's borders; cf. Hdt. 6.56.

τοὺς τὸν ἥλιον κατοικοῦντας: an inhabited Sun may sound absurd, especially considering that even ancient Greek philosophers, as noted above, described the Sun as a fiery rock (Anaxag. 59 A 42 (6) DK). Still, and even ignoring Iambulus' fanciful tale and his people of the Sun, the question seems to have been debated by the Stoics; see Lact. *Div. inst.* 3.23.14.

ἁπάντων εὐδαιμονέστατα...καταβιώσεσθε: one of the most common aspects of philosophy in the imperial period is addressing the question of what constitutes a good or happy life; though of course this question is quite old, as we see in the famous dialogue between Croesus and Solon regarding who was the happiest man in the world in Herodotus (1.30–2). Philosophers, to whom one pays a fee for instruction, are supposed to help.

τοὺς ἀπορωτάτους: the distinction between the rich and the poor is noted more than once in Lucian's celestial voyage (cf. *VH* 1.22, 25, and 29).

ἀποικίαν: colonizing and founding new cities is a common topic in early Greek history, and modern writers have often attributed colonization to shortages of food, land, and materials. Lucian provides no details, but simply focuses on the moving of the poorest people to accommodate Edymion's desire (ἐβουλήθην) to establish a colony. Tsetskhladze (2006), in order to move away from the notion of colonization as simply a result of shortages, focuses on the evidence of forced migration and specifically migration in the context of conflict. Lucian designates the colony as an ἀποικία, a proper city (as opposed to an ἐμπόριον, a trading station or port).

Ἑωσφόρον: the Morning star (the "Bringer of the Dawn" and its dampness) or Venus (cf. *VH* 1.12). West (1966) on Hesiod *Th.* 381 observes, "Because its [Venus'] orbit lies inside that of Earth, it is never visible all night, but only for a few hours after sunset or before sunrise, as the Evening Star (ἕσπερος, *Il.* 22.318) and the Morning Star (Ἑωσφόρος, *Il.* 23.226)."

γῦπας...τῶν βασιλικῶν: that is, from the king's stables.

1.13–17 The defeat of the Selenitai in the war between Endymion and Phaethon

In his *You are a Literary Prometheus* Lucian, in the role he assumes as the creative god Prometheus, defends his combination of comedy and dialogue and mentions creatures such as *hippokampoi* (that combine the body of a horse and the tail of a fish) and *tragelaphoi* (compounds of goats and stags). Lucian's *True History* is filled with such grotesque compounds. Most are *hapax legomena*. This kind of word-building is also common in Old Comedy (Cloudcuckooland, Νεφελοκοκκυγίαν, is a classic example), and Lucian is perhaps responsible for creating all of them, though it is impossible to be certain. For the cloud-centaurs, in particular, influence from Aristophanes' *Clouds* (347–9) is clear, where the clouds liken themselves to centaurs.

On the orbs of the Moon and Sun we find the following creatures:

Of Endymion and the Moon

Ἱππόγυποι	horse-vultures
Λαχανόπτεροι	cabbage-wings
Κεγχροβόλοι	millet-slingers
Σκοροδομάχοι	garlic-brigade
Ψυλλοτοξόται	flea-archers
Ἀνεμοδρόμοι	air-runners
Στρουθοβάλανοι	ostrich-acorners
Ἱππογέρανοι	horse-cranes

Of Phaethon and the Sun

Ἱππομύρμηκες	horse-ants
Ἀεροκώνωπες	air-mosquitoes
Ἀεροκόρδακες	air-trotters
Καυλομύκητες	mushroom-stalkers
Κυνοβάλανοι	dog-nutters
Νεφελοκένταυροι	cloud-centaurs

Signatories of the treaty between Phaethon and Endymion:

For Phaethon

Πυρωνίδης	Fire Son
Θερείτης	Summer Son
Φλόγιος	Flame

For Endymion

Νύκτωρ	Night Watchman
Μήνιος	Moon Man
Πολυλάμπης	Brilliant

1.13 τὰ δὲ ὠκύπτερα ἔχει θριδακίνης φύλλοις μάλιστα προσεοικότα: these wings with long quills (Aristoph. *Av.* 803 and Luc. *Icar.* 10) are like leaves of lettuce on earth.

ἐτετάχατο: Ionic (third-person plural, pluperfect middle-passive) instead of Attic, though the form is found in Attic authors such as Thucydides (5.6 and 7.4).

ἀπὸ τῶν ὑπὲρ τὴν Καππαδοκίαν ἀστέρων: this region in Asia Minor is the home of the Ἱππογέρανοι, the horse-cranes. It could be, as is sometimes suggested, that the horse-cranes come from Cappadocia because of its fame for producing fine horses and mules; cf. Apul. *Met.* 8.24 and the Lucianic *Lucius or the Ass* (36).

1.15 ἀράχναι παρ᾽ αὐτοῖς πολλοὶ καὶ μεγάλοι γίγνονται, πολὺ τῶν Κυκλάδων νήσων ἕκαστος μείζων. τούτοις προσέταξεν διυφῆναι τὸν μεταξὺ τῆς σελήνης καὶ τοῦ Ἑωσφόρου ἀέρα: Endymion's spiders are larger than an island of the Cyclades. Perhaps Lucian is once again outdoing Herodotus (3.102), who tells of ants bigger than foxes. There is also a philosophical context, since at *Pseud.* 24 Lucian associates the spider's web with a sophist's obscure words; see the lengthy note ad loc. in GL.

1.16 ἐμάχοντο... ἀλλὰ καὶ αὐτοὶ μάλιστα τοῖς κέρασιν: in Greek the ants make use of their horns in combat. In English we would say antennae.

ἐσφενδόνων ῥαφανῖδας ὑπερμεγέθεις: the air-trotters wound the Selenitai with the huge radishes they hurl from their slings. Their wounded opponents die from the stench of their wounds. The radish has a distinct reputation in classical Greece. What is called ῥαφανίς must be larger than our radish, as K. J. Dover suggests in his note to Aristoph. *Nu.* 981 (1968); see too his note on *Nu.* 1083–4. In Athens a man caught in adultery was punished by having a radish thrust up his rectum; he could be killed if adultery was a matter of seduction and not rape, as is clear from Lysias 1 (*Against Eratosthenes*).

μαλάχης ἰῷ: as Jerram notes, the joke is that the mallow is not poisonous. Rather it is known as a healing plant (Plin. *HN* 20.222–30; Diosc. 2.118 and 3.146; Athen. 58e). GL notes that mallow was also used in cooking (Luc. *Alex.* 25; *Merc. cond.* 26) and for making walking sticks (Theophr. *HP* 1.3.2; Plin. *HN* 19.62).

οἱ τὸν Σείριον κατοικοῦντες: with the Dog Star comes the summer heat; Manilius even says that its brightness is close to that of the Sun (1.396–411).

As for its dog-faced inhabitants, one might immediately think of Ctesias' dog-faced men, since Ctesias is constantly censured by Lucian. But dog-like men are found elsewhere, e.g. Hdt. 4.191 and Plin. *HN* 7.2.14. And, of course, as GL notes, if this is a battle between philosophers, the dog-faced men might be the Cynics.

Γαλαξίου: the Milky Way is typically a place of souls; see Cic. *De rep.* 6.16, Manil. 1.758–808, Porph. *De ant.* 28 [75]. The Pythagoreans believed the Milky Way was formed by Phaethon's chariot ride (cf. Manil. 1.729–49): Phaethon attempted to drive the chariot of his father, Helios, but fell from the sky to the earth.

1.17 ὠγκήσαντο ἑκατέρων οἱ ὄνοι—τούτοις γὰρ ἀντὶ σαλπιστῶν χρῶνται—ἐμάχοντο: the braying of donkeys of both armies serves as the trumpet signal to begin battle. The σάλπιγξ is a war-trumpet. One pedestrian Byzantine reader is outraged by this passage. Lucian's description of the donkey trumpeters provokes the imprecations of γοής ("imposter") and τερατολόγε ("wonder monger") (*sch. in Luc.* 17 p. 19 Rabe). The scholiast not only read without the willing suspension of disbelief that Lucian's fantasy deserves, but he also has forgotten, or is unaware of, Herodotus, where the braying asses of the Persians confuses the Scythian cavalry. In Lucian's *Dionysus* (4) the braying of Silenus' donkey announces the battle between Dionysus and the Indians. Yet, not to leave philosophers out, the Cynic in Lucian's *Pseudol.* (3) is said to bray. Cf. also the lengthy note in GL ad loc.

ἐπὶ τῷ τοῦ Σαρπηδόνος θανάτῳ: Sarpedon was the king of Lycia, killed by Patroclus (Hom. *Il.* 16.458–61).

1.18–20 The capture of Lucian and his crew and a treaty of peace

1.18 τοῦ Ῥοδίων κολοσσοῦ: in the *Natural History* (34.41) Pliny the Elder describes the Colossus of Rhodes as the work of the sculptor Chares of Lindus. The Colossus was a statue of Helios erected after Demetrius Poliorcetes (the Besieger) gave up his siege of Rhodes in 303 BCE. It measured 70 cubits (in Roman measures) or *c.*90 feet and was toppled by an earthquake fifty-six years after it was erected. Its debris was carted off to Emessa in Syria.

ὁ ἐκ τοῦ ζῳδιακοῦ τοξότης: the archer of the zodiac is Sagittarius, the Greek zodiac of course being the twelve groups of stars, i.e. constellations, that could be seen in the night sky by the naked eye. The constellation of stars is part of the star catalogue of Ptolemy (*Alm.* 8.1). As Beck notes, the signs of the zodiac can also be divided into four seasonal quadrants, and in the context of the path of the Sun and the cycle of seasons the signs can be indicators of time. Sagittarius would then be the end of the autumn equinox and the beginning of the winter solstice (Beck (2007)).

τρέπουσιν...τρόπαια: τρέπω is commonly used in the sense of "to turn" and thus "rout" troops on the field of battle. A trophy is literally a monument erected to celebrate the turning or retreat of the enemy, usually made of wood; cf. Diod. 13.24.

1.19 ἀπετείχιζον: the walling of the Moon to cut off the light of the Sun is likely inspired by Pisthetaerus' plan in Aristophanes' *Birds* (*Av.* 550–2) and the establishment of the city of Cloudcuckooland. It is probably Lucian rather than Aristophanes who inspired Swift's island of Laputa in *Gullivers' Travels*. Laputa is a floating island that can wall off the light of the Sun from the land below it.

σαφὴς ἔκλειψις τῆς σελήνης: on the eclipses of the Moon and Sun, see especially Plin. *HN* 2.43–58 and [Plut.] *De plac. phil.* 891e–f. Eclipses are not uncommon in battle narratives, particularly as an omen regarding the outcome, on which see Pritchett (1979).

1.21–6 The Selenitai described

Lucian describes the "strange and surprising" (καινὰ καὶ παράδοξα) things he observed during the last seven days he spent on the Moon before returning to the sea on earth: the inhabitants of the Moon (they are all male despite the dim presence of the goddess of the Moon, Selene); the tree-people and their manner of reproduction; and the esteem in which bald men are held there.

1.21 ὑπισχνούμενος δώσειν πρὸς γάμον τὸν ἑαυτοῦ παῖδα: commonly seen as a parody of Alcinous' offer of Nausicaa to Odysseus (*Od.* 7.311–12). And since the surreal battle has now concluded, and it very much seems a parodic battle of philosophical schools, GL cleverly reminds us that in his

Symposium (5) Lucian uses the marriage of a host's daughter as the occasion—rather than the conclusion—for a philosophical contest.

ἀποπέμπει: the "historical present" (Smyth §1883 b).

1.22 γάμοις... γαμεῖται... γαμεῖ: in Lucian both the noun and the verb do not have their usual association of marriage or a wedding feast. It seems to mean sex for reproduction (or simply to have sex—one of the meanings of γαμώ in modern Greek). Up to the age of 25 the males are passive sexual partners. After that age they are active. (Rhadamanthus reduces the age of a sexual partner from 25 to 18 in *VH* 2.28.) On the Moon children are not born of mothers but of younger males, who have no wombs but conceive in what Lucian calls the γαστροκνημία, i.e. the soft muscle of the calf of the leg, a word still in use in the medical profession; this is clear from its use in the Hippocratic corpus (Hippoc. *Art.* 60), Aristotle (*HA* 494a7), and Pseudo-Galen (Gal. 2.316). Children are born dead but are revived by the wind, much as Sarpedon's soul was returned to his lifeless body by a blast of the North Wind (Hom. *Il.* 5.694–8); this may also reflect the Pythagorean notion that the soul is born by the winds and may enter a new body via breath (Arist. *De anim.* 410bc = Orph. F 27 Kern), or even the common ideas of rebirth after death. We should also recall that the third human form described by Aristophanes in Plato's *Symposium* (189e–190b), which have both male and female genitalia, are born of the Moon. See also the lengthy and informative note by GL ad loc. As for the strange race of Δενδρῖται, they are produced by cutting off a man's right testicle and planting it in the ground. A tree springs up from it that is fleshy and resembles a phallus. Once the trees are ripe (ἐπειδὰν πεπανθῶσιν) their acorns are harvested from which men are extracted; the form πεπανθῶσιν is aorist subjunctive of πεπαίνω. The notion of people springing up from non-human entities is not unique to Lucian. The scholiast (*sch. in Luc.* 22 p. 20 Rabe) on this passage notes the Theban tale of the men who came to life from the teeth of the dragon killed by Cadmus.

Giving birth from the back of the leg or calf should immediately bring to mind the birth of Dionysus from Zeus' thigh; in Lucian's *Dialogues of the Gods* (12.1) Poseidon indeed jokes about Zeus being pregnant in multiple areas of his body. And, of course, in the context of the Δενδρῖται we can look to Uranus in Hesiod, who sidesteps the female role in reproduction entirely by using the blood and semen from his severed testicles to create Aphrodite. Lucian is perhaps having fun with the idea of phallocentric monogenesis, which reaches far back into Greek culture. It is Apollo's words in Aeschylus' *Eumenides* (658–63) that stand out as an early and strong Athenian example. The "one called mother" (μήτηρ ἡ κεκλημένη) is not the nominalized agent or "begetter" (τοκεύς, from τίκτω). Although she is clearly the receptacle, her identity and function is external; she is the "nurse" (τροφός) and in fact an "other" (ξένη). Instead, "He, the one who mounts, gives birth... there can be a father without a mother" (τίκτει δ' ὁ θρῴσκων... πατὴρ δὲ γείναιτ' ἄνευ μητρός). See also Deriu (2017).

This description of the sex life and reproduction of the all-male inhabitants of the Moon was excised in the Victorian edition of Jerram (1879), but restored in the reprint of Bolchazy-Carducci (2000).

οἷον φαλλός· ἔχει δὲ καὶ κλάδους καὶ φύλλα: in comparing the tree to a penis, note that it is also common in Greek to use such arboreal language as euphemisms for pubic hair; cf. Aristoph. *Lys.* 89 and 100.

αἰδοῖα μέντοι πρόσθετα ἔχουσιν, οἱ μὲν ἐλεφάντινα, οἱ δὲ πένητες αὐτῶν ξύλινα: prosthetic genitals. Lucian makes another distinction based on wealth: ivory for the wealthy, wood for the poor. In *D. mer.* 5.4 Lucian's Megilla wears something akin to a modern strap-on dildo. Prosthetic limbs are attested in Greco-Roman antiquity (Luc. *Ind.* 6; Hdt. 9.37; Plut. *De frat. amor.* 479b), as is the dildo, for which Miletus was a famous producer (Aristoph. *Lys.* 107–12).

1.23 ἐπειδὰν δὲ γηράσῃ ὁ ἄνθρωπος, οὐκ ἀποθνήσκει, ἀλλ' ὥσπερ καπνὸς διαλυόμενος ἀὴρ γίνεται: perhaps not so much a parody as a simple use of Epicurean atomism to further define this celestial world in which earthly philosophers and philosophy covertly lurk. At death the soul is dissolved into atoms (Lucr. 3.838–9), a process which is described as smoke or mist by Epicurus according to Sextus Empiricus (*Math.* 9.72).

βατράχους ὀπτῶσιν ἐπὶ τῶν ἀνθράκων... τὸν ἀναθυμιώμενον καπνόν: the smoke (τὸν... καπνόν) from frogs roasted on coals provides nourishment for the Selenitai. It is like the κνίση or the savory odor of roasting meat that arises from altars to the eager nostrils of the gods in Homer (*Il.* 1.66); κνῖσα also describes the vile smell of burning human flesh on the Island of the Impious (*VH* 2.29). In his apparatus Macleod compares Herodotus' description of the Issedones inhaling the smoke of nuts from certain trees as they sit about a fire (2.202). It is not evident that Lucian had this passage from Herodotus in mind. The scholiast refers not to this passage but Herodotus' description of the Scythians' use of roasted cannabis seeds (Hdt. 4.75, *sch. in Luc.* 23 p. 20 Rabe).

οὐ μὴν ἀπουροῦσίν γε καὶ ἀφοδεύουσιν: the Pythagoreans believed that the creatures of the Moon do not defecate. Yet this is due to their diet, which produces no waste (Philolaus DK 44 A 20). Ctesias' dog-heads also do not defecate, but that is because they have no rectum (*FGrHist* 688 F 45).

ἐν ταῖς ἰγνύσιν ὑπὲρ τὴν γαστροκνημίαν: cf. Orph. F 80 KERN, where the deity Phanes has his genitals in the rear around his buttocks.

Καλὸς δὲ νομίζεται παρ' αὐτοῖς ἥν πού τις φαλακρὸς καὶ ἄκομος ᾖ: the paradoxical appreciation of lunar beauty contradicts the Greek sense of male beauty as exhibited by the honourific epithet given the Achaeans in Homer's *Iliad*: "long-haired Achaeans" (κάρη κομόωντας Ἀχαιούς). On the eve of the battle of Thermopylae, the Spartans under the command of Leonidas are occupied in combing their hair (Hdt. 7.208.2). Long hair was commended by the long-haired Apollonius of Tyana in Philostratus' *Life of Apollonius* (2.8.7). It was left for the sophist Synesius of Cyrene (fourth–fifth century CE) to praise baldness (*calvitii encomium*). The Moon men certainly hate long hair (τοὺς δὲ κομήτας καὶ μυσάττονται). In Lucian's *Dialogues of the Dead* all the dead are bald—meaning skulls (4).

κομητῶν ἀστέρων: the Greek word for comet is κομήτης, because it is considered a star (ἀστήρ) that has hair (κόμη). See especially Aristotle's discussion of comets in *Meteor.* 343a–b.

1.24 ἔλαιον δὲ ποιοῦνται, ἀπὸ τῶν κρομμύων...εὐῶδες ὥσπερ μύρον: this is immediately an affront—and perhaps a very laughable one—to Greek sensibilities. The onion was notoriously smelly. Aristophanes (*Lys.* 798) even mentions that bad onion breath is very much a turn-off for women. The onion itself is also associated with the Moon; it supposedly grew when the Moon waned and shriveled when it waxed (Aul. Gell. 20.8.7; Plut. *De Is. et Os.* 353f.).

πρὸς ἡμᾶς καταπίπτει ἡ χάλαζα διαρραγέντων τῶν βοτρύων: jokes concerning the source of hail and rain are found in Aristophanes, where hailstones come from the slingshots of the clouds and rain is caused by Zeus urinating through a sieve (*Nu.* 373 and 1125). This of course utterly opposes the scientific explanations that had been proposed, e.g. Plat. *Ti.* 59e; Arist. *Meteor.* 347b–349a; Plin. *HN* 2.152.

τῇ μέντοι γαστρὶ ὅσα πήρᾳ, χρῶνται: the stomachs which serve as satchels and whose fur provides warmth for newborn children is one of the most marvelous descriptions of Lucian, who was writing in an age when the marsupials of Australia and South America were unknown. But the idea of animals using parts of their bodies as pouches has some precedent: Ael. *NA* 1.16–17; Arist. *HA* 566b17–18. The scholiast on this passage even claims Lucian is referencing reports about certain sea creatures (*sch. in Luc.* 24 p. 20 Rabe).

1.25 τοὺς ὀφθαλμοὺς περιαιρετοὺς ἔχουσι: the removable eyes of the Selenitai must be inspired by the single eye that the three Graeae share among themselves. They do the same with their single tooth. The Graeae, "old women," are part of the genealogy of the gods of the sea (Phorcys and Ceto) in Hesiod (*Th.* 270–5), but the tradition of the shared eye and tooth is first found in Pherecydes of Athens (*FGrHist* / *BNJ* 3 F 11). They are described in connection with Perseus' search for the Gorgon in Apollodorus (*Bibl.* 2.4.2).

1.26 κάτοπτρον μέγιστον: the mirror on the Moon. Viewing the world from high above is often a moment of laughter in Lucian: *Char.* 6, 13–17; *Icar.* 15–19; *Herm.* 5. Here we see the "real" world from above but reflected in a mirror. The tradition of the Moon as a mirror of Earth or mirror-like is an old one, going all the way back to Anaxagoras (DK 59 A 77); cf. also Plut. *De fac.* 920f, 936d–937c; [Plut.] *De plac. phil.* 891c. Anaxagoras (DK 59 A 71), Democritus (DK 68 A 40 (4)), and Chrysippus (*SVF* F 1049) even speculated that the Moon was formed from the Earth's substance. See the lengthy note in GL ad loc. Of course, in the broad context of Lucian's literary *mimesis*, we should not forget Plato's use of the mirror as a metaphor for mimetic art (*R.* 10 596d4–e4) and its significance in his notions of truth and falsehood (the reflection is an inferior copy); on this see especially the discussion by ní Mhealleigh (2014, 216–27). This incredible mirror over a wellhead in the palace of Endymion provided one of the many sources for Jorge Luis Borges's *Aleph*, a source he acknowledges in the postscript to this strange tale.

φρέαρ: for the well as a point of communication between humans and Zeus, see Luc. *Icar.* 25.

ὅστις δὲ ταῦτα μή: The lack of distinction between οὐ and μή in later Greek has been mentioned a few times. Still, Jerram is right to note that in this statement regarding truth and belief Lucian correctly uses μή with the indicative in an indefinite relative clause (conditional force; see Smyth §2505 b); no one will actually get to the Moon to verify his claim.

1.28–9 Descent down to the Ocean, arrival at the island of Lychnopolis, and the trip past Cloudcuckooland

Before Lucian and his crew touch down on the sea, the celestial trajectory is clear enough. He locates Lychnopolis midway between the Pleiades and the Hyades (both constellations signaling the rainy season at their setting), and both are closer to Earth and below the Zodiac. The ship, after being swept up to the Moon and even navigating close to the Sun, is now descending back to Earth.

Commentators are hard pressed to find an exact source for Lucian's Lychnopolis, and perhaps it is the product of his own vivid imagination. Nevertheless, Lucian is possibly creating based upon earlier sources and traditions. Jerram suggested the Feast of Lanterns at Sais in Egypt mentioned by Herodotus (2.62) as one possible source. GL offers a comprehensive and informative note: e.g. the personification of lamps in poetry, especially Aristoph. *Eccl.* 1–29; the lighting of the lamps ritual (λυχναψία), and the cult of the dead (Ahen. 701B; *P.Oxy.* 1453; *P.Amh.* 2.70.11); and astronomical sources (Teucer of Babylon (*CCAG*) and a ninth-century Arabic work that uses Teucer) in which lamps are associated with stars and even speak; see the extensive treatments in GL and Möllendorff ad loc. Sabnis (2011) has also shrewdly argued that Lucian's lamps, in fact, symbolize household slaves, living in their own refracted form of society, and reference a long tradition of personified lamps in Greek literature; the fact that Lucian encounters his family's lamp, his family's possession, unlike Odysseus who encounters an actual family member, provides Sabnis' very firm ground upon which to argue. On Lychnopolis the distinction between the diminutive size of thc poor lights and the size and brilliance of the wealthy is clear and clever, especially since the adjectives λαμπροὺς καὶ περιφανεῖς can describe conspicuous people; λυχνεῶνες (lampfolds) is also attested only here in Greek. And, of course, the death sentence for disobedient lamps is to be snuffed out (σβεσθῆναι, aorist passive infinitive of σβέννυμι). After this glowing encounter, for the final stage of Lucian's return to the sea on Earth, his Cloudcuckooland is clearly that of Aristophanes' *Birds*, as he acknowledges (*VH* 1.29–31).

1.28 παρῄειμεν τὸν ἥλιον, ἐν χρῷ τὴν γῆν παραπλέοντες· οὐ γὰρ ἀπέβημεν καίτοι πολλὰ τῶν ἑταίρων ἐπιθυμούντων: as previously noted, there is a long tradition of the stars, Moon, and Sun as fiery rocks. Even with the discussion of the Sun possibly being inhabited, a joke might be implicit to some, or perhaps even a parody of Iambulus—if we had more. Lucian treats his passing of the Sun as if he is on the water, hugging the coastline. More importantly, the Sun is described as green and well watered (τὴν χώραν εὐθαλῆ τε καὶ πίονα καὶ εὔυδρον). Considering Lucian's companions greatly wanted to go ashore (genitive absolute with adverbial accusative πολλά), this must be an allusion to the fate of Odysseus' companions on the Island of the Sun (Helios). Odysseus warned his crew not to land on this island, but his companions persuaded him. Despite his warnings, they slaughtered some of the cattle of the Sun and all, save Odysseus, perished at sea after they left the island (*Od.* 12.260–390).

1.29 ἄραντες: aorist active participle of αἴρω ("to lift") in the sense of to raise the sail.

βασιλεύειν μέντοι αὐτῶν ἐλέγετο Κόρωνος ὁ Κοττυφίωνος. καὶ ἐγὼ ἐμνήσθην Ἀριστοφάνους τοῦ ποιητοῦ, ἀνδρὸς σοφοῦ καὶ ἀληθοῦς καὶ μάτην ἐφ' οἷς ἔγραψεν ἀπιστουμένου: Koronos son of Kottyphion. Κορωνός is masculine for a crow (κορωνή); Κοττυφίων is formed from κόσσυφος (a blackbird), meaning the son of Blackbird. Both are *hapax legomena*. Lucian's nod to *Birds* and its comic aerial journey is quick but pointed, and he names Aristophanes, describing the poet as "a wise man and truthful, and not believed for no reason on account of what he wrote"; this is at once a confirmation of the "truth" of Aristophanes' comic poetry and fantasy and perhaps even a confirmation of Lucian's veracity, since Old Comedy is an essential component in Lucian's literary inventiveness. Bowie (2007, 39) also notes how Lucian blends the "birdy" Homeric name Coronus (*Il.* 2.746) with a patronymic in good Attic spelling (*kottuphos* and not Koine *kossuphos*).

1.30–42 In the belly of the whale (continued in *VH* 2.1–2)

There is an entire world in the belly of the whale (κῆτος). It could accommodate a city of ten thousand inhabitants (*VH* 1.31). As Erich Auerbach (1953) saw clearly, this long passage in Lucian (*VH* 1.30–2.2) was Rabelais' inspiration for the world he installs in Pantagruel's mouth. The belly of Lucian's whale contains an island plateau 240 stades in circumference, with trees and birds perching on them. (Again, a *stadion* is *c.*600 feet, so *c.*144,000 feet.) The only human inhabitants of this inner island are the sole survivors of the whale's swallowing a merchant ship from Cyprus. Lucian discovers the ship's captain, Scintharus, and his son, Cinyras. The Cypriots farm a plot on the island. Their plot even produces vines, a sign of Greek civilization. The other marine creatures that inhabit the belly of the whale are both monstrous compounds and hostile. In entering this enclosed space, or even prison as Lucian refers to it, it is principally Homer's cave of the Cyclops in the *Odyssey* (9.105–542) and Plato's cave in the *Republic* (514a–520a) that scholars and commentators cite as the most likely sources of inspiration (see also the treatment of GL and Möllendorff ad loc.).

The idea of a person being swallowed by a whale is much older and not limited to Lucian. Hansen (2002) covers the topic briefly. Since Lucian and his crew just "passed" through Old Comedy, it is noteworthy that Aristophanes (*Nu.* 555–6) mentions an old woman swallowed by a sea monster or whale (κῆτος), a reference to a comedy of Phrynichus, who seems to have parodied the story of Andromeda and her rescue by Perseus by substituting an old woman for the young princess. The traditions of Perseus (Lyc. 834–41) and Heracles (Hellanicus *FGrHist* 4 F 26; Lyc. *Al.* 31–7; Tz. *Ad Lyc.* 34) included killing sea monsters from the inside out. In the Old Testament there is the Hebrew tale of the prophet Jonah who spent three days in the belly of a whale. And in a *Thousand and One Nights* Sinbad encounters a giant fish that is about to swallow the ship.

1.30 θηρία καὶ κήτη: on whales and sea-monsters, see Plin. *HN* 9.8, Str. 15.2.12–13, Arr. *Ind.* 30.1–6.

ἐπῄει δὲ κεχηνός: κεχηνός is the neuter perfect active participle of χάσκω, i.e. with the mouth wide open.

τοὺς ὀδόντας ἐκφαῖνον πολὺ τῶν παρ' ἡμῖν φαλλῶν ὑψηλοτέρους: the teeth of the whale are compared to the Greek phallus. Lucian perhaps has in mind the giant phalluses he describes in *On the Syrian Goddess* (16 and 28). Lightfoot (2003) notes that these pillars, which are called φαλλοῖ, are 300 ὀργυιαί or 1,800 feet tall.

ἡμᾶς αὐτῇ νηΐ: "us and the ship along with us." νηΐ is a dative of accompaniment (Smyth §1525).

οὐ μέντοι ἔφθη συναράξαι τοῖς ὀδοῦσιν: φθάνω is usually accompanied by the participle, which conveys the action done beforehand or first, and not the infinitive; yet the infinitive is found at Aristoph. *Nu.* 1384.

1.31 ἐκ τῆς ἰλύος ἣν κατέπινε συνιζάνουσα: the emendation (συνιζανούσης) of D. A. Russell, noted in Macleod's apparatus, is adopted in the translation;

though this is not the text Russell prints in his *Anthology of Greek Prose* (1991). The genitive participle συνιζανούσης describes the sediment of the slime (τῆς ἰλύος) as it settles in the mouth of the whale, thus forming both the land mass and the hills; the prepositional phrase with ἦσαν conveys the transition from slime to both states of being (cf. Smyth §1688 c). Left in the feminine nominative, the participle only modifies γῆ.

λάρους καὶ ἀλκυόνας, ἐπὶ τῶν δένδρων νεοττεύοντα: Jerram points out that the kingfisher (ἀλκυόνας) does not nest in trees.

1.32 εἴ ποτε ἀναχάνοι: the aorist active optative denotes repeated action in the past, Goodwin §176 A, i.e. "whenever the whale opened its mouth."

ἐπιγραφὴ... στήλας: the inscription in the sanctuary of Poseidon is reminiscent of the bronze inscription Lucian discovers on the Island of the Vine-Maidens, but the στήλας they discover inside the whale mark the graves of the people who had died trapped inside it. When exactly Lucian enters the underworld is not perfectly clear, and these grave stones certainly muddy the waters in that respect. As for a sanctuary of Poseidon in general, certainly within a moving creature of the sea it has its logical place. But perhaps it is also a nod to the god who is the root cause of Odysseus' tall tale.

1.33 ἡσθέντες οὖν ἅμα καὶ φοβηθέντες: aorist passive deponent participles (Smyth §356 c).

συννηχόμεθα τῷ περιέχοντι τούτῳ θηρίῳ: συννήχομαι, "to swim with" (+ dat.), is common, even though Lucian and his crew are not literally swimming.

νεήλυδες: The adjective is formed from ἤλυθον, the aorist of ἔρχομαι, and the accusative of νεός used adverbially, meaning "newcomers."

ὅτι μὴ... καθείργμεθα: as Jerram notes, in a negative of fact after ὅτι we would expect οὐ.

ὁ δὲ οὐ πρότερον ἔφη ἐρεῖν... πρὶν ξενίων τῶν παρόντων μεταδοῦναι: the Cypriot, Scintharus, observes the very Homeric rules of hospitality (ξενία). It is a breach of these rules to question a stranger before offering food and drink.

1.34 μέχρι μὲν οὖν Σικελίας εὐτυχῶς διεπλεύσαμεν: the voyage from Cyprus to Sicily and beyond would take Scintharus and his crew beyond Cape Malea at the southern tip of the Peloponnesus, a passage notorious for its danger to mariners. The dangers of turning this cape and the world of wonders that lay beyond it are brought out in Clay (2007).

τριταῖοι ἐς τὸν ὠκεανὸν ἀπηνέχθημεν: the Atlantic Ocean. The adjective τριταῖοι, meaning "on the third day," is used with the main verb and modifies the subject. The use here conveys that they were swept up by the storm for three days and on the third day reached the Atlantic. ἀπηνέχθημεν is the aorist passive of ἀποφέρω.

βραγχία: unlike Pliny (*HN*. 9.19), Lucian assumes whales have gills.

1.35 ἄμικτοι: "not mixing or mingling" with others and thus unsociable and even hostile (as in *VH* 2.27).

τὰ μὲν γὰρ ἑσπέρια καὶ οὐραῖα: The precision of western (the tail) and eastern (the mouth) parts of the woods within the belly of the whale makes no sense, since the whale moves about in all directions. It is also noteworthy that Lucian uses neither "northern" nor "southern" but right and left to complete his points of the compass.

A list of the names of the compound creatures in the belly of the whale:

Ταριχᾶνες	gefulte-fishers
Τριτωνομένδητες	triton-lizards
Καρκινόχειρες	crab-claws
Θυννοκέφαλοι	tuna-heads
Παγουρίδαι	crab-tails
Ψηττόποδες	sole-feet

1.36 Σκινθάρῳ: the Cypriot merchant's name seems to be derived from the rare word σκίνθος, a sea bird, the so-called diver. In Anaxandrides (F 28 KA) σκινδάριον seems to be the diminutive of some kind of fish.

1.38 ἐκείνην μὲν οὖν τὴν ἡμέραν καὶ τὴν νύκτα ἐπηυλισάμεθα: the accusative is used adverbially to indicate extent of time.

τῇ ὑστεραίᾳ: a common elliptical expression, i.e. ἡμέρᾳ is omitted.

1.39 καὶ ὅλως: adverbial καί introducing an appositionally related idea. There is freedom in translation, since καί is stressing the idea of the clause that follows and is perhaps best omitted in translation. With ὅλως the sense conveyed is "really" or "actually."

1.40 τῷ δ' ἐνάτῳ μηνὶ πέμπτῃ ἱσταμένου: not surprisingly Lucian reckons the time he spent in the belly of the whale by the Attic calendar that divides the month into three "decades" or ten-day periods: ἱσάμενος, μεσῶν, and φθίνων (the "rising," the "middle," and the "perishing" phases of the Moon). Thus, on the ninth month, at the period of the Moon's "rising."

ἅπαξ γὰρ δὴ τοῦτο κατὰ τὴν ὥραν ἑκάστην ἐποίει τὸ κῆτος: γάρ, "since," is parenthetic (Smyth §2812) and thus its explanatory clause is grammatically an aside. κατὰ τὴν ὥραν expresses an interval or lapse of time, though the exact measurement of time is uncertain. By Greek time-reckoning it can mean "once every hour" if the Egyptian and Babylonian system of time reckoning is adopted. In this system there were twelve hours to the day and twelve to the night (Hdt. 2.109; cf. E. J. Bickerman (1968)).

ἄνδρας μεγάλους, ὅσον ἡμισταδιαίους τὰς ἡλικίας: these fleets of giants riding islands, as if they were ships, are of course an unbelievable sight. τὰς ἡλικίας is an accusative of respect and here seems to mean "in size," not age; though stature of the body, i.e. size, remains generally correlated with signs of age. These sailors would then be around 300 feet tall.

οἶδα μὲν οὖν ἀπίστοις ἐοικότα ἱστορήσων, λέγω δὲ ὅμως: in *VH* 2 Lucian will make no more apologies for describing things still more incredible as if they were true. In this case the oars the crew employed on these island-ships were giant cypress trees, their branches, foliage, and all (αὐτοκλάδοις καὶ αὐτοκόμοις). The bronze tiller of the helmsman is five stades in length. The ruddy hair of the giants is lambent fire; the flaming hair instead of helmets likely recalls *Il.* 5.4, where Athena makes the helmet and shield of Diomedes ignite to make him a conspicuous figure on the battlefield, one to clearly fear. Moving islands also have precedence in Greek literature. The island of Aeolus in the *Odyssey* is said to float (*Od.* 10.1–3). Both Herodotus (2.156) and Hecataeus (*FGrHist* 1 F 305) mention a floating island in Egypt, Χέμμις and Χέμβις respectively; Hecataeus in particular notes that it moves on water, ἐστὶ μεταρσίη καὶ περιπλέει καὶ κινέεται ἐπὶ τοῦ ὕδατος.

1.41 πολλαὶ δὲ καὶ ἐμβληθεῖσαι κατεδύοντο: to ram a ship at its side (ἐμβολή) as opposed to the prow (προσβολή).

συμπλεκόμεναι: συμπλέκω is often used for the grappling of a wrestling match. Lucian also uses it in the context of a philosophical contest at *Symp.* 30. Yet the verb does have precedence for describing the entanglement of ships in naval combat; cf. Hdt. 8.84; Plb. 1.23.6.

ἀντὶ δὲ χειρῶν σιδηρῶν: the iron "hands" were grappling hooks, a term known from the descriptions of sea battles; cf. Thuc. 4.25.4 and 7.62.3.

πολύποδας μεγάλους: the "many footed" or octopus, which is described at Aelian *VH* 1 and Oppian *Hal.* 4.281–99. Pliny (*HN* 9.29) mentions one with tentacles 30 feet long.

1.42 Αἰολοκένταυρος: an unusual name. As Jerram notes, αἰόλος probably means "nimble" in this compound, and is perhaps loosely based on πόδας αἰόλος in Homer: the "darting" or "quick centaur."

ἀγκύραις... ὑαλίναις: strong anchors made of glass sound rather absurd; anchors were usually made of wood or iron. Harmon (1913), in his Loeb, suggests that ὑαλίναις may be a pun on ξυλίναις, i.e. wood.

Book 2

The Episodes of *True History* Book 2

2.1–2 Escape from the belly of the whale

2.1 The plan Lucian devises to escape from the belly of the whale with his ship and companions is inspired by Odysseus' escape from the cave of the Cyclops. After Odysseus had blinded the drunken Cyclops, the Cyclops had blocked the entrance to his cave by a huge boulder. There seemed to be no way to escape, but Odysseus devises a means to get out. In the morning, after the Cyclops had removed the boulder to pasture his flock, Odysseus rides out attached under the belly of one of the Cyclops' rams. The first attempt of Lucian to escape from the belly of the whale has nothing Odyssean about it. Lucian and his men excavate a hole deep into the "right wall" of the whale, but get nowhere; therefore the use of the imperfects (διεκόπτομεν and οὐδὲν ἠνύομεν) to convey ongoing action. Then they light a fire in the tail of the whale to kill the beast, but Lucian and his companions realize that the whale is slowly dying and opening his mouth less frequently. Moreover, he is opening and closing quickly. The only way to escape is to prop up the mouth; otherwise they will be trapped inside to await their doom.

2.1 Τὸ δὲ ἀπὸ τούτου μηκέτι φέρων ἐγὼ τὴν ἐν τῷ κήτει δίαιταν ἀχθόμενός τε τῇ μονῇ μηχανήν τινα ἐζήτουν: τὸ δὲ ἀπὸ τούτου is another common elliptical expression, "from that [time/moment]." The subjunctive force of μηκέτι is likely retained, "I could no longer endure." With δίαιταν, which conveys a mode of living and in Plato has a philosophical context (cf. *Phdr.* 265a–b), GL suggests a possible connection to Plato's cave, i.e. the desire to escape into the light (knowledge and truth). μηχανήν is possibly a reference to Odysseus and his epithet πολυμήχανος.

ὕλην καῦσαι διέγνωμεν: in the Cyclops episode, Odysseus realized that if he killed the Cyclops with the burning stake, the stone covering the entrance to the cave would remain permanently. In a kind of parodic reversal, Lucian's fire will kill the whale, but, unlike Odysseus, he and his men have the ability to prop open the whale's mouth and thus escape.

ἀναισθήτως εἶχε τοῦ καύματος: in this common ἔχω with an adverb construction, note that the adverb (ἀναισθήτως) retains the verbal force of αἰσθάνομαι and so takes the genitive (Smyth §1437).

ἐνενοήσαμεν ὡς...κινδυνεύσομεν: instead of the expected optative, the indicative in a dependent clause is used in another example of the so-called vivid construction; this example shows the simple logic for why the future easily replaced the optative in Koine Greek.

2.2 Τῇ δὲ ἐπιούσῃ: another common elliptical expression; supply ἡμέρᾳ.

ἐπαναβάντες δὲ ἐπὶ τὰ νῶτα καὶ θύσαντες τῷ Ποσειδῶνι αὐτοῦ παρὰ τὸ τρόπαιον: αὐτοῦ is adverbial, "there." Sacrificing to Poseidon in and of itself is not strange in context.

πᾶν ἐπάγη τὸ πέλαγος: the entire ocean froze (ἐπάγη is the aorist passive of πήγνυμι). For frozen seas, cf. Hdt. 4.28; Ov. *Tr.* 3.10.29–53; Plin. *HN* 4.104; Str. 1.4.2. The arctic or at least the North Sea appears in Greek and Latin literature, especially travel-literature. Whole months are dark (Pytheas F 13a and Ant. Diog. Phot. 110b), which we now refer to as polar nights. We also find the sea resisting the movement of ships, which might suggest ice (Pytheas F 7a, Tac. *Ag.* 10, and Sen. *suas.* 1.1).

2.3 The sacred island of Galatea

2.3 Lucian and his men land on a deserted island where they take on water and discover two strange wild bulls. The horns of these creatures are placed below their eyes, not above. This prodigy calls to mind the fable of Momus, the god of fault-finding, and the defect he discovered in Zeus' (or Poseidon's) creation of the bull with horns above his eyes; he could not see the object as he was goring it, ὥσπερ ὁ Μῶμος ἠξίου ("as Momus recommended"). Lucian had in mind Aesop's Fable 102 HAUSRATH (cf. Babrius 59). He often returns to this fable, since Momus is particularly congenial to his sense of humour: *Nigrinus* 32 *Hermotimus* 20, and most prominently in *The Assembly of the Gods*, in which Momus plays the central role. In Hesiod, Momus is the son of Night (*Th.* 214), not an illustrious pedigree. Night is the sister to Death, Sleep, and the race of Dreams (*Th.* 211).

πέλαγος...οὐχ ὕδατος, ἀλλὰ γάλακτος· καὶ νῆσος ἐν αὐτῷ ἐφαίνετο λευκὴ πλήρης ἀμπέλων. ἦν δὲ ἡ νῆσος τυρὸς μέγιστος συμπεπηγώς: as GL observes, the sea of milk and Island of Cheese are perhaps physical manifestations for what the island of the Cyclopes was famous: milk and cheese (*Od.* 219). Of course, since milk is γάλα and cheese is τυρός, it is rather appropriate that this island has a temple of Galatea and Tyro as its queen.

Γαλατείας τῆς Νηρηΐδος: another possible link to the island of the Cyclops. Polyphemus attempts to woo Galatea with his milk and cheese in Theocritus (11.34–7); Lucian also uses this very topic at *D. mar.* 1 and thus seems to allude directly to Theocritus.

Τυρὼ ἡ Σαλμωνέως: Tyro, the daughter of Salmoneus; Poseidon took advantage of her love for the river-god Enipeus and assumed his appearance in order to lay with her (Hom. *Od.* 11.235–59; Soph. *Tyro TrGF* 648–99; Apollod. *Bibl.* 19.8); this is, in fact, the subject of discussion between Enipeus and Poseidon in Lucian's *D. mar.* 13.

μετὰ τὴν ἐντεῦθεν ἀπαλλαγήν: "after her departure from there." Here ἐντεῦθεν seems to mean "from this life." Odysseus encounters Tyro in the underworld (*Od.* 11.235–52).

2.4 The men with feet of cork on the island of Phello

2.4 Φελλόποδες... Φελλώ: both of Lucian's inventions come from the Greek word for cork, φελλός, the Quercus Suber (quercus, therefore cork), which grows in the Alentejo north of the Tagus in what is now Portugal. Cork was known to Greek writers of the fourth century (Plat. *Plt.* 288e; Theophr. *CP* 1.2.7 and 1.5.2). In Lucian's age Portugal was the Roman province of Hispania Lusitania. In describing the island as round (πόλις ἐπὶ μεγάλου καὶ στρογγύλου φελλοῦ κατοικουμένη) Lucian is perhaps referencing, generally, actual geography. GL notes an Aeolian island called Στρογγύλη along with six others, some of which were known for their volcanic nature (Diod. 5.7.1; Str. 6.2.11). Lucian not only mentions six more islands, but also five that have fire blazing upwards.

οὐ βαπτιζομένους, ἀλλὰ ὑπερέχοντας τῶν κυμάτων καὶ ἀδεῶς ὁδοιποροῦντας: the motif of walking on water is also found in Lucian's *Philops.* 13. Walking on water in dreams is also a good omen for safe travel on a ship (Artem. 3.16). And, of course, Jesus walks on water in the New Testament (Matt. 14:22–36); cf. Betz (1961, 167). There is also an analogy between a cork's ability to float straight and those souls that do not yield to and are dragged by their passions (Plut. *De gen.* 592a–b).

2.4–19 Arrival at the Island of the Blest and the banquet on the Elysian Fields

Lucian does not give the location of his Island of the Blest (νῆσος Μακάρων, *VH* 2.6), except to say that it was the island he encountered after passing the Island of Cork. The tradition of the Island of the Blest as the destination in death of some of the heroes who fought at Thebes or Troy is found in Hesiod's *Works and Days* (*Op.* 156–73) and Pindar (*O.* 2.68–80). Of course, in the prophecy of Proteus to Menelaus (Hom. *Od.* 4.561–9) we find mention of the "Elysian Field" to which Menelaus is destined in death because he is the son-in-law of Zeus by his marriage to Helen, the daughter of Leda and Zeus. The island is identified as being the realm of "fair-haired Rhadamanthus" (Hom. *Od.* 5.564). Both the Islands of the Blest and the Elysian Field are located remotely at "the ends of the earth" near its ultimate limit, the all-encompassing River Ocean (encased by Hephaestus on the rim of the shield of Achilles at Hom. *Il.* 18.607–8).

In Lucian these two traditions merge. His Island of the Blest contains an Elysian Field on which the heroes not only banquet, but this banquet is also very much a symposium of the dead (*VH* 2.14). The variegated population on this island also seems unique to Lucian. In Hesiod, as noted, and implicitly in Homer's *Odyssey*, the Islands of the Blest (plural) are the unique destiny of the heroes who fought at Thebes and Troy (Hes. *Op.* 159–60). Many of these were heroes in that they had become objects of cult in their communities. Lucian refers to his blest in Hesiodic terms both as ἥρωες (*VH* 2.10, 17, 23) and "the ἡμίθεοι who fought at Troy" (*VH* 2.17). We discover on Lucian's island Ajax, Menelaus (but not Agamemnon), Nestor, and Achilles. But the Athenian culture hero Theseus is prominent among the heroes and second only to Achilles. And besides other great men, Lucian remarkably admits two famous women: Lais and Helen. Furthermore, this ιsland may be traditionally a place of heroes, but this is a symposium and they thus need entertainment. Enter the poets of archaic Greece. The legendary Eunomus and Arion are named, as are Anacreon and Stesichorus. The most important poet among them, however, is—of course—Homer.

History too is present on Lucian's island. Here again Lucian manages to surprise us. He is notably not as negligent of the Hellenistic and Roman worlds. Lucian thus avoids the archaism typical of the Greek culture of the Second Sophistic, the archaizing tendency to elide the "recent" history of Greece after Demosthenes and Alexander, which is especially notable in Pausanias' *Guide to Greece* (Paus. 1.6.1; see also Simon Swain, *Hellenism and Empire* (1996) and Habicht, *Pausanias' Guide to Ancient Greece* (1988, 134)). Most surprisingly, and perhaps even as a shock to his readers, there are barbarians on the island: the two Cyruses (the Great, the subject of Xenophon's *Cyropaideia*, and Cyrus the Younger, the subject of Xenophon's *Anabasis*) and Zalmoxis and Anacharsis—Anacharsis is, of course, very familiar to Lucian's readers from his dialogue entitled *Anacharsis*. As for Rome, we find only Numa and Italy's invader, Hannibal.

And then there are the philosophers. That philosophers make up a good number of the island's population should come as no surprise to the reader of Lucian. Philosophers are everywhere in Lucian's corpus. One only has to recall especially his *Lives on Auction*, the *Fisherman*, and *Dialogues of the Dead*. As noted often, before arriving back on Earth, under the costumes of Lucian's war in space scholars see a nonsensical, hyperbolic war among philosophical sects. Yet their presence amongst the notable dead seems unique to the Syrian; even in Virgil's underworld there are Greek poets (notably the legendary Orpheus and Musaeus, *A.* 6.645–7, 661–5) and

Romans to be distinguished in the future (6.756–892), but no philosophers. Here we first discover all the seven sages, save Periander (*VH* 2.17). Socrates is present, intimately conversing with handsome young men and idly chatting with Nestor and Palamedes. As lovers of pleasure (ἡδεῖς), the followers of Epicurus and Aristippus of Cyrene are also prominent. Diogenes of Sinope appears, but has notably abandoned his pretensions to Cynic austerity and misanthropy; he has taken up with Lais and is now devoted to drink and dancing. Aesop is here as the jester (γελοτοποιός) to entertain the company. Pythagoras too is present, though the blest are in doubt about what to call him: Pythagoras or Euphorbus, as he was in the incarnation when he killed Patroclus with the aid of Apollo and Hector (*VH* 2.21; *Il.* 16.806–87). Members of some notable schools of philosophy, however, are nowhere to be found. Plato is absent but survives in the afterlife in his own state making his own laws; while the name Socrates gives his ideal city in the *Republic* (7 527c) is Kallipolis, Kidd (2017, 362) notes the pun in τῇ πολιτείᾳ καὶ τοῖς νόμοις, as "constitution" (usually translated as *Republic*) and "laws" are the titles of Plato's most famous works. Yet Lucian observes that males on the Island of the Blest are most "Platonic" (Πλατωνικώτατοι) because they enjoy the women in common (*VH* 2.19). The Stoics have no representative here; they had yet to make the steep climb to the summit of the Mountain of Virtue. The philosophers of the Skeptical Academy could not decide if there was such a thing as an Island of the Blest. Empedocles arrives half-baked from his plunge into the crater of Aetna, but is not admitted to the island, obviously because he must have been mad to have made the plunge. Aristotle and his school are sedulously ignored.

Lucian not only has created an island out of Greek literature and history, but also, as ní Mhealleigh (*per litteras*) has noted, the kind of compendium or encyclopedia in vogue during the imperial period, as the works of Strabo and Pliny the Elder, for example, convey. But in this literary encyclopedia constructed on Lucian's Island of the Blest, he also places himself, the author. In that context, Lucian has precedent: Simonides (F 22 West^2). Another, which he may or may not have known, is possibly Horace. In *Epode* 16, Horace, speaking as a poet who had fought on the losing side at Philippi in 42 BCE, promises to lead an expedition away from Rome and its civil wars to prosperous islands and blessed fields (41–2):

> Nos manet Oceanus circumvagus; arva, beata
> petamus arva, divites et insulas.

It could be, as one ancient commentator noted, that Horace remembered the tradition that Sertorius heard the reports of Islands of the Blest in the Atlantic lying off the coast of Luisitania (Portugal), which we find in Plutarch (*Sert.* 8.2–3). Horace casts his escape from Rome in terms of Hesiod's Ages of Man. He will flee the Iron Age of the civil wars of Rome and return to a Golden Age. Like the Elysian Field of Proteus' prophecy, these islands of Horace's imagination suggest the divinely favored fertility we find in descriptions of the Golden Age and in Lucian *VH* 2.5 and 12–13, passages reminiscent of the description of the Gardens of Alcinous in *Od.* 7.114–32. It is telling that Iambulus cites lines 120–1 of this Homeric passage to describe the spontaneous productivity of the Island of the Sun (Diod. 2.56.7). Lucian's description of the Island of the Blest certainly evokes Hesiod's description of the Golden Age (*Op.* 118–19, 172–3; cf. *Od.* 19.109–14.

2.5 θαυμαστή τις αὔρα περιέπνευσεν ἡμᾶς, ἡδεῖα καὶ εὐώδης, οἵαν φησὶν ὁ συγγραφεὺς Ἡρόδοτος ἀπόζειν τῆς εὐδαίμονος Ἀραβίας: the reference is to Hdt. 3.113. This is perhaps a precursor or foreshadowing of the foul smell of the Island of the Impious at 2.29, where Herodotus is placed and punished for being a liar (*VH* 2.31). Souls, evidently, have a sense of smell according to Heraclitus (DK 22 B 98). GL note the philosophical sense of εὐδαιμονία, "being happy," referencing back to *VH* 1.12, where Endymion explains that Lucian and his crew, if he succeeds in his war, will live the happiest of lives. Lucian is indeed concerned with how philosophers define a happy life (*Menippus* 4)—particularly the contradictory notions of the various sects. Yet note that the use of the adjective is common in historiography to define visibly wealthy people; cf. LSJ. It is also used specifically to define Arabia (*Peripl. M. Rubr.* 26), and we must remember travel literature certainly informs Lucian's *True History*.

ἐγινόμεθα: from γίνομαι, the common form of γίγνομαι after the fourth century BCE.

ῥόδων καὶ ναρκίσσων καὶ ὑακίνθων καὶ κρίνων: these flowers are used in the context of death: roses were laid on graves (Theophr. *HP* 6.6.4–5; Plin. *HN* 21.14–21; Athen. 682b–c); in mythology the death of young men generates the narcissus and hyacinth (Theophr. *HP* 6.6.9 and 6.8.2); the lily is also used as a symbol of death (Diph. F 98 KA).

ἐοικότα τοῖς ἐπ' ἐρημίας αὐλήμασι τῶν πλαγίων αὐλῶν: this music is produced by the "cross flute" held horizontally. It could be, as Jerram suggests, that the expression ἐπ' ἐρημίας refers to shepherds dedicating their pipes to Pan in the countryside, citing Vergil (*Ecl.* 7.24).

2.6 λειμῶνος εὐανθοῦς: the general symposiastic nature of Lucian's Island of the Blest and his ability to engage and ask questions—especially of Homer—suggest Lucian is parodying Plato's meadow in the myth of Er in the *Republic* (614e–615a), in which souls greet each other and interact in a festival-like atmosphere.

οἱ δὲ δήσαντες ἡμᾶς ῥοδίνοις στεφάνοις: the gentle restraint of binding by garlands is reminiscent and repetitious of the binding of Lucian and his crew when they landed on the Moon (*VH* 1.11). Roses, as noted above, are associated with death; additionally the ship on which Cinyras and Helen escape from the Island of the Blest is hauled back by a rose cable (*VH* 2.26).

ὁ Κρὴς ῾Ραδάμανθυς: the Cretan Rhadamanthus, the son of Zeus and Europa, is one of the three judges of the underworld. Lucian does not mention the others, Minos and Triptolemus, as being present, although there is the month of Minos on the island (*VH* 2.13). In *De luct.* 7, however, Lucian does have Minos and Rhadamanthus paired as judges. In the *Odyssey* (4.564) Rhadamanthus is an inhabitant of Elysium.

2.7 Αἴαντος τοῦ Τελαμῶνος...κατηγορεῖτο δὲ αὐτοῦ ὅτι μεμήνοι καὶ ἑαυτὸν ἀπεκτόνοι: with the passive κατηγορεῖτο the genitive (αὐτοῦ) expresses who is accused. After the death of Achilles his armour was not awarded to Ajax, the second-best warrior, but to Odysseus. In order to stop his rage, which was directed at Odysseus and the other leaders of the Greek expedition, Ajax was driven mad by the gods. The madness and suicide of Ajax is most vividly dramatized in Sophocles' *Ajax*.

τοῦ ἐλλεβόρου: the supposed antidote for madness (Aristoph. *Vesp.* 1489; Theophr. *HP* 9.10.1–4; Hippoc. *Vict.* 1.35), which grew in Anticyra (Hor. *Sat.* 2.3.166).

2.8 κρίσις ἐρωτική: The rivalry of Menelaus and Theseus over Helen. Here Lucian exploits the tradition that Theseus, the Athenian culture hero, had kidnapped Helen when she was a girl and left her with his mother; Castor and Pollux later returned her to Sparta where she would marry Menelaus. On the various traditions regarding the kidnapping of Helen, see Plutarch (Plut. *Thes.* 31).

τήν τε Ἀμαζόνα καὶ τὰς τοῦ Μίνωος θυγατέρας: the Amazon is Hippolyta (possibly Antiope), and the daughters of Minos are Phaedra and Ariadne. Ariadne, who helped Theseus escape the labyrinth of the Minotaur, was abandoned on Naxos. Phaedra's disastrous love for Hippolytus, Theseus' son by Hippolyta (or Antiope), is the subject of Euripides' *Hippolytus*.

2.9 τρίτη δ' ἐδικάσθη περὶ προεδρίας: the dispute between Alexander and Hannibal is over the honour of sitting on the front seat, typically in reference to the theater, the arena of athletic contests, or the public assemblies. Lucian staged the debate in his *Dialogues of the Dead* (25 (12)); his version is a parody of an alleged postwar conversation between Hannibal and Scipio at Ephesus, a story preserved by Livy (35.14), Appian (*Syr.* 10), and Plutarch (*Flam.* 21). In this dialogue, persuaded by Scipio Africanus, Minos gives precedence to Alexander, then to Scipio, and third to Hannibal. On Lucian's Island of the Blest there is no theater, only this sympotic assembly and, as we shall see, a few athletic contests. Alexander, as the winner, is notably seated next to the elder Cyrus, and his seat is not a seat of honour (προεδρία) but a throne (θρόνος).

2.10 Ἀριστείδης ὁ δίκαιος ὁ Ἀθηναῖος: Aristides "The Just." The subject of one of Plutarch's *Lives*, Aristides lived in the period of the two Persian invasions of Greece. His epithet, ὁ δίκαιος, is perhaps best exemplified by the story of Aristides being presented with a shard (ὄστρακον) on which to scratch the name of a citizen to be exiled from Athens. Aristides asked the illiterate individual whose name he should incise. The answer was Aristides, and he thus wrote his own name on the ostracon (Plut. *Arist.* 7.5–6). He was ostracized in 483/2.

φιλοπραγμοσύνης: this is the only time Lucian uses this word. It is the equivalent of πολυπραγμοσύνη, which carries the bad connotation of meddlesomeness; it is specifically used in this context of Philip of Macedon by Demosthenes (1.14; 4.42).

δοῦναι τὰς εὐθύνας: political terminology for the rendering of accounts, whereby an elected official's actions would be evaluated at the end of his term; cf. Aristoph. *Pax* 1187. In Lucian's underworld, it is notable that the comic poet Alexis (F 264 KA) barrows this terminology as a metaphor for "rendering the accounts" of one's life.

μὴ πλέον μηνῶν ἑπτά: the limitation of seven months finds parallel with Iambulus' journey, though in his narrative it is seven years (Diod. 2.60.1).

We should also note that in Plato's myth of Er souls stay in the meadow for seven days and then depart on the eighth (*R.* 616b).

2.11 ἐλελύμεθα: the pluperfect tense with the genitive absolute is described in Smyth (§1953) as the "pluperfect of immediate occurrence." Chains or bonds falling off on their own appear as early as Euripides (*Ba.* 634 and 642); cf. also Xen. *An.* 4.3.8.

ἡ πόλις πᾶσα χρυσῆ...: Lucian's imaginary city of gold with its emerald wall and its beryl temples of the gods recalls Euhemerus of Messene's description of the temples on the sacred island of Panchaea (Eus. *PE* 2.2.59B–61A; Diod. 6.1 and 5.41.4–46.7); the fragments of Euhemerus are translated by Clay and Purvis in Winiarczyk (1991). There is also similarity with the description of the City of the Sun in Ps.-Call. *Alex. rom.* 3.28 and of Hierapolis in *De Syr.* 10 and 30–2. The scholiast on this passage takes Lucian to be mocking the Jerusalem of Revelations of John (21.1–5) and the holy prophets of the church (*sch. in Luc.* 11 p. 21 Rabe); see also Betz (1961, 92–4) and Möllendorff ad loc. The Greek Septuagint (the Hellenistic translation of the Hebrew Scriptures) was certainly available in Lucian's age, but it is hard to assess any influence on him; it is certainly important in a passage of Timarion (9), a dialogue considered to be falsely attributed to Lucian.

πήχεων ἑκατὸν βασιλικῶν: according to the Herodotus (1.178 and 7.117) the royal cubit is three fingers longer than the normal cubit.

2.12 ἀλλ' ἀναφεῖς καὶ ἄσαρκοί εἰσιν...ἔοικε γυμνή τις ἡ ψυχὴ αὐτῶν περιπολεῖν τὴν τοῦ σώματος ὁμοιότητα περικειμένη: the scholiast on Lucian's description of the insubstantial bodies that appear on the Island of the Blest takes our author to be "mocking the bizarre tales told of the regions beyond Thule" (*sch. in Luc.* 12 p. 21 Rabe); see also Stephens and Winkler (1995, 120–1). Overall, Lucian's intangible, fleshless, and shadowlike dead are in the tradition of what we find in Homer and Vergil (cf. *Od.* 11.14–15; *A.* 6.292–4). That the dead wear their wraithlike bodies as if they were garments might also be a part of Lucian's general use of the "life as theater" metaphor (see above n. 1.2), i.e. even souls are costumes to be worn in the theater that is the underworld (an observation of ní Mhealleigh *per litteras*).

οὐδὲ νὺξ...οὐδὲ ἡμέρα...τὸ λυκαυγὲς...τοιοῦτο φῶς: as mentioned above Lucian seems aware of polar nights (when night lasts more than twenty-four hours within the polar circles). Here he also seems aware of polar days, or the so-called midnight Sun (when the Sun stays above the horizon for more than twenty-four hours in areas north of the Arctic Circle (as well as south of the Antarctic Circle)), which provides a suitable atmosphere for the Island of the Blest, as the light experienced is neither truly day nor truly night. In Plutarch, λυκαυγές (*De fac.* 931e and 941d) is similarly used to convey an atmosphere of twilight, one particularly similar to the sky during an eclipse.

2.12–13 On Lucian's Island of the Blest spring is eternal in this half light, as it seems to be on the island of Alcinous (*Od.* 7.114–32); Jerram notes that the passage reads like a parodic version of Alcinous' gardens. There are twelve months that all bear crops, but there are no seasons. For some crops, the month of Minos produces two; perhaps this is because Minos is a king of the underworld, yet he is not present on Lucian's Island of the Blest, or, as GL suggest, a kind of joke based on Minos' rules (Plat. *Min.* 320a) against excessive drinking (thus in his month other crops overshadow the vines); for vines bearing fruit twelve times per year, cf. Iambulus ap. Diod. 2.56.7; Hom. *Od.* 7.117–20; Hes. *Op.* 174–5. The Zephyr or West Wind is the fecundating wind of a perpetual spring, associated with the month of March; this spring is described by Ovid in his account of the Golden Age (*ver erat aeternum, placidique tepentibus auris mulcebant Zephyri natos sine semine flores, Met.* 1.107–8). The fecundating power of the West Wind in spring is also evoked by Lucretius in the opening of the *De rerum natura* (1.1–20). But the Zephyr is also a wind capable of carrying the dead to the Island of the Blest or elsewhere (cf. Hom. *Od.* 4.567; Pind. *O.* 2.78; Apul. *Met.* 4.35).

2.13 φυτοῖς ἡμέροις τε καὶ σκιεροῖς: it could be, as Harmon suggests in his Loeb edition, that Lucian is contrasting Sun loving and shade loving plants and intends to pun on ἡμέροις, as if it is derived from the Greek word for day and daylight, ἡμέρα.

2.14 διακονοῦνται δὲ καὶ παραφέρουσιν ἕκαστα οἱ ἄνεμοι πλήν γε τοῦ οἰνοχοεῖν: the description of the winds as servants at this symposium recalls Apuleius' description of the winds that serve Psyche in the episode of Cupid and Psyche (*Met.* 4.35 and 5.3). But in a sympotic context, the image is also close to Simonides F 25 West[2] in which the poet is in want of the cold wind to pour snow down to cool his warm drink.

2.15 That Homer is seated behind Odysseus in what is now called a "double occupancy couch" means that Odysseus—meaning the *Odyssey*—was not his ἐρώμενος but his favorite poem. The erotic implication of such reclining arrangements is well brought out in von Blanckenhagen (1992, 51–68).

Four famous poets are named: Eunomus of Locris, Arion of Lesbos, Anacreon of Teos, and Stesichorus of Himera in Sicily. Eunomus and Arion are legendary. Eunomus was famous for the story of how he played alongside the tune of a grasshopper, after a string of his lyre snapped during a performance (Clem. Al. *Prot.* 1.1); Strabo notes that a statue of Eunomus and the grasshopper was erected at Locris (4.1.9). We know the legend of Arion, the supposed inventor of dithyrambic poetry, as well as the dolphin that saved his life mainly from Herodotus (1.23–4; cf. also Ov. *Fast.* 2.83). Anacreon is famous for his sympotic poetry, as are the poems attributed to him (the *Anacreontea*). Stesichorus was said to have been blinded by Castor and Pollux for his unsavory depiction of Helen. His "Palinode" (an ode in which the author retracts views expressed in a previous poem) directed to Helen not only regained his eyesight (ἤδη τῆς Ἑλένης αὐτῷ διηλλαγμένης), but also claimed that she never went to Troy, despite her dramatic appearance on the walls of Troy from which she identifies the Greek warriors for Priam in Homer (*Il.* 3.130–242). Three lines of the famous "Palinode" of Stesichorus are cited by Socrates in Plato's *Phaedrus* (243a): "This was no true tale, you did not enter ships with their sturdy benches, nor did you go to the citadel of Troy" (F 91 FINGLASS = F 15 *PMG*). The negative vs. positive portrayals of Helen are very distinct in Euripides (*Andr.* 103–4, 248, 594–5, 626; *Tro.* 881; *El.* 213–14), Gorgias' *Encomium of Helen*, and Isocrates' *Helen*.

2.16 πηγαὶ . . . ἡ μὲν γέλωτος, ἡ δὲ ἡδονῆς: perhaps a parody of the springs of pleasure and sorrow in Theopompus (*FGrHist* / *BNJ* 115 F 75).

2.17 πλήν γε δὴ τοῦ Λοκροῦ Αἴαντος: the exception is the "lesser Ajax" of Locris (to distinguish him from the more famous Ajax, son of Telamon), whose bad reputation is confirmed by both the *Iliad* (his rude exchange with Idomeneus, *Il.* 23.473–98) and by the *Odyssey* (his drowning by Poseidon, *Od.* 4.499–511). More serious is the tradition that he dragged the suppliant Cassandra from the altar of Athena at Troy and raped her (in the *Il. Pers.*, *Homeri Opera* ALLEN). Lucian condemns him to his Island of the Impious (*VH* 2.23).

τὸν Σκύθην Ἀνάχαρσιν: Anacharsis (sixth century BCE) was a famous traveler who visited Greece. He is referred to as a student of Solon, and sometimes even included among the Seven Sages (Hdt. 4.76). Anacharsis is, of course, Lucian's principle interlocutor in the eponymous dialogue (see Branham (1989, 81–104)).

τὸν Θρᾷκα Ζάμολξιν: tradition holds that Zamolxis was a slave of Pythagoras, from whom he learned about the heavenly bodies and the doctrine of the immortality of the soul. He is described as the lawgiver of the Getae in Thrace (Icar. 16; J. Trag. 44), and supposedly lived in a cave from which he gave advice (Hdt. 4.94–6; Str. 7.3.5). Zamolxis is treated as Scythian by Lucian in *The Scythian* 1 and 4, and the Getae are considered Scythians in *Deor. conc.* 9.

Νομᾶν τὸν Ἰταλιώτην, καὶ μὴν καὶ Λυκοῦργον τὸν Λακεδαιμόνιον: Numa Pompilius was the second king of Rome and founder of Roman law and religion. Lycurgus is the celebrated lawgiver of Sparta and author of the Great Rhetra or Spartan constitution. Although the two are syntactically and ethnically separated, the near pairing recalls the deliberate pairing by Plutarch in his parallel lives.

Φωκίωνα: Phocion, the Athenian general and statesman, was put to death in Athens during the democratic revolution under Polyperchon in 318 BCE. Like Aristides, he had an honourific epithet: The Good (ὁ χρηστός). As a rhetorical opponent of Demosthenes and a favorite of Macedon, he was eventually charged with treason by the Athenians. His fame lasted, as he is the subject of one of Plutarch's biographies.

Τέλλον τοὺς Ἀθηναίους: in Herodotus' account of the interview of Solon of Athens with King Croesus in Sardis, the wealthy Croesus asks the Athenian statesman and philosopher whom he takes to be the happiest of mortals (ὀλβιώτατος). Croesus expects that Solon will nominate Croesus himself, but Solon nominates Tellus, who enjoyed a good reputation in Athens. He had two fine sons and grandsons from them. He fought for Athens at Eleusis, died in the battle, and was given a public burial (Hdt. 1.30).

τοὺς σοφοὺς ἄνευ Περιάνδρου: the Seven Sages: Thales, Pittacus, Bias, Solon, Cletobulus, Periander, and Chilon. Perhaps it is the description of his monstrous crimes by Diogenes Laertius (1.94–9) that would justify his exclusion from Lucian's Island of the Blest. Plato notably replaces Periander with Myson (*Prt.* 343A; cf. also D.L. 40.108). Yet in Plutarch's *The Banquet of the Seven Sages* (*Mor.* 146B–164D) Periander of Corinth hosts this fictional banquet.

Σωκράτη τὸν Σωφρονίσκου: we discover Socrates chatting with Nestor and Palamedes. Nestor of the *Iliad* was famed for this garrulity. Palamedes was, like Socrates, sentenced to death on a false charge—not that of impiety and corrupting the youth of Athens, but of treason to the Greek army at Troy; Palamedes' father, Nauplius, is Lucian's pilot on his voyage to the Island of the Impious, *VH* 2.29–32. In his final address to the jury who had sentenced him to death for impiety, Socrates speaks of the judges in the afterlife, Rhadamanthus, Aiacus, and Triptolemus, and expresses the hope that in the afterlife he would meet Ajax and Palamedes (*Ap*. 41 A–C). Both were victims of the eloquence of Odysseus who won the contest with Ajax over the arms of Achilles and with the arms the title "best of the Achaeans."

Ὑάκινθός τε ὁ Λακεδαιμόνιος καὶ ὁ Θεσπιεὺς Νάρκισσος καὶ Ὕλας καὶ ἄλλοι καλοί: Socrates' companions are handsome young men: Hyacinthus of Lacedaemon, Narcissus of Thespiae, and Hylas. All died young. Hyacinthus was struck by a discus thrown by his divine lover, Apollo. Narcissus drowned because of his fascination with his own image in a pool of water. And Hylas was drowned by a water nymph in Mysia (so Apoll. Rhod. 1.1229–39). It struck Lucian that Socrates must have been in love with Hyacinthus because he spent most of his time probing him with difficult questions (τὰ πολλὰ γοῦν ἐκεῖνον διήλεγχεν; the verb obviously references the ἔλεγχος, the name given to Socrates' method of cross-examination). The imperfect, ongoing action perhaps conveys Socrates' insistence; γοῦν offers confirmation of a previous general assertion, e.g. "certainly" or "at any rate." Lucian alludes to Socrates' pederasty in *Lives on Auction* (15).

τὴν εἰρωνείαν: Socrates (especially the Socrates of the Platonic dialogues, as opposed to the Socrates in the works of Xenophon and Antisthenes) was notorious for what is called his "irony." His tactic was to play the role of the ignorant learner in his dialogic exchange with others. The word εἰρωνεία is used only once in Plato; it is hurled at Socrates by the exasperated Thrasymachus of Calchedon (*R*. 1.337A). On the Island of the Blest Rhadamanthus seems to have the same reaction as Thrasymachus.

Πλάτων δὲ μόνος οὐ παρῆν: see Introduction 2.3.

2.18 οἱ μέντοι ἀμφ' Ἀρίστιππόν τε καὶ Ἐπίκουρον...συμποτικώτατοι: the Cyrenaic and Epicurean schools. Aristippus, a student of Socrates, founded the Cyrenaic school around 370 BCE. Due to his focus on pleasure as the primary goal in life, of course his disciples would be great guests at a party. Epicurus' focus on pleasure, though defined by φρόνησις (wisdom) and ἀταραξία (peace/tranquility of mind), is thus also easy to parody in an incongruent party context. Lucian mentions Aristippus and especially Epicurus in a favorable light elsewhere (e.g. *Demon*. 62; *Bis. acc*. 13; *Vit.*

auct. 19; *Herm.* 25); see also Tackaberry (1930, 25); Caster (1937, 84–106); Branham (1989, 189–210).

Αἴσωπος ὁ Φρύξ . . . γελωτοποιῷ χρῶνται: Jerram notes that ὁ Φρύξ is used to ensure that he is not confused with Aesop the actor and friend of Cicero. Although Aesop is well known as both a slave and an author of fables, what has been passed down under his name has been considered spurious; the rewriting of his fables is evident, as in the versified versions of Barbrius and Phaedrus. In Aesop's biographical tradition, *P.Oxy.* 1800 (= *FGrHist* 1139) details his unjust death and the subsequent honours he received at Delphi (see the text and commentary by Meccariello in *FGrHist* 1139); these honours received after death perhaps, as Möllendorff notes (ad loc.), legitimize his place on the Island of the Blest. On Lucian and Aesop, see Bompaire (1958) 460–1.

Διογένης μέν γε ὁ Σινωπεὺς . . . ἑταίραν τὴν Λαΐδα: Diogenes of Sinope is the notorious Cynic best known from Diogenes Laertius' account of him in his *Lives* (*VH* 6.26–81) and Lucian's own characterization of him in *Lives on Auction* (7–11). From Diogenes' account of his life it is clear that his Cynic scorn extended to all of humankind. Lais of Hycara was a notorious courtesan from Corinth, a seaport famous for its courtesans—whence the proverb "it is not the luck of every man to sail to Corinth." Lais was reputed to have had a sexual relationship with Diogenes, but she would not take money from him; she was also closely attached to Aristippus and Demosthenes. Here Diogenes has comically abandoned the Cynic life and has engaged in matrimony, drinking, and even dancing.

τῶν δὲ Στωϊκῶν οὐδεὶς παρῆν . . . τὸν τῆς ἀρετῆς ὄρθιον λόφον: the virtuous life as a steep ascent up a hill appears in Hesiod (*Op.* 286–92). In a philosophical context, it does appear in Pythagoras and in the so-called *Tabula Cebetis* allegory ascribed to Cebes of Thebes, and it was extensively used by the Stoics to convey the long challenge that virtue poses. The Mount of Virtue appears in Lucian's *Hermotimus* (2–4), where he also happens to make fun of the Stoics for their apparently unending and thus pointless training. So here the Stoics are not present because, even in death, they are still trying to find virtue.

περὶ Χρυσίππου: the Stoic Chrysippus, who was a student of Cleanthes, the founder of the Stoic school, is waiting for admission to the island, but not before he had been treated by a dose of hellebore for the fourth time. Lucian, in *Lives on Auction* (20–5), notably has Chrysippus say that no one can be a philosopher unless they consume a triple dose of hellebore. Hellebore was used to treat madness. Chrysippus' madness seems to be suggested by the account Diogenes Laertius gives of his death (7.185); he died of a fit of laughter while asking an old woman to give an ass a cup of unmixed wine, since the ass was eating his figs. Three doses, evidently, was not enough for the madness of philosophy.

Ἀκαδημαϊκοὺς...τὴν ἐπὶ τοῦ ῾Ραδαμάνθυος, οἶμαι, κρίσιν ἐδεδοίκεσαν, ἅτε καὶ τὸ κριτήριον αὐτοὶ ἀνῃρηκότες: Lucian, like Aristophanes in *Clouds*, is good with jokes at the expense of philosophers and their sects, especially in the context of incongruity. Here, the Academicians, philosophers of the Middle and New Academy—predominately represented by Arcesilaus and Carneades—, applied academic skepticism and claimed that there could not be a standard of truth, resulting in a "withholding of judgment" (ἐποχή). Without such metric, they essentially nullified the role of Rhadamanthus—and thus naturally feared his judgement in Lucian's underworld.

2.19 περὶ δὲ συνουσίας καὶ ἀφροδισίων...οὐδαμῶς τοῦτο αὐτοῖς αἰσχρὸν δοκεῖ: sex in public is noted usually amongst non-Greeks, so the scholiast conjectures an illusion to this practice among the Indians (*sch. in Luc.* 19 p. 22 Rabe; Hdt. 3.101); there are also others stigmatized by this practice (cf. Megasthenes ap. Str. 15.1.56; Xen. *An.* 5.4.33–4; Apoll. Rhod. 2.1015–25). For philosophers, we of course must note Diogenes' Cynic behaviour and the story of Crates and Hipparchia having sex in public (though Zeno eventually hid them with his cloak) in Apuleius (*Fl.* 14). In death, everyone has apparently embraced the advice given by the Cynic in *Vitarum auctio* 10.

Πλατωνικώτατοι: Lucian has in mind the second of the three "waves of paradox" that Socrates proposes in Plato's *Republic*: that the guardian class should have wives, children, and property in common (*R.* 5.449c); Lucian also mentions this in *Vitarum auctio* 17. We also find this idea in Iambulus (ap. Diod. 2.58.1) and Herodotus (1.216; 4.104 and 180).

2.20 The interview with Homer

Homeric questions, which were addressed in scholastic treatises, consisted of problems in Homeric scholarship and were very common by Lucian's time; the *Homeric Questions* of Porphyry in the third century CE is a good example. Ultimately this type of inquiry reflects earlier works such as Zoilus of Amphipolis' *Against Homer's Poetry*, Aristotle's now fragmented and possibly entitled *Homeric Problems*, and in particular Hellenistic scholarship at Alexandria and Pergamum. Here Lucian focuses on a few critical issues: Homer's origins, the authenticity of certain passages, and the poetic composition and relationship between the *Iliad* and the *Odyssey*. In meeting Homer face to face, as GL observes, Lucian fulfills an academic and intellectual fantasy, one even mentioned by Socrates himself (Plat. *Ap*. 41a).

The most important of Lucian's questions concerns Homer's birthplace (in general see [Plut.] *Vita Homeri* ALLEN). He lists three cities that were the main contestants for this honour: Chios (usually taken to be Homer's birthplace) and both Smyrna and Colophon in Asia Minor. Lucian's question was of pressing concern in the Antonine age. Many cities (including Salamis, Rhodes, Argos, and Athens) actually contested for not only the honour of being the birthplace of Homer, but some, like Ios in the Cyclades, claimed to be the site of his burial and hero cult as well. In the *Contest between Homer and Hesiod*, the emperor Hadrian is said to have put Lucian's question to the oracle of Delphi (*Certamen Homeri et Hesiodi* ALLEN). The Delphic answer the emperor received (he was born in Ithaca; his father was Telemachus and mother Epicaste (the daughter of Nestor)) did not satisfy Lucian. Homer's claim that he was a Babylonian and called (by the Armenian name) Tigranes is most certainly an unexpected response; see the Introduction (3.3.2.) for the literary and larger cultural interpretations. Lucian might also be simply parodying this general cultural contest by introducing another seemingly shocking option. It was not just Greek cities in the fray, but the *Suda* (s.v. Ὅμηρος ADLER) claims that some assigned him a Lydian and Egyptian origin, and even the Alexandrian scholar Zenodotus himself suggested he was Chaldean (*schol. in Il.* 23.79b (MSS AT) ERBSE); Lucian, though in a Pythagorean transmigration of the soul context, also seems to parody this debate at *Gall.* 17, where Homer was actually a Bactrian camel during the Trojan War.

As for Homer's name, there is a simple linguistic joke that Lucian might be exploiting in making him Babylonian: ὅμηρος means "hostage," and thus he might not even be Greek. Jerram notes the uncertain derivation: "It is supposed to be from the root ὁμ- in ὁμ-οῦ, etc. and ἄρ-ω, i.e. 'the fitter' or 'composer'; or more probably in a passive sense 'the fitted' or 'united,' in reference either to the union of various lays in one poem or to the mingling of different grammatical forms and dialects." There were attempts to rationalize this as more of a nickname, whether he had to be led around like a hostage because of his blindness or because he once was a hostage (cf. [Plut.] *Vita Homeri* ALLEN; Ephorus *FGrHist* / *BNJ* 70 F 1; Arist. F 20.1 GIGON).

2.20 περὶ τῶν ἀθετουμένων στίχων: the Alexandrian editors Zenodotus and Aristarchus prepared critical recensions of Homer's text, which was done by collating the copies of Homer's poems in the Library. Zenodotus marked his text with the obelus (a short line) to indicate the passages that he would "set apart" from their text of Homer as later additions; see Schironi (2018, 49–52). Zenodotus of Ephesus was born *c.*325 BCE and served as head of the Library of Alexandria from *c.*284. He also created a Homeric glossary that defined difficult words. Aristarchus of Samothrace (*c.*216–144 BCE) was the tutor of Ptolemy VII and head of the Library at Alexandria from 153 BCE. His recension of the Homeric epics is historically important, as it is greatly responsible for Homer as we know him today. It is not exactly certain whether it was Zenodotus or Aristarchus who divided the epics into twenty-four books.

Lucian also asks Homer why he began his *Iliad* with the word μῆνιν. Homer's response was the last response a critic of Lucian's age would have expected: it was the first thing that came to his mind. The question itself may pertain to exact word choice or perhaps, as Jerram notes, whether or not the work was originally meant to be an Achilleid (a poem dedicated strictly to Achilles). As for the order of composition of the Homeric epics, Lucian observes that some believed that the *Odyssey* was written first; some even asserted that the epics were written by different authors, a theory that perhaps originates in Xenon and is later found in Hellanicus. Again Lucian's Homer denies his later literary critics. The view that Homer wrote the *Iliad* before the *Odyssey* is well expressed in the treatise *On the Sublime*, where the author (often called Longinus) claims that Homer wrote the *Iliad* at the height of his poetic powers and the *Odyssey* in the blazing sunset of his poetic decline (9.11–13). Longinus notes that garrulity is a symptom of old age and describes the *Odyssey* as a "comedy of manners" (κωμῳδία τίς ἐστιν ἠθολογογένη). This comment might illustrate the appeal that the *Odyssey* held for Lucian. Finally, as for Homer's blindness, Lucian did not have to ask the question. It was clear that Homer could see. That Homer was blind is mentioned in the *Homeric Hymn to Apollo* (172), quoted by Thucydides (3.104), and in Pseudo-Plutarch's *Life of Homer* (*Vita Homeri* ALLEN). In Lucian's age and earlier, Homer was portrayed blind with his eyes lifted up to a reality he could only contemplate with his mind's eye, an attitude well captured by Rembrant in his portrait of a very Dutch and contemporary Aristotle contemplating the bust of Homer now in the Metropolitan Museum of Art in New York. Swift must have appreciated this passage in Lucian for he gives Homer "Eyes [that] were the most quick and piercing I ever beheld" in chapter 8 of Book 3 of *Gulliver's Travels*.

Of course, one should bear in mind the possible joking play here that, whereas Tiresias in Homer's underworld provides Odysseus with no information on how to get home—even though he was supposed to—Homer in Lucian's underworld also provides the *wrong* kind of information.

γραφὴ…ὕβρεως ὑπὸ Θερσίτου: Thersites' complaint is for the rough treatment he is given in Homer's *Iliad* (2.211–77). The case (in terms of Attic law) is a public and not a personal indictment for the public and demeaning abuse of both Homer and Odysseus. At Lysias 10 *Against Theomnestus*, for example, a δίκη κακηγορίας is a personal indictment. But, as Jerram notes, a γραφὴ…ὕβρεως is not the expected legal terminology for libel or verbal abuse: λοιδορία or κακολογία. Although Thersites has brought forward charges because Homer "mocked" (ἔσκωψεν) him in the *Iliad*, the legal use of γραφὴ…ὕβρεως refers to the physical violence he suffered at the hands of Odysseus, who here has served as Homer's συνήγορος (he pleaded Homer's case before Rhadamanthus). Thersites' inclusion amongst those of the Island of Blest is indeed curious, since he is in no way a hero of the Trojan War. However, he gives Lucian the opportunity to continue comically a story across literary space and time, as he does with Odysseus and Calypso (*VH* 2.35–7).

2.21 Pythagoras of Samos

2.21 Πυθαγόρας ὁ Σάμιος: Pythagoras is a new arrival, since he has returned to the Island of the Blest after seven reincarnations into different forms of life. In his human incarnation as Pythagoras he had a golden thigh (also preserved in Diog. Laert. 8.2–11). While Lucian mentions his golden thigh in *Philosophers for Sale* (*Vit. auct.* 6)—clearly to increase his value—here his entire right side is now hyperbolically golden (ἦν δὲ χρυσοῦς ὅλον τὸ δεξιὸν ἡμίτομον). Pythagoras claimed to have undergone four or five transmigrations, and the second was that of the Trojan Euphorbus (who was in part responsible for killing Patroclus and killed by Menelaus: *Il.* 16.779–809; Diog. Laert. 8.4). He is also reported to have stopped a man beating a dog because he recognized in the dog's yelp the voice of a friend (Xenophanes DK 21 B 7 and Diog. Laert. 8.36). Lucian also has great fun with Pythagoras in *Alexander of Abonouteichos* and in *Dialogues of the Dead* (6). Pythagoras' transmigrated soul also appears as the cock in Lucian's *The Cock.*

Ἐμπεδοκλῆς: Empedocles of Acragas in Sicily was also associated with the Pythagoreans. His suicide by plunging into the crater of Mt. Aetna is reported by Diogenes Laertius (8.69 and 75). Lucian also speaks of his incineration in *Icaromenippus* (13–14). Surviving evidence thus far documents Empedocles speaking only of the successive forms of his life: "a boy, a girl, a bush, a bird, and a fish" (DK 31 B.117).

2.22 The games of the dead

2.22 τὰ Θανατούσια: Lucian's games are typically seen as a parody of the athletic contests of the Phaeacians in the *Odyssey* (8.104–235) and the funeral games of Patroclus in the *Iliad* (23.257–897). Lucian alludes to a great number of events, but the summary he provides (wrestling, boxing, running, and the pancration) is closest to the number of games in the *Odyssey* (no pancration (see below), but jump and discus are also included). Lucian also adds a contest of poetry.

Κάρανος ὁ ἀφ' Ἡρακλέους: a mythical founder of the Argead dynasty (Theopompus *FGrHist* 115 F 393). In one tradition Caranus is also the first king of Macedon. He is the son of Temenus, the son of Aristomachus, and principle player in the tradition of the return of the Heraclids. Gronovius is responsible for emending the text here, as Lucian's manuscripts transmit κάρος and κῦρος. On the possibility of κάρος, see Forbes (1939) and Fiedler (1987, 253–9).

Ἀρείου τοῦ Αἰγυπτίου: we know of Areius the philosopher in Alexandria when Octavian takes Egypt; he is later responsible for instructing Augustus in philosophy and also said to be a writer of rhetoric (Suet. *Jul.* 89; Quint. *Inst.* 3.1.16). But this Areius is surely different. Fiedler (1987, 259–61) suggests an athlete of the Hellenistic period.

Ἐπειοῦ: Epeius, the son of Panopeus, won the boxing match against Euryalus during the funeral games of Patroclus (*Il.* 23.664).

παγκρατίου: the pancration event is later than Homer and thus not part of the Phaeacian games in the *Odyssey*. Due to its popularity, it is unsurprising that Lucian includes it in the games of the dead. It is typically treated as a no-holds-barred fight, in which one could mix boxing and wrestling skills, let alone any other techniques.

ἐνίκησεν δὲ ὅμως Ἡσίοδος: this captures the tradition of Hesiod's victory over Homer as they are pitted against one another in a poetic contest at Chalcis (*Certamen Homeri et Hesiodi* ALLEN). It is uncertain how old this story is. Attempts to treat Homer and Hesiod as near contemporaries is evident as early as the fifth century BCE (Hdt. 2.53). Common tradition held that the two poets were not contemporaries.

2.23–4 The impious escape and attack the Island of the Blest

2.23 The battle of the heroes of the Island of the Blest and of the impious, who had broken out of their prison, seems to be Lucian's invention; though GL suggests a parallel with Theopompus for the escape of the impious (*FGrHist* / *BNJ* 115 F 75) and one for their desire to go to the Island of the Blest in Plato (*R.* 615d–616a). Here Lucian names some of the most notorious villains of antiquity: Phalaris of Acragas in Sicily, Busiris of Egypt, Diomedes of Thrace, Sciron, and Sinis. The tradition of Phalaris is well known. He had a bronze smith, Perilaus, make a bull into which Phalaris would insert his victims and light a fire under the bull to roast them. Perilaus was to be the first victim of his cruelty; in two pieces entitled *Phalaris* (1 and 2) Lucian actually defends him against the charge of cruelty and even has the tyrant send the bronze bull to Delphi as a dedication to Apollo. Busiris of Egypt would sacrifice any Greek who reached his shores; he met his end at the hands and club of Heracles. Diomedes of Thrace fed his victims to his carnivorous mares—a scene carved in the throne of Amyclae near Sparta (described by Paus. 3.18.2). Sciron the Megarian and Sinis, called Πιτυκάμπτης ("The Pinebender"), were robbers; both were killed by Theseus (Plut. *Thes.* 8 and 9). As an Atticist *par excellence*, it is, perhaps, appropriate that Lucian should name Theseus, hero of Athens, first of the heroes to confront the impious before Achilles and Ajax; though Achilles had the greatest impact on the battle. Socrates was notably positioned on the right flank, and he distinguished himself even more than he had in the battle of the Athenians and the Thebans at the sanctuary of

Apollo in Boeotia (the Delion). The reference is to Socrates' conduct in the battle and in the Athenian retreat in 424, something we owe to Alcibiades' praise of Socrates in Plato's *Symposium* (220D–221C). Although his valor is mentioned by numerous later authors (e.g. Antisthenes *SSR* 5A, 200 = Athen. 216b–c; Diog. Laert. 2.22–3; Str. 9.2.7), there is some evidence of dissent (cf. Athen. 215c–216c). In the battle with the impious, Socrates was awarded the prize for valor (ἀριστεῖον). In this case the award was the Academy of the Dead, a lovely garden spot in the suburbs of the Island. (Plato's Academy, named after the hero Academus or Hecadmus, was located outside the Dipylon Gate of Athens on the way down to the Piraeus in the Gymnasion).

2.24 τοῦ ποιήματος: On Lucian's departure from the Island of the Blest Homer gave him his epic of the battle between the blest and impious. Unfortunately, Lucian lost it on his voyage home (cf. *VH* 2.47), but he has memorized its first line.

Νῦν δέ μοι ἔννεπε, Μοῦσα, μάχην νεκύων ἡρώων.

As ní Mhealleigh has observed, this line is essentially a parody of the opening line of the *Odyssey* (see Introduction 3.3.2): ἄνδρα μοι ἔννεπε, Μοῦσα, πολύτροπον, ὃς μάλα πολλά.

τὰ ἐπινίκια: the accusative of respect or cognate accusative with εἱστιῶντο. The substantive use of this adjective is common, here understand ἱερά for the sacrificial feast in honour of the victory.

μυσαττόμενος τὴν κυαμοφαγίαν: the reason for Pythagoras' aversion to beans—he also forbade his disciples—was a mystery in antiquity. Speculation, however, was by no means wanting (cf. Porph. *Vit. Pythag.* 44). Lucian has Pythagoras explain his prohibition against eating beans in *Lives on Auction* (6), in which his abstinence is based on four observations: (1) beans are holy and wonderful by nature; (2) they are essentially male seed and its internal structure resembles male genitalia; (3) they can produce blood under certain cooking conditions; (4) the Athenians use them to cast votes. Regarding the last, perhaps we should bear in mind that, according to Xenophon's accuser (*Mem.* 1.2.9–11, 12, 58), one of the emphasized charges against Socrates was his ridiculing of the democratic system of voting by lot (though typically associated with pebbles or stones). When Lucian uses Pythagoras in his works, his abstinence from beans is usually the running joke. For modern conjectures, see the note ad loc. in GL.

2.25–7 The flight of Helen revisted

2.25 ὁ Κινύρας ἁρπάσας τὴν Ἑλένην: in the context of Greek epic, Cinyras is a known figure: the king of Cyprus who gave armour to Agamemnon (*Il.* 11.20–3). There is also a priest of Aphrodite named Cinyras (Pind. *P.* 2.15–16) whom Lucian says erected a sanctuary of Aphrodite at Byblos (*Dea Syr.* 9). For the characterization of Helen, who is willing to run off, see Hdt. 1.4. On rebooting the story of Helen, see also Introduction 3.3.2.

2.26 βοήν τε ἠφίει: Lucian's parody of the Homeric epithet for Menelaus, βοὴν ἀγαθός ("Menelaus of the terrible war cry"; e.g. *Il.* 12.408).

ναῦν μονόξυλον ἀσφοδελίνην: the asphodel is an important plant in the topography of the afterlife, but the size of the single stem of the asphodel is, of course, far too small from which to build a ship.

παρὰ τοσοῦτον: here the preposition conveys motion and the prepositional phrase the overall distance achieved during Cinyras and Helen's attempted escape, i.e. they almost made it.

Τυροέσσης: possibly a parody of the White Island, on which Helen lives with Achilles and from which she informs Stesichorus how to regain his sight (Paus. 3.19.11–13).

ἐκ τῶν αἰδοίων δήσας: Cinyras and those that helped him abduct Helen are bound by their genitals.

2.27–8 The decree of exile against Lucian and his companions

2.27 ἐμπροθέσμους: within the time allotted for their stay, i.e. before their time was up.

τὴν μεγάλην ἤπειρον τὴν ἐναντίαν: the "large land opposite" ours. There is no exact reference regarding direction: to the east or west? That a large and vast land or lands existed beyond the known world was a part of the Greeks' geographical consciousness, whether in imagination alone or based on some tradition. According to information from actual journeys over land and sea, Aristotle seems to indicate that there is nothing but sea between the Pillars of Heracles and India (*Meteor.* 362b). Pseudo-Aristotle (*Mu.* 392b) too indicates the possibility of many inhabitable lands opposite the intervening seas. And, of course, Aelian, citing Theopompus (*FGrHist* / *BNJ* 115 F 75) tells of an immense mass of land beyond the world (κόσμος), where the inhabitants are large and have strange customs.

2.28 παρῄνεσε δέ: Rhadamanthus' instructions to Lucian seem to be a subtle parody of Pythagoras' *symbola* or enigmatic sayings intelligible only to fellow Pythagoreans (Diog. Laert. 8.17 and 19). The first, "stir not the fire with iron," and second, "abstain from beans" (see also above in the note to 2.24), are found among Pythagoras' precepts preserved by the third-century CE Neoplatonist Iamblichus (*Protr.* 21 = DK 58 C 6; the first is also preserved in Plut. *Mor.* 12e). As for the third precept, the order not to make love to a boy over 18 seems to be a comic jab at the stereotypical portrayal of philosophers as pederasts; it is also a precept anticipated during his stay on the Moon (*VH* 1.22), where the age limit is given as 25.

δίστιχον ἐπίγραμμα: the moment Lucian's name is revealed, which finds a comparison in Homer's *Odyssey* (9.19) where Odysseus must ultimately reveal his name and tell his tales. Homer is treated as the inventor of the epigram in Pseudo-Plutarch's *Life of Homer* (*Vita Homeri* ALLEN), and epigrams attributed to him are preserved in Pseudo-Herodotus' *Life of Homer* (*Vita Herodotea* ALLEN). The epigram, of course, is also the poetic form associated with death and tombs.

δίδωσιν ἐπιστολὴν εἰς Ὠγυγίαν τὴν νῆσον Καλυψοῖ κομίζειν: on the letter to Calypso, see Introduction 3.3.2.

πορθμέα Ναύπλιον: descendant of Poseidon and father of Palamedes. Nauplius is also the navigator on the Argo in Apollonius Rhodius (1.138; 2.896). The two mariner heroes, however, are likely not the same individual.

2.30–2 The Island of the Impious

There is no Greek tradition of Islands of the Impious. However, this place of punishment finds a parallel with the myth of Er in Plato (*R.* 615a–616a). In Homer, the souls of the dead are discovered by Odysseus on the shores of Oceanus. In Odysseus' account, dead souls are attracted to him by the offerings he pours down to them in a pit he has excavated. He adds to these the blood of the slaughtered sheep that provides "blood for the ghosts." Three branches of the Styx feed into Homer's underworld: the Acheron, Cocytus, and Pyriphlegethon. Lucian encounters three rivers on the Island of the Impious, which seem to recall the rivers of Hades in Plato (*Phd.* 60): one of mud, one of blood, and one of fire. Only one of Homer's infernal rivers is relevant to Lucian's Island of the Impious: the Πυριφλεγέθων—the River of Lambent Fire (*Od.* 10.513; Plat. *Phd.* 114A). The underworld is the lowest realm of Socrates' cosmology in *Phaedo* 110–115A.

2.30 λυχνίσκους: the diminutive of λύχνος, a "lamp." But, in terms of translation, this refers to the fish that apparently glow like torches and burning coal.

2.31 Τίμων ὁ Ἀθηναῖος: Timon the Athenian, the famous misanthrope of Athens who lived during the time of the Peloponnesian War. He appears to be the subject and the title (Τίμων) of an Old Comedy play by Antiphanes (F 204 KA, see also Phryn. F 19.2 and Plat. Com. F 237 KA), and, of course, is the principal character in Lucian's *Timon*, where his misanthropy is the direct result of having been abandoned by his friends after spending lavishly on them. His fate was invoked by Mark Anthony, when he was abandoned by his friends in defeat and thus assumed a sort of self-exile on an island near the famous Lighthouse of Alexandria (Plut. *Ant.* 70). The story preserved in Lucian's *Timon* might have been influenced by or is directly based on Antiphanes' play; it is also the essential foundation of Shakespeare's play *Timon of Athens*.

2.32–5 The Island of Dreams

This episode is inspired by Penelope's account of dreams to Odysseus, whom she takes to be a stranger in *Od.* 19.560–9 (imitated by Virgil in *A.* 6.893–9) and referred to by Socrates in Plato's *Charmides* (173A). Her distinction is between the Gate of Ivory by which false dreams come to the dreamer and the Gate of Horn by which true dreams come to the sleeper. Here Lucian describes the Island of Dreams as "an island that behaved [ἔπασχε in the imperfect tense] hazy and indistinct in the distance, as it retreated from sight, something like what we experience in dreams: it fled from us as we approached, but we caught up with it." On the island Lucian and his crew land at the Gates of Ivory. This suits Lucian's project, since, as noted many times, Lucian openly professes the lie that is *True History*. Homer is recognized, but both criticized for his inaccuracy (οὐ πάνυ ἀκριβῶς συνέγραψεν) and corrected.

2.32 τὸ τοῦ Ἀλεκτρυόνος ἱερόν: the connection with sleep may be a reference to the story of Alectryon, which Lucian tells in his *Gallus* (3). The boy was the lookout for Ares, while he was with Aphrodite, but he fell asleep. After Hephaestus discovered them, Ares transformed Alectryon into a cock. Also, just as dreams are things to be interpreted, so cocks were used in divination.

2.33 μήκωνες ὑψηλαὶ καὶ μανδραγόραι: mushrooms (poppies) and the mandrake were thought to be narcotic plants.

τοῦτο γὰρ μόνον ἐν τῇ νήσῳ γίνεται ὄρνεον: note that the bat is classified as a bird.

Νυκτιπόρος: "Nightford" or "Sleepwalker"; Oppian (*Cyn.* 1.441) uses this adjective to describe a she-wolf.

Νήγρετος: "Wakeless." The name of this spring, of course, recalls the deep sleep into which Odysseus falls after finishing his tale and leaving Alcinous (*Od.* 13.80). He remained "wakeless" until he reached home: Ithaca.

Παννυχία: "All-Night-Long." All-night rituals (παννύχιαι) are not uncommon in Greek religion, such as those of the Eleusinian Mysteries. Herodotus (4.76) also mentions in the context of Anacharsis, a figure prominent in Lucian's work, all-night rituals performed in honour of the mother of the gods at Cyzicus in Anatolia.

τὸ τῆς Βλακείας πεδίον: the "Plain of Stupidity," which is likely a parody of the Plain of Forgetting in Plato (*R.* 621a), where souls prepare to be reincarnated.

Νυκτῷον: the "precinct/temple of the Night"; Night is a deity in Hesiod (*Th.* 123, 211–12).

σατράπας... Ταραξίωνά τε τὸν Ματαιογένους καὶ Πλουτοκλέα τὸν Φαντασίωνος: "Confusion, son of Failure" (the nightmares) and "Fabulous Wealth, son of Fantasy" (the good dreams).

πηγή τίς ἐστιν, ἣν καλοῦσι Καρεῶτιν: "The Spring of Deep Sleep." Lucian's scholia (*schol. in Luc.* 33 p. 24 Rabe) note that he appropriately named this spring from the deep slumber that follows sleep (ἀπὸ τοῦ κάρου τοῦ ἐπιγινομένου τοῖς ὑπνοῦσι τὴν πηγὴν καταλλήλως ὠνόμασεν).

Ἀντιφῶν ὁ τῶν ὀνείρων ὑποκριτής: Antiphon the interpreter of dreams was roughly a contemporary of Socrates, whose dates are 469–399. Not much survives of Antiphon's *Interpretation of Dreams*, though Cicero gives an account of his interpretations in *Div.* 1.20.39 and 2.70.144.

2.35 ἡμέρας μὲν οὖν τριάκοντα καὶ ἴσας νύκτας: long slumbers, even lasting six months to many years, are not uncommon in the Greek imagination; cf. Hdt. 4.25; Epimenides DK 3 B 1; Ant. Diog. ap. Phot. 110b29–111a19.

βροντῆς μεγάλης: cf. Plato's use of the thunderclap in the context of sleeping souls at *Republic* 621b.

2.35–6 The island of Ogygia

Ogygia might be connected with Ὠγύγιος, the name of a mythical king of Athens, and, if it has a meaning other than being a place name in Homer, it might mean "the mythical island." This distant island is the home of the lonely goddess, Calypso (whose name derives from the verb καλύπτω, "to hide"). Her cave is described in *Od.* 5.55–74. In his letter to Calypso (introduced by the elliptical and common expression in Greek letter-writing Ὀδυσσεὺς Καλυψοῖ χαίρειν: "Odysseus sends greetings to Kalypso") Odysseus gives a summary of his *Odyssey*, but adds one detail: after he had killed all the suitors on Ithaca, Telegonus, his son by Circe, killed him; the story is told in Eugammon's (560 BCE) *Telegonia*, a continuation of the *Odyssey* and part of the Epic Cycle. The name Telegonus ("born far from home") shows some similarity to the name of Odysseus' son by Penelope, Telemachus ("he who fights from afar").

2.36 περὶ τῆς Πηνελόπης: Penelope's epithet is περίφρων (1.329, 4.787). Her prudence and discretion in avoiding remarriage, even after the twenty-year absence of her husband, are most evident by her ruse of weaving a shroud for Odysseus' father, Laertes, during the day and unweaving it at night (*Od.* 24.128–45); she promised to marry one of the suitors who had flocked to Ithaca in Odysseus' long absence once she had finished weaving the shroud. On Odysseus' eagerness to return to Calypso, see the Introduction 3.3.2.

2.37–9 The assaults on Lucian and his crew

2.37 ἐξελόντες τὴν ἐντεριώνην: meaning once the pumpkin-pirates (Κολοκυνθοπειραταῖς) had removed the soft pulp of the pumpkin.

ἱστοῖς μὲν χρώμενοι καλαμίνοις: καλαμίνοις is an adjectival form from κάλαμος and means "made of reed." To serve as masts the reeds on the nearby islands must have been enormous and thick if they were to be used in pumpkins 60 cubits long; the flower of the pumpkin must have been correspondingly long to serve as a sail.

2.38 Ἐπεὶ δὲ ἀπεκρύψαμεν: in the sense of "once we had lost sight of them."

2.39 ἄνδρες ἐπὶ δελφίνων: for dolphins carrying men on their backs, cf. the story of Arion (Hdt. 1.23).

2.40 A halcyon day

2.40 γαλήνης οὔσης...ἀλκυόνος: the halcyon appears in Greek poetry, notably Alcman of Sparta (F 26 *PMG* = F 26 *PMGF* Davies) and Aristophanes (*Av.* 1594). Lucian had already observed halcyons nesting in the trees growing in the belly of the whale (*VH* 1.31); though Jerram objected to this ornithological observation, since halcyons do not nest in trees. The halcyon was supposed to build her nest in the short spell of fair weather in winter when an agitated sea could not destroy it (cf. Plin. *HN* 10.90). A dialogue attributed to Lucian is entitled *Halcyon*. It is likely not by Lucian, but it reproduces a great deal of halcyon lore. The closest parallel to Lucian's description of the halcyon's nest comes from his much younger Roman contemporary, Aelian of Praeneste (*NA* 9.17). In his *Historia animalium* (5.542b) Aristotle quotes Simonides on the fourteen days of calm (or Halcyon days) at the winter solstice (yielding Simonides F 17 Poltera = F 3 *PMG*). Jerram also notes, "The reader will remember the story of the Roc and its egg in the *Second Voyage of Sinbad the Sailor*. Whether Lucian may have barrowed from the *Arabian Nights* (or rather from the common material out of which those tales were composed) is a fair question."

ᾠὰ πεντακόσια: according to Pliny (*HN* 10.90), the halcyon lays five eggs.

2.41–6 New marvels

2.41 χηνίσκος: the ornamental prow of a ship in what can be taken as the form of the neck of a goose. For its shouting, cf. the speaking stern of the Argo (Apoll. Rhod. 4.580–3). This entire passage seems to be inspired by the *Homeric Hymn to Dionysus* and the description of the transformation of the mast of his ship that had been captured by Etruscan pirates into a vine stalk heavy with grapes.

2.42 καταπεφυτευμένον: the κατά is, as Jerram notes, intensive, and thus conveys the sense of overgrowth. Trees are said to grow in the Indian Sea (Antig. 132 (*PGR* p. 90)).

ἀνιμησάμεθα: aorist middle of ἀνιμάω: "to draw/pull up," here by means of the large rope (κάλῳ μεγάλῳ).

τὸ Ἀντιμάχου τοῦ ποιητοῦ ἔπος: sailing on this forest brings to Lucian's mind a line from Antimachus of Colophon describing just such sylvan sailing (F 77 Matthews). Antimachus wrote a *Thebaid* around 400 BCE.

2.43 χάσματι... διαχωρίσματα: cf. the chasms in the myth of Er in Plato (*R.* 614c).

ναῦς... παρ' ὀλίγον ἐλθοῦσα κατενεχθῆναι: the expression consisting of a prepositional phrase with παρά + ἔρχομαι + infinitive is common in the sense of "to come close within/near," e.g. Eur. *Heracl.* 296 and Plut. *Pyrrh.* 10. κατενεχθῆναι is the aorist passive infinitive of ἐκφέρω, meaning that the ship barely managed to come to a halt before it was carried down into the chasm in the sea.

2.44 Βουκέφαλοι: the Island of the Bull-Heads. To describe the appearance of the vine-women, Lucian had earlier referred to paintings of Daphne (*VH* 1.8). οἷον παρ' ἡμῖν τὸν Μινώταυρον ἀναπλάττουσιν: the use of ἀναπλάττω situates Lucian's reference in both the realm of building with the imagination and sculpture. It is possible that Lucian has a sculpted representation in mind. Pausanias saw a statue of Theseus and the Minotaur on the Athenian acropolis (1.24.1). There is possibly some allusion to the Laestrygonians in the *Odyssey* (10.82–132), and even some parody of Ctesias' dog-heads of India (*FGrHist* 688 F 45).

συμπεφύκεσαν: an instance in which the augment of the pluperfect has been omitted. Omission is not without precedent, especially in Homer, the lyric poets, Attic tragedy, and under specific circumstances in Herodotus. For Lucian's Atticism, there are also instances in Thucydides, Xenophon, and especially in Plato. See Smyth §238.

2.45 ναῦται... τὰ αἰδοῖα... ἔπλεον: on using the penis as a nautical instrument, cf. Trygaeus and his "oar" in Aristophanes' *Peace* (142).

2.46 νῆσος ἐκαλεῖτο Κοβαλοῦσα, ἡ δὲ πόλις αὐτὴ Ὑδαμαργία: perhaps something like "Witchery" and "Watertown," as translated by the brothers Fowler (1905). The confusion over these names in the manuscripts of

Lucian and the confusion they cause for Lucian's editors are tributes to Lucian's inventiveness; for a concise treatment of the problems at hand, see the note in GL ad loc.

τὰ σκέλη οὐ γυναικός, ἀλλ' ὄνου ὁπλάς: the ass-shanks of this island, like the women of the Island of the Vine-Women, address our mariners in Greek. In this, the final scene of Lucian's "Odyssey," he skirts two scenes from Homer's *Odyssey*: the scene of Odysseus brandishing the μῶλυ plant that Hermes had given to protect him from Circe (*Od.* 10.302–479) and the human remains he sees as he passes the Island of the Sirens (*Od.* 12.39–54 and 184–91). The ass-shanks greet Lucian and his men in the manner of courtesans (ἑταιρικῶς), and there is a tradition that the Sirens were courtesans (Heraclit. *Incred.* 14).

Ὀνοσκελέας: ass-shanks. We should note the story of the misogynistic young man who had sex with a female ass, which subsequently gave birth to girl named Ὀνοσκελία (Aristocles *FGrHist* / *BNJ* 831 F 3). The specter Empousa, who devours men, is also called Ὀνοσκελίς (cf. Aristoph. *Ra.* 285–95 and the scholion to *Ec.* 1085).

ἡ δὲ αὐτίκα ὕδωρ ἐγένετο: the shape-shifter Proteus was also capable of turning into water (Virg. *Georg.* 4.10).

2.47 An account of further adventures promised

2.47 τὰ δὲ ἐπὶ τῆς γῆς ἐν ταῖς ἑξῆς βίβλοις διηγήσομαι: Lucian finds himself in the same position as had Iambulus (Diod. 2.60.2.) when he alone was shipwrecked on the north-east coast of India, except that most of Lucian's original crew, now reduced by nine, survive. Rhadamanthus had prophesied that Lucian would reach the great "opposite" continent at *VH* 2.27. He does. Yet the promised story of that adventure goes without fulfillment. Here Lucian might be playing with the very compositional structure of the *True History* itself. Kidd (2017) observes that the episodic nature of the Greek novel, including the *True History*, is indicative of their playful and even comic nature. Moreover, journeys to the underworld in Greek literature have been treated typically as episodes or digressions from the principal plot structure (Lye 2016). Lucian has thus not only made a "digression" the focus of his comic (*VH* 1.2 ἀκωμῳδήτως) story, but he seems to omit or lose information regarding greater tales and journeys, namely Homer's now "lost" epic of the battle between the dead heroes and the impious and this great mysterious continent, the one whose inhabitants he specifically set out to find (*VH* 1.5). These are the tales, the major story arcs, that would have typically encompassed a digression to the Moon and especially to the underworld.

Index